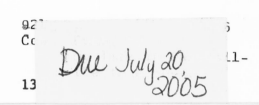

D1293363

MY LIFE IN BASEBALL
The True Record

MY LIFE IN BASEBALL
The True Record

by TY COBB, with Al Stump

y. m.

Doubleday & Company, Inc. Garden City, New York

1961

Contents

Foreword

Few names have left a firmer imprint upon the pages of the history of our times than has that of Ty Cobb. His life as baseball's most aggressive competitor is chronicled in this volume.

This great athlete seems to have understood early in his professional career that in the competition of baseball, just as in war, defensive strategy never has produced ultimate victory and, as a consequence, he maintained an offensive posture to the end of his baseball days. Thus, for nearly a quarter of a century his aggressive exploits on the diamond, while inviting opposition as well as acclaim, brought high drama to the sports pages of the land. They did much to give pre-eminence to baseball as a great American competitive sport. They brought the urban centers of population into friendly competition, provided absorbing relaxation to tens of millions of onlookers and vitalized the competitive spirit among the youth of the land from sand lot to college campus.

Still holder of many of baseball's records which may never be equalled or surpassed, Ty Cobb injected much of his own fighting spirit into that aspect of the American character which has put inspiration and direction behind our progress as a free nation.

Douglas MacArthur

March 6, 1961

Ty Cobb as I Knew Him

by E. A. Batchelor

As the oldest active member of the Baseball Writer's Association of America, in point of continuous service dating back to October 1908, it was my privilege to see a very large percentage of the baseball games in which Tyrus Raymond Cobb appeared during his tenure of 22 years with the Detroit Tigers. This, I believe, lends some authority to my appraisal of his talents and accomplishments. It has established that, in my considered opinion, he was, all things considered, the greatest ballplayer that ever lived and the most valuable piece of property ever owned by any ball club, because he had the longest and best-sustained record of stardom.

Ty's claim to greatness is sustained by the numerous records that he holds. Among these are: twelve times American League batting champion, including nine consecutive years; highest lifetime batting average in the major leagues (.367); most hits (4191); most games played (3033); most runs scored (2234); 1901 runs batted in, with no records available for this feat for his first two years; most total bases (5863 against 5793 for Babe Ruth); most stolen bases (96 in one season and 892 over-all).

Imposing as these tangibles are, they do not give the whole picture of the man. They were supplemented by a group of intangibles that only he possessed in such generous measure; the greatest combination of qualities of body, heart, and mind ever given to a professional ballplayer. These assets cannot be reduced to cold figures as can his physical accomplishments but they were what did the most to set him above all the rest.

Nature gave him a superb body, wiry, rangy, all-muscled, and perfectly co-ordinated. His top playing weight was about 190. It gave him also keen eyesight and lightning reflexes. It gave him a quick and active brain that enabled him to size up any situation that developed in a ball game, instantly and accurately. Equally important, it gave him an intensely competitive disposition that caused him to fight for everything he wanted to do.

Early in his baseball life, a canard developed that Ty was a brawler who constantly sought trouble. This misconception seems to have started when he first joined the Tigers, as a slender youth of eighteen, a well-brought-up boy inclined to be friendly with everybody and anxious only to make good on his own merits. Unfortunately for him, there then were among an otherwise fine group of men on the Detroit roster, a few who were contemptible bullies. These rowdies immediately started to pick on the stripling from Georgia and did everything their disordered minds could think of to make life miserable for him.

Among other things they provoked two fist fights between Ty and Charlie Schmidt, one of the regular catchers, a mature, muscular man who far outweighed him. There was no way that Cobb could avoid these encounters except by actually running away and he wasn't a coward. In fact, the way he stood up to the powerful Schmidt earned him that man's respect and they became good friends.

As Ty developed into stardom, he was subjected to a lot of the annoyances that are the portion of conspicuous men. Most of these he took with good grace but a few got so unbearable that he resented them with his fists when there was no other courageous course possible.

On the ball field, he insisted on his rights at all times but he avoided brawls. He made less trouble for the umpires than did a lot of players with less than half his talent. He was smart enough to realize that umpires are human beings (though some of the fans don't think so) and that, being so, they might be inclined to guess some of the close ones in his favor. In fact, Ty did so little kicking on called strikes that when he did protest, the umpire gave him credit for being not only sincere, but perhaps right.

Because Ty was the most daring and successful base-runner that the American League ever knew, another myth developed that he was constantly trying to spike men who were covering the bases. There even were stories that he used to file his spikes to razor sharpness to aid in this base line manslaughter. The truth is that Ty insisted on the right to the base line that the rules give the runner and if the fielder didn't recognize this fact or made his play in a clumsy manner, he was in some danger of getting cut. But Ty told me that only twice in his life did he ever deliberately spike a player, and that only after repeated warnings to yield the right of way.

When Ty was setting records for base stealing, some of the fans attributed his success to great speed. As a matter of fact, speed was only a part of the story. There have been faster runners in baseball who hardly ever stole a base. Where Ty shone was in getting the jump on the pitcher—in determining when he was going to throw to the plate rather than to a base occupied by the Georgian. It was said that he could "read" any pitcher he ever faced, including some of those who specialized in holding runners, among them Nick Altrock and Ed Walsh. Cobb supplemented his ability to get the jump by mastery of the hook slide. When he hit the dirt to go into a base, the only target he offered the fielder was the tip of one shoe.

Unlike some of the home-run sluggers of today, who have to wait for a pitch particularly to their liking, Ty could hit any ball that he could reach, pulling to right field, slicing to left, or driving it through the middle as the case might be. Because of this ability to hit to all fields, defensive players could not station themselves with any degree of certainty in spots where he was most likely to drive the ball. Among other things, he was a most accomplished bunter and he got a lot of safe hits by "legging out" slow grounders.

Because of his smooth, level swing and his keen eyesight, Ty was very hard to fool with any kind of a pitch. Although he didn't go after home runs, he ranks fourth in the American League in extra-base hits and tenth in total bases on long hits. It should be borne in mind, in this connection, that most of Ty's career came in the days of a very "dead" ball and that, furthermore, pitchers were allowed a great deal more liberty in the way of freak deliveries than is the case today. The "spitter," the "emery ball," the "shine ball," and some others now prohibited were in common use.

So much of the Cobb saga has to do with his hitting and base-stealing that many fans forget his accomplishments as a fielder. He was one of the best, with speed enough to cover ground, good judgment on fly ball, sure hands, and an adequate arm. In fact, in his early days his arm rated excellent but he impaired it somewhat by insisting on trying to develop into a pitcher and spending a lot of time throwing curves and various trick deliveries.

We read in a magazine not long ago that Cobb could not be classed as a truly great ballplayer because he was not a "team man" and that consequently the Tigers didn't win pennants consistently during his tenure. Nothing could be more ridiculous. In the first place, baseball, in spite of a lot of printed matter to the contrary, is not a team game in the sense that one man's efforts are dependent in large degree on the help he gets from others. It is as highly individualized as any sport in the world; everything a player does he does alone. Even in a double-play, everyone who handles the ball does it all by himself—getting possession of a batted ball by one man, his throwing it to another man who will be in a predetermined spot on the play, and the second man's throwing it to a third unless it is a fly ball.

Baseball games can be won in only one way—by scoring one or more runs. That being so, the best "team man" must be the one who contributes most to the scoring of runs, either by completing the round of the bases himself or driving teammates home. Well, Cobb scored 2234 runs, an all-time major league record, and batted in 1901. That makes a total of 4135 runs that he produced. Which, we would say proved not only that he was a great "team man" but probably the greatest of all time.

Cobb was by far the greatest gate attraction that the Tigers ever had and he shares with Babe Ruth, an entirely different type of player, the honor of being the greatest in the history of the game. Although not a "show-off," many of Ty's feats were spectacular. There never was a completely dull ball game if he was on the field. No matter what the score or the position of the Tigers in the pennant race, he always did his best and in the course of the game usually contributed something that sent the fans home talking about him. In his day, ball parks generally had much less seating capacity than some of the huge stadiums today. Otherwise, he certainly would have been instrumental in creating new attendance records.

In his six-year term as manager of the Tigers, his club finished in the first division four times—attaining second place in 1923, even though the personnel was not of championship caliber. He made a reputation as a hard task-master in the managerial role but that was largely due to the fact that he had no patience with a player who was satisfied just to get by, rather than putting forth maximum effort. Ty so loved the game of baseball that it was incomprehensible to him that anybody in it ever should do less than his very best, try to make the most of such talent as he had, and work to improve on it.

There will never be another Ty Cobb, because there never again will be the type of baseball in which he starred, where science, speed, and intelligence brought big results. His game has been supplanted by one in which slugging is at a premium and its exponents get the big money. Base-running has all but disappeared from today's game—Ty stole more bases in a single season than any entire club is doing today. A whole generation of fans has grown up since he quit and it is a generation to whom the niceties of the game would be misunderstood and maybe even boring. In my opinion, this transition from skill to power has taken much from the game but so long as the fans will crowd the parks to see ordinary fly balls turned into cheap home runs by the lively ball and the restricted playing areas, there is nothing that anybody can do about it.

MY LIFE IN BASEBALL
The True Record

1

First Inning:
Hits, Errors, and Heartache

One of my first clear-cut memories is of a buggy, bumping along a red clay road between Commerce and Carnesville, Georgia. I seem to recall that I was barefoot and wore a hickory shirt under a pair of bib overalls. With my legs dangling over the tailgate, I was busy winding yarn around a small core ball. It was slow work.

But I kept at it. In the next village, where my schoolmaster father was to become principal, I knew I'd find a leathermaker who for the price of a few errands run would make a cover for my ball. And the new kid in town who owned a hittable ball could overcome social obstacles faster than the boy who didn't.

At eleven and twelve, I liked to play cow-pasture baseball—what we called town ball. Still, I had no fiery ambition to make a career of the game. Professional athletics were something I'd scarcely heard of down there in the backwoods of northeastern Georgia.

Move ahead just six years, and I have another clear memory—of sitting alongside manager Bill Armour on the Detroit Tigers' bench, realizing that in a few minutes I'd play my first major league game. That Tyrus Cobb had jumped from that buggy tailgate all the way into Bennett Park, Detroit, at the age of eighteen, seemed to me the No. 1 miracle of creation.

The evidence that I'd rushed things was all around me . . . I scarcely heard Armour's soothing words.

Warming up for the New York Highlanders was the legendary

Wee Willie Keeler, only 5 feet 4½ inches and 140 pounds, but a placement hitter beyond compare. With his choked-up bottle bat, Keeler had averaged as high as .432. A fourteen-year veteran, he had yet to hit under .300. At second base was the great Kid Elberfeld, himself. The New York pitcher was Jack Chesbro, the original master of the spitball who'd won a record 41 games the season before. On our side was Wahoo Sam Crawford and Bobby Lowe, first man to hit four home runs in one game. And Germany Schaefer, who stole bases in reverse to demonstrate his genius. Until that day—my first in a big-time park—I'd never dreamed that men could field and hit so wonderfully. Such speed, class, style, speedy maneuvering, and lightning thinking! It seemed miles beyond anything I could ever do. When the bell rang, I found myself involved in a duel by artists at the art of extracting every last inch of opportunity from every situation. And they went at it with a red-eyed determination I couldn't believe. On one play, Kid Elberfeld tried to bump Schaefer off his running line as he raced for third, and Germany dumped the Kid on his head for it. "Rowdy Bill" Coughlin, our third baseman, flew at umpire Silk O'Loughlin and was thrown out. Frank Delahanty of New York made a diving, somersaulting catch that left me wide-eyed. Later, Delahanty was carried away after tearing ankle tendons while trying to stretch a double into a triple. He was through for the season.

When Chesbro cranked and fired his overhand spitter—loaded with slippery elm—it came up to the plate like a standard fastball, and then took a diabolical dive under your bat.

Armour had me, a babe-in-the-woods, batting fifth in the line-up!

What did they say about me next day? The Detroit *Journal* of August 31, 1905, wasted few words: "Cobb, the juvenile outfielder from Augusta, made his first appearance and was given a hospitable hand. He comes up to expectation."

The *Free Press* had a little more to say:

"Cobb got away well. For a young man anxious to get along in the world, it was not an auspicious situation as he faced Mr. Chesbro, the American League's finest twirler. In addition, Tyrus had the bad luck to confront Chesbro on two occasions when two men were out and a man waiting to score—a base hit being the only thing of value. First time up, Chesbro poured two fast strikes past the uneasy lad. But then the Georgian whaled the next one over Eddie

Hahn's head and off the center field wall for a delightful double that scored his man. Second time up, he drew a walk and was thrown out stealing. In the field, he was adequate.

"Tyrus was well-received and may consider a two-base pry-up a much better career opener than usually comes a young fellow's way."

We beat Chesbro, 5–3, and I actually made a clean hit off the meanest delivery in the business. That night I was floating a foot off the ground.

But next day came the lesson. The country kid had his plow cleaned, as we said down home. As the runner at first base, I went sprinting to second and slid head-first at the bag. Kid Elberfeld was waiting to give me the professional "teach"—which he did by slamming his knee down on the back of my neck, grinding my face untenderly into the dirt. Spluttering and spitting dirt, I heard Umpire O'Loughlin's well-rounded baritone—"Owwwwtttt!"

I walked, or sort of crept, away from there with some skin scraped off. And with the Kid grinning at me.

Armour and the Tigers didn't have to tell me I'd pulled a dumb, sandlot slide that could have finished me before I was started. The Kid could have broken my neck. Food for thought—and I pondered a lot on Elberfeld and sliding before we played New York again. The scab on my nose reminded me that the head-on method of stealing bags I'd thought such hot stuff in the Georgia minor league was suicide up here.

During our next Highlander series, I banged into Elberfeld feet-first, caught him by surprise and knocked him kicking onto the grass, while I slid in safely. The Kid was known as a tough number. He got up, shot a stream of tobacco juice, and looked me over reflectively.

"Son, that's how it's done—you've got it," he said. "More power to you."

Nothing that happened in my short rookie season of 1905 or my first full big league campaign of 1906 gave me a greater lift than Elberfeld's spontaneous gesture of sportsmanship. Because I had almost everything in the book to learn. I didn't suspect then, for instance, that some of my own clubmates would soon hate me for the aggressive style I adopted. I wasn't prepared to be hazed and ostracized and jockeyed into fist fights with men bigger and older. On the technical debit side, I knew nothing about hitting left-handed pitching, in fact had no real concept of stance, grip, swing, and the adaption of position in the box to the particular pitcher involved. Being so young, I was a scatter-brained base-runner who didn't know that you could steal more bases on the pitcher than on the catcher. Much circulation has been given the story that I was a prodigy, a baseball natural. That story couldn't be more untrue—unlike Larry Lajoie or Joe Jackson or Babe Ruth, who came fully equipped to hit well as beginning players, I was a walking study in faults. The proof of it is that in the Sally League, in 1905, I'd been a mediocre .260 hitter until late season, when I improved past the .300 mark. As a Detroit rookie, I was scarcely able to stick on the roster. Another young Southerner named Mel Ott averaged .383 as a freshman major leaguer. Rogers Hornsby averaged .313 and .327 in his first two full seasons. Honus Wagner opened with .344, Al Simmons with .308, and Paul Waner with .336.

My own rookie mark of .240 looks pale alongside those performances. To set the record straight, I was anything but a born ballplayer. The ax hung over my neck, ready to drop, for quite a while. Why it didn't—after one game in which Doc White, a southpaw White Sox pitcher, made a bowknot of me, while striking me out four times—I'm still not sure.

I am deliberately jumping ahead of my childhood days and family origins in telling the story of my life because my break-in period with the Tigers was the most miserable and humiliating experience I've ever been through. In dealing with the heartache first, perhaps some glaring misconceptions about me will be cleared up. This book came very close to never being written. For upward of thirty years, I've turned away from all offers to speak my piece. I have not wanted to unburden myself of a great many facts directly opposed to what Americans have been led to believe is the truth. I felt no need to justify or defend any act of mine. I feel none now. In no way is this book an apologia.

But my time is running short and I find little comfort in the popular picture of Cobb as a spike-slashing demon of the diamond with a wide streak of cruelty in his nature. The fights and feuds I was in have been steadily slanted to put me in the wrong. There comes the moment when a man must speak—not in rebuttal, and certainly not in anger, but as a simple duty to himself and those who carry his name. My critics have had their innings. I will have mine now.

To backtrack a bit, I arrived in Detroit from Augusta the night before the Highlander game I've just described at around 10:30 P.M. No one met me at the depot. I went looking for a hotel, carrying my total possessions of the moment: one suitcase, a uniform roll containing my suit, spare underwear and dirty laundry, my pancake-style Spalding glove and a couple of favorite bats. I found a lodging place that was no chinch-bug emporium, but definitely on the third-class side. It cost $10 a week, American plan, for I had to nurse my slim bankroll. Next day, I was to sign a Tiger contract for $1800 per season. But it was now August 29—I'd been jerked out of the minors suddenly when the Detroit outfield ran into injuries—and I could count on only a month's pay before the season ended.

I don't believe I looked, or felt, like too much of a rube. The Cobbs were people of position and property in the South; I knew whick fork to use and I wore a presentable dark suit and neat bow tie. At eighteen, I was about 5 feet 10 and weighed 155. I was light complexioned with plenty of reddish-blond hair then, parted in the middle. Baptist-reared, I neither smoked nor drank, or chased women or used the oath. Until a few days earlier, I'd been playing the outfield for Augusta in the Sally League. I had a total experience of about 150 professional games which could be counted as such. My proudest possession, and it was in my pocket, was a gold watch. That handsome turnip had been recently presented to me by Augusta fans in token of a late-season batting spurt that had brought me the league lead at the moment Detroit called me up.

Awed? No, I wasn't that. Apprehensive, yes. I'd started playing baseball originally because I loved the competition, the matching of muscle and wits. It was a joust and a challenge, and, although my father—a state senator as well as a teacher—had me scheduled for West Point, somehow the military life seemed like total bondage. Going against my father came hard. But I had a burning zeal in me to find out what I could do on my own. I had followed an urge he never quite understood, but was willing to tolerate.

And all at once this game I'd only been experimenting with had caught me up and propelled me far above the Mason-Dixon—my first time out of the South. The thing had gone much too far for me to retreat.

The next morning, I inquired the way to Bennett Field, then the Tigers' park, and hiked over there. Old Bennett, at Michigan and

Trumbull avenues, seated only 8500. But it looked gigantic to me. It was named for a much-loved 1894 Tiger catcher named Charley Bennett, who slipped on a railroad platform in Kansas, fell under the train and lost one leg at the knee. A nice, sentimental touch, I thought. I'd learn how much sentiment there was in the Big Show before much longer.

After signing the contract, I met Bill Armour, the manager. He was a fashion plate, with an impressive walrus mustache, who never wore a uniform in the dugout. I thought he was one of the most elegant men I'd ever seen. He was affable and covered up any fear he had that I was too young and green for the job he needed done. Detroit had paid Augusta the grand sum of $750 for my services.

"Meet Jimmy Barrett," said Armour, introducing a well-set-up player. "His knee's on the bum, and I'm using you in his place in center field."

Armour added nonchalantly, "We have a way of stealing New York's signs. Jimmy will give you the dope."

As Barrett explained, during games he sat in the center field stands with a pair of spyglasses strong enough to pick out the fillings in the opposition catcher's teeth. Nearby was a fence sign reading: *THE DETROIT NEWS—BEST NEWSPAPER IN THE WEST.*

"Keep your eyes peeled on the letter 'B' in that sign," said Barrett, "You'll notice that little slots in it open and close. If the slot is open in the upper half of the 'B,' it means I've stolen their signal from the catcher for a fast ball. If the bottom slot is open, you can expect a curve. One of the boys is back there working the slots after I give him the office."

I thought it over and decided I didn't want the espionage working for me. "I'm not used to it," I told Armour. "Can't I just get up there and hit?"

Armour shrugged. "Suit yourself." But there was the ominous undercurrent that I'd *better* hit.

After my debut against Chesbro and the Highlanders, and my forceful lesson from Kid Elberfeld, it became evident that I'd set no rookie records. In the first big-time game of my life, I'd hit that double. In game No. 2, I twice hit safely off the portly Jack Powell of the Highlanders. In game No. 3, I went hitless. And then I began to get goose-egged regularly. In the outfield, I was glaringly weak on ground balls. Armour was forced to use me, since Barrett was

22

hurt. His only other replacement, Dick Cooley, had stiffened from age and looked like a man running on stilts. So I stepped into a starting opportunity mostly by forfeit. My .240 average for 41 games made it highly dubious that I'd return in 1906. For some reason, Armour gave me another chance the next spring.

If modern players battle fiercely for starting assignments, I have to say that the old-timers were even more wolfish. Over that 1905-6 winter, Detroit acquired Davey Jones, a fleet outfielder and a great lead-off man. That meant that the three outfield jobs were up for grabs among Sam Crawford (a cinch), Matty McIntyre, a light hitter but a good ballhawk, Jones, and Cobb. Who'd sit on the bench? It wouldn't be McIntyre, if a tightly organized clique on the Detroit club could help it. McIntyre and his chums began a systematic, carefully schemed campaign to break my spirit and make me the fellow who picked his teeth with bench splinters while they made the money.

At first, there were no open clashes. McIntyre and his roommate, Twilight Ed Killian, a pitcher, began by locking me out of the hotel bathroom the players shared. I'd stand shivering in a towel or bedsheet while they hogged the tub for hours. At batting practice, I'd be jostled aside and told, "Get out to the outfield, sand-lotter. This is for men only." In restaurants, and there were no hat-check girls then, I'd dine, and find my hat impaled on the rack, minus its crown. It got to the point that I walked up to my tormentors and said, "Whoever did this to my hat, stand up, you ——!" They just grinned at me. I could never prove a thing.

It was clear that they intended to razz me off the team and back to the bushes, and that they had endless methods to accomplish it. During Pullman rides, a soggy wad of newspaper would fly down the aisle and smack me in the neck. After wiping off the water, I'd stalk down the aisle, raging mad, and yelling, "Get on your feet, the —— who threw that!"

But they wouldn't fight—not quite yet.

It was a war of nerves. My only support came from Wild Bill Donovan, the pitcher, and a few others, who urged me, "Stick up for your rights. If it comes to a showdown, we'll back you up."

Armour, the manager, rightly, saw that it was my personal problem to win or lose and did nothing in particular to stop the hazing. It was a routine hazard in the early century for rookies to be worked over. But usually it was done more in a joshing spirit than with malevolent intent . . . this feud was for keeps.

Social ostracism was introduced. I found myself eating alone, cold-shouldered in the clubhouse and unable to find a permanent roommate. In Detroit, the veterans stayed at a half-hotel, half-burlesque house called the Brunswick, while I roomed at a sedate hostelry a few blocks away. It was a bleak, lonely time for a boy not yet nineteen. For a while, Edgar (Eddie) Willett, a rookie pitcher from Norfolk, Virginia, moved in with me. He was a big, good-looking farm boy with a world of promise. But the high-living McIntyre crowd put pressure on Eddie.

"We're going to run Cobb off the club," they warned him, "and you, too, if you stay friends with him. Either move out and hang around with us, or you're finished."

Eddie told me this. I said, "You're at the crossroads. These men just want to make a beer-drinker out of you, like them. Edgar, they are *not* driving me off this team. I'd tell them to go to hell, if I were you."

But Eddie packed up and left, and soon the sporty life caught up with him. In six seasons he was finished.

My enemies were a sneaky lot, always operating behind a façade of innocence, because, by now, they knew that I always went armed. I kept a weapon of a lethal nature close by me at all times and I had eyes in the back of my head. If they jumped me some dark night, they'd find one Georgia boy who wouldn't hesitate to even the odds with extreme means, if fists failed to save me. One of the most under-handed stunts they pulled was to break my bats. I cherished the fine ash bats I had collected. I found them smashed, and had excellent rea-son to believe that the man who'd done it was Charlie Schmidt, a powerfully built catcher.

Schmidt—in time—became my good friend. A burly ex-miner from Coal Hill, Arkansas, he was most likable, except when conned by the anti-Cobbs into provoking me into fighting him, which was what the faction wanted. Weighing well over 200, Schmidt once had boxed Jack Johnson, the world's heavyweight champion. For amusement, he'd drive spikes into the clubhouse floor with his fist.

We first clashed during a spring training trip down South, more of a wrestle than a fight. Moving into Mississippi, my tormentors

THIS IS the earliest known photograph of me—and note that I seem to have been born with a hitter's eyes!

I'M NOT quite sure when this study photograph was taken—I think I was in my mid-20's. But it's always been a traditional picture of me.

NORMAN ARTHUR (KID) ELBERFEL
one of the toughest infield scrapper
ever lived. He gave me "the teach"
early in my rookie season when I
sliding headfirst into second, later
plimented me when I knocked
kicking.

THE PERFECT HITTER—Shoeless Joe
son. My stance and swing had to be
ioned—Joe's was purely natural. Lif
average: 356.

WAHOO SAM CRAWFORD—the hero of Detroit before I arrived. We had some hard words, wound up fine friends.

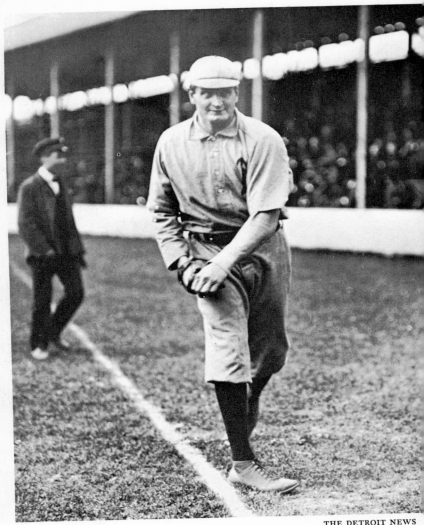

THE DETROIT NEWS

I ONCE touched Rube Waddell for a historic home run and Mr. Connie Mac
right off the Athletics' bench. But, oh, how Rube could wing 'em in when he h

ONE OF THE most underrated managers of all time: Hughie Jennings of Detroit. Note, in second photo, how managing aged this fine baseball man. Hughie died young.

THEY DON'T make baseball cut-ups like Herman (Germany) Schaefer any more. He stole bases in reverse! He was my teammate and a great pal.

You COULD tuck Willie Keeler into your hip pocket, but he lasted nearly 20 years and had a batting average with his punch-hitting style that modern stars can't touch —.345 in more than 2100 games.

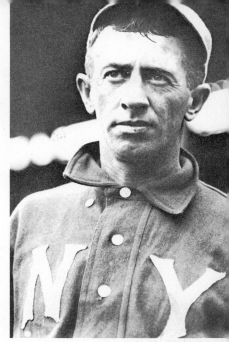

JOHN McGRAW, left, the Little Napoleon, took it hard when I fist-whipped one of his Giants—Buck Herzog—in a Dallas hotel room. Mr. Connie Mack, right, was the man I most admired in baseball. Here they meet at the 1911 World Series, which the Macks won, 4 games to 2.

TAKE A SQUINT at that oversized driving glove Napoleon Lajoie is wearing. We had no factory-customed ball traps in 1910. That year Nap fought me down to the wire for the batting title—with explosive results.

told Charlie, "Cobb is going around claiming he licked you. You going to let him get away with that?"

In Hattiesburg, I had just laced my shoes and was walking toward the field when I heard a voice growl:

"Cobb."

I turned, and Schmidt's punch caught me with both hands at my side, a crushing wallop that knocked me flat and broke my nose. From then on, a terrible anger was in me. Anger, hatred, and humiliation. I hadn't been raised to brawl like this. I could see no reason why ballplayers should lower themselves to an animal level and I felt ashamed of the game and these men who would stop at nothing to ruin a youngster's spirit.

On the field, toward late season of 1906, the thing became so bitter that the Tigers were dropping games because of it. Davey Jones pulled a Charley horse and I played center field regularly, with McIntyre in left field. Outfielders back each other up on all possible plays, and I obliged whenever McIntyre had a chance to handle, and I could get over behind him. But McIntyre wouldn't back up Cobb. It came to the point in a game with St. Louis that George Stone drove a ball between us—a shot which either of us might catch. I broke for it, and saw that McIntyre hadn't budged. The ball had split our positions and his responsibility to try for it was as great as mine. So I stopped dead-still. The ball bounced between us and on to the fence for a home run.

Pitching that day for our side was Ed Siever, one of the anti-Cobb ring. I'd saved more than one game for Siever with glove and bat, but back in the dugout he cursed me.

I jumped up and stood over him. Where I came from, men had been killed for saying what Siever did. "Get up! Get on your feet!" I shouted at him. Dimly, but almost obliterated by my rage, was the realization that I hadn't been brought up for such hooligan exhibitions, and even as I challenged Siever I felt the shame my parents would have felt had they witnessed the scene.

He didn't get up . . . for I was ready.

But that night at the Planter's Hotel in St. Louis, I came down the staircase and wandered over to the cigar counter, thinking that a smoke would relax me. I was studying the cheroots when Siever edged up close. Wild Bill Donovan put a hand between us. "Let's not have any trouble, boys," he said.

"I want no trouble," I answered.

Siever muttered something and retreated to a corner of the lobby, where he huddled with McIntyre and others. They stood there, talking. Feeling something was up, I eased over behind one of the lobby columns to listen in. But they spotted me.

Suddenly, around the column, and moving fast, came Siever. He was a left-handed puncher, as well as pitcher, and he started one that would have removed my head had it landed. But I smothered the blow and then let go all my pent-up emotion. I hit him a right to the jaw that started him down and connected several times more as he was staggering and falling. Siever went down in a badly damaged condition. Sensible heads, such as Donovan's broke it up.

"Let's get out of here," urged Donovan. "The police might come."

"Let them come. I'm innocent of anything except defending myself," I said.

"Sure, sure," said Bill, "but you'll land in the cooler, anyway. These guys *hate* you. They'll prefer charges, or do anything to hurt you."

I didn't run out. I waited a spell, and then I took a long and lonely walk down to the railway station. Only two games remained in the season. I wished I didn't have to play in them. I was sick at heart and disillusioned. I'd dreamed of becoming a part of the Detroit organization, and all I'd known, so far, was jealousy and persecution. I had a hunch that the enemy would expect me to pull out for Georgia and pass up the last two games. But to force an issue that was thrust upon me, and then follow up, had been part of my training as a boy.

I surprised them by showing up for the train leaving St. Louis next morning. I ran into Tom McMahon, our trainer. "You did only one thing wrong," he remarked. "You kicked Siever after you had him down."

"I didn't have to kick him," I replied. "He was well-licked when he went down. Get your facts straight, Tom."

To reach my berth, I had to pass through a narrow aisle, and there, stretched out on a seat, with some players holding a beefsteak to his face, was Siever. He was groaning and looked like he'd been in a mangler.

"Siever," I paused to say, "they tell me I kicked you. I don't

26

recall any such thing. But if I did, I apologize for that part of it."

He mumbled something about, "I'll get you . . ."

In bed, I stretched out, but I didn't sleep. It was more than possible that I'd be attacked during the night. If so, I was armed and ready. And I remained ready until the day came when I was established as a Detroit regular and, one by one, my antagonists dropped away.

Readers might be interested in the later-day resolvement of my relationship with these men.

Matty McIntyre died in 1920 without ever shaking my hand and letting bygones be bygones.

Charlie Schmidt died in 1932, and we parted friends. Before then, Charlie would even weep a few tears when he thought of how it had once been with us. The Dutchman was a grand man, and he knew how much I liked him.

Twilight Ed Killian wrote to me one day years after his big league days were ended. He was working in a Studebaker plant in Detroit and thought there might be enough snap left in the old soupbone to pick up a few dollars in an industrial league. "Ty, it's been tough for me," he wrote. "If I had a pair of shoes and a glove, I could make this team and it would help."

"Ed," I wrote back, "present yourself at the Spalding's sports good store in Detroit and order the best—anything you need. I'll phone them and make sure your order is filled. I hope you win every game."

How small seem these events of the past weighed against the long haul of life . . . yet how large they loomed for me at the time.

It has been widely written that the hazers turned me from a cheerful young fellow into a lone wolf. My rugged style of play is supposed to date from my baptism at Detroit. The fact is that the clique did me a tremendous favor. Although I hated them as much as they hated me, in driving me off by myself, they gave me time to think. I ate alone, roomed alone, and walked alone. In off hours, I couldn't take in a vaudeville show every night. Pool halls, bowling alleys, and saloons didn't interest me. And I wasn't much of a reader in those days. Sitting in my room or taking long hikes, I had only baseball to think about—in particular, pitchers who were handcuffing me at the plate. In an exhibition game, Rube Manning, later of the Highlanders, had fanned me three times. Doc White of the White Sox threw a drop I couldn't fathom—he whiffed me four times running. There were others, mostly left-handers, who threatened to drive me out of the league.

What's more, the attitude of my teammates gave me the extra incentive of becoming a top player in order to show them up. There were a lot of things I couldn't do on the field that even some minor leaguers I'd seen could do. More than ever, I wanted to improve.

So, stretched on my hotel bed or walking the streets, I thought . . . and all at once I could picture Doc White on the mound as plain as day. In my mental conjuring, I suddenly saw what he was doing to me, and how I could counteract it.

With a left-hander throwing to a lefty batter, the ball curves away from you, leaving little time for a good look at it. I'd been standing well up in the batter's box. By dropping back as far as possible, I'd have an extra split-second to judge the pitch. White had to pitch to the plate. Two feet of advantage would be mine if I moved back. Furthermore, I saw that the edge would increase still more if I could hit the ball in the direction it was breaking—in other words, poke it into left field instead of pulling it to right. To hit to the opposite field, I'd have to close my stance, dropping my rear foot back a couple of inches, choke the bat and punch the ball rather than take a full cut at it.

I caught up with White, finally. Using the new style, I got under the ball as it broke over the plate and touched him for four base hits in one game. He never bothered me again. I didn't exactly feast on all lefties, but I began to get my share of safeties. By mid-1906, despite the hazers, I was above .300 in the averages, and climbing. A game against the Beaneaters of Boston sticks in my mind as a turning point. Cy Young—who'd thrown the first big league perfect game in 24 years not much earlier—was blazing them in with his usual needle-threading control and shrewd ability to discover a man's weakness. Cy had been a rail-splitter as a kid. He'd developed an arm as wonderful as any ever hung on a pitcher. Cy had set a record of 23 hitless innings in '04. He'd pitched both ends of a double-header and won both. He'd won 30 or more games in five seasons. Until now, I'd had little luck against the amazing Mr. Denton True Young—who finished his career with more victories (511) than any pitcher who ever lived.

Cy allowed us just seven hits that day. In the opening frame, with a Tiger on base, he nicked the corner of the plate for two

28

strikes on me. Standing deep in the box, I waited for the curve ball and put it against the right-center boards for a double. That extra instant to time the ball was the difference. Two singles followed, and I'd had a day against Cy Young to treasure forever.

A yellowed clipping also reminds me of "Red John" Powell, and a game at Sportsman's Park, St. Louis. I'd never been able to reach the spitballing Powell for an extra base hit. The Detroit *Journal* told it like this:

TIGERS SWALLOW
THE BROWNS WHOLE

"The crowd of 11,000 bade Tyrus to hit 'er out. Obedient lad. He took a strike. Big Powell handed him another whizzer in the same spot. Bow-ee! The ball shot over Bobby Wallace's head at shortstop, buzzing like a swarm of bees. It hit the left-field fence like an 8-inch bullet hitting a battleship. When the high-salaried Mr. George Stone passed the ball into the higher-salaried Mr. Wallace, the low-salaried Mr. Cobb was heading for third. Mr. Wallace shot the ball to Mr. Joe Yeager, but the low-salaried Mr. Cobb came a low-down trick. He slid into the high-salaried Mr. Yeager so hard that that prehensile gentleman was jarred loose from the ball.

"Meanwhile, Mr. Dee Jones of the Tigers had scored and a 10–2 rout of the Browns had begun."

I see by that ancient clip that in the ninth inning I had a home run on top of the triple off Powell . . . breaking my famine, and convincing me I was on the right track. As my sophomore season ended, I'd upped my average 80 points to .320. The men who'd guyed me into living a friendless life had been my benefactors—most unwittingly. From then on, a poor hitter became a pretty good one.

But I still had the problem of killing the long hours between games. I came up with several solutions. I loved dancing, and enrolled in a school of ballroom terpsichore. The veteran Tiger infielder, Bobby Lowe, and his wife, took pity on a kid and invited me to dinner. One night we were strolling past a St. Louis store window and I stopped short. On display was a gorgeous watch, made of three kinds of gold. A sign under it read: "TO BE AWARDED THE BATTING CHAMPION OF THE AMERICAN LEAGUE, 1907."

I thought of my .320 mark of the current season—quite a bit short of the .422 and .381 posted by Larry Lajoie and the .376 of Ed Delahanty that had captured the prize in the past.

"Bob," I said to Lowe, "if hard work will do it, I'm going to win that watch."

"Don't be in a hurry, Tyrus," said Lowe. "It took me ten years to learn to be a ballplayer. You've only been up here for two."

"I'm going to win it," I repeated.

Maybe it was then that I chose baseball, forever, irrevocably, as a career. I'd aspired to be a surgeon, a composer, or a scholar, like my father, in my 'teen years, but that glittering challenge in the window seemed to me a guiding star, pointing the course of my life.

With a goal to reach, I felt I could take anything the Tigers or the opposition dished out to me.

As another way to beat loneliness, I buddied around with a cigar-store owner, Frank Dean. Frank could get free passes for the Detroit Opera House—I heard my first Chopin, Bach, and Beethoven concerts, and thrilled to them.

But the best time-killer of all was to reach Washington, Boston, or New York on a road trip and map out a sightseeing tour for myself. Each morning, armed with an itinerary, I'd start out. I gawked my way through Ford's Theater, Mount Vernon, the Statue of Liberty, the Boston Tea Party docks, and every museum and art gallery I could find. Once, old man Moran, head of the Secret Service, invited me to visit the Subtreasury vaults at the Bureau of Engraving.

"How'd you like to hold seventeen million dollars in your hands?" he asked.

I did, and it got into the newspapers, pictures and all. There was hell to pay. Federal officials put through a rule against visitors fondling the government's cash.

Meanwhile, I was beginning to kick up my heels on the base paths, using a technique I'd worked out through observation and deduction. Runners, it seemed to me, were leaving their feet too soon when sliding. With those long take-offs at the bag, they surrendered maneuverability and sometimes failed to reach the base for lack of momentum. My idea was to hold the initiative to the last instant. Then I'd give it the bing-bing—a fast fallaway slide either to the right or left. You could hook with a toe, or swing your body far out and sweep your hand over the base, or use any of many variations. I went at base-running boldly—and on that subject, more later.

However, in 1906 my 23 stolen bases didn't impress the Detroit critics as a ticket to longevity in the league. One of them prophesied just before I packed my bags for the October trip home to Georgia:

"With his zany, neck-risking style, young Cobb will burn himself out within very few seasons. Unlike the phlegmatic Sam Crawford, who will be around long after Cobb is forgotten, he is much too wild and reckless to keep his arms, legs and head intact.

"He behaves as if he was fighting the Second Battle of Bull Run."

Remembering who won *both* battles at Bull Run, in '61 and '62, I didn't mind the criticism too much. I headed for the Georgia homeland with far more confidence than I'd had fourteen months earlier.

2
My Father Makes a Point

"Proud with the proud—yet courteously proud."

My father, a lifelong scholar and educator, was determined to drum that precept of Lord Byron into me when I was a shirttail kid. "Hell is paved with big pretensions, Tyrus," he'd lecture me. "Always be on the side of right, always play it square, always be modest."

He spotted the false pride that was growing in me as early as my twelfth year. Cobb—originally spelled Cobbs in England and with a coat of arms to herald it—was an illustrious name in Georgia, North Carolina, and Virginia from the earliest Colonial days on. Years before I saw the light of day, twenty-seven Cobbs had achieved varying degrees of note in the law, military, medical, mercantile and agricultural fields. This fact I knew all too well.

Our community of Narrows, Banks County, Georgia, where I was born December 18, 1886, was a struggling place—corn and cotton were the subsistence crops and the hellish damage of a great war only twenty years earlier was far from repaired. My own family's lot was happier. We had status. Somehow the idea of staring at the rump of a balky mule while I steered a plow behind him didn't strike me as fitting work.

However, my father, Professor William Herschel Cobb, was more than the respected schoolmaster and mathematics instructor in the towns of Lavonia, Harmony Grove, Carnesville, and Royston. Recently he'd become a landowner. With upward of one hundred acres of tillable bottom soil, he had Negroes to work it . . . and also a son whom he saw needed some comeuppance.

"Ten acres," he said, pointing to a plot of land that seemed to me to stretch to Tennessee. "Eight of cotton, two of corn. Tyrus, I want you to get that ground ready for crop-planting."

A certain young lady had attracted my attention, in a vague sort of way, and whenever I saw her coming, I picked the lowest spot on the field I could find. I'd hide out there until she had passed. I was ashamed to have her see me in overalls doing manual labor.

I plowed for miles behind a gray horse and a mule. By now I was coming on fifteen, but as a "townie," rather than a farm boy, I needed instruction in keeping the plowshare straight and the reins untangled. My teacher was Uncle Ezra, a patient old black. I'd never been required to do such mean and grimy work. You can bet my father stayed close to make sure I didn't cut and run.

For there was always a ball game going on nearby, and I could hear the yells . . . but I wasn't in it.

At around this age, I was well-enough versed in Cobbian history to know that in 1611 Joseph Cobb had arrived from England to settle on the James River in Virginia, where his home "Cobham" had been a Southern mansion of note. In Britain stood a village named Cobham. In Albemarle County, Virginia, there was, and still is, a village of Cobham, named for an early ancestor of mine. Among these personages was Thomas Willis Cobb, an emigré from Virginia to Georgia who held a colonelcy in the Revolutionary War and lived to be one hundred and eleven years old, with his great-great-great grandchildren at his side. His son, Thomas, became a United States Senator in 1824. Cobb County, Georgia, was laid off in 1832 in his honor. The bloodline that had produced George Washington had blended with Cobb blood in marriage. We had everything on our family tree, including dashing Indian fighters, pro- and anti-slavery exponents, and generals. One I'd especially admired in reading about was Thomas Reade Rootes Cobb, born in 1823, and *facile princeps* at the University of Georgia—a phenomenal student, author of *Cobb on Slavery*, first codifier of Georgia's laws and commander of Cobb's Legion in the War between the States. A brigadier general famed for his flaming bravery, he was defending a field across the road from his family home at Fredericksburg when a shellburst severed his femoral artery.

33

General Robert E. Lee said at his burial, "Know ye not that there is a prince and a great man fallen this day?"

I was a Cobb and stuck behind a mule that broke wind when the breeze was the wrong way. I resented it deeply.

Unhappily, then—but fortunately over the long pull—I had a stern and strong father. He was a big, impressive, fine-looking man with eyes that bored through you. He was remarkably versatile—mayor of Royston, a state senator, county school commissioner, and editor of the Royston *Record*, in addition to his teaching. My father was born in rural North Carolina. In his early twenties, he met my mother, Amanda. She was a woman of warmth, grace, and strength, the daughter of Captain Caleb Chitwood of Banks County, a well-to-do plantation owner. I was their first child. John Paul came two years later. Then Florence Leslie, about five years later.

How my father came to pick my given name I'm not entirely sure, but the story that it stems from Tyr, the Norse god of war, is false. Father was an avid reader of ancient history. And the Tyrians of Tyre, the ancient Phoenician seaport, appealed to him. Cleopatra wore a silken gown of famous Tyrian purple. Tyrus, a Tyrian leader, resisted the Roman invasion, before Alexander slaughtered the population, and from him comes my name.

There was still another powerful male influence in my early life: my grandfather, John Cobb—the squire of a section of the Blue Ridge Mountains near Murphy, North Carolina. Summertimes I was allowed to visit Grandpa and Grandma Cobb. I couldn't wait to make the 100-odd-mile trip.

From miles around, settlers came to John Cobb, who held no official office, to arbitrate their disputes. He was a legend in his time—an anti-slavery Republican, although he'd fought for the Confederacy, a farmer by vocation, a wise and eloquent soul. He settled everything from wife disputes to boundary feuds. Short and lean, about 5 feet 6, he had a bad back which stamped an expression of pain permanently on his face. Yet he was always ready to jump into an adventure with me.

"Let's go track us a bear," he'd say to me. Grandpa had killed twenty-five bear and over one hundred deer, and, although we might not find one, he'd dramatize past hunts for me until I shivered with excitement. "There he was, glaring at me red-eyed," he'd say, "—a slavering monster 12 feet tall, fangs as long as a corncob, claws on him the size of a scythe . . . looked like a field piece couldn't bring him down . . . and me with just a long-rifle."

"What happened?" I'd gasp.

Grandpa would light his pipe slowly. He'd look down at me solemnly.

"Tyrus, if I'd missed—you wouldn't be here today."

Before his vivid description of the battle with the bear ended, I'd be exhausted and watching the woods fearfully. Grandpa couldn't talk without being dramatic. I don't think we ever stumbled on a bear—but possum and squirrel were plentiful, and I owned a little old bench-legged hunting hound named Old Bob. He lived with me at my folks' home in Royston. Which meant smuggling him aboard the train to Grandpa's place across the North Carolina border.

Once, I remember, the conductor stopped to punch my ticket. "You're quite a reader, young man," he observed.

Newspapers and copies of the *Police Gazette* were piled on the floor of my seat to the height of my knees. A regular blizzard of literature.

"All my family reads a lot," I replied, with one foot on Old Bob's head, under the paper. "My father's a professor."

The conductor wanted to discuss the subject, but I fell into a coughing fit, which covered up the *whuffs* coming from half-smothered Old Bob. By the skin of our teeth, the two of us made it once more to Grandpa's place.

John Cobb—somehow, on his slim farmer earnings—put all four of his sons through college. And they came back to his Republican stronghold as Democrats. The arguments! The boys had book-learning to back their political beliefs, but Grandpa, without formal schooling, destroyed them with his logic. It became evident to me that book-education wasn't everything—not when my wonderful grandsire was elected foreman of the County Grand Jury and rode down from his mountain throne 23 miles to the railhead and on to Asheville, North Carolina, to render verdicts on the flatlanders below. A decision I'd have to make before long—between college and a career no other Cobb had elected—began to take shape here.

Grandpa was an opportunist, too—a trait I was later alleged to have displayed on the diamond. Nights, I'd huddle snugly under

Grandma's homemade comforters, and I'd hear Old Bob bellering in the woods. I knew what it meant, but I coveted my warm bed.

But at 2 or 3 A.M., here would come the candle . . . with Grandpa's nightcap and beard behind it. His wife wove the family clothes from homespun; with vegetable dye of her own mixing she colored their garments. Grandpa's ax and drawing knife had formed oaken furniture that would last for generations. Nothing was wasted—especially food.

"Tyrus," he'd say, shaking me as I faked sleep. "He's calling you. Old Bob's out there just begging for your help. Up you get, son."

So I'd have to drag myself out there, chop down the tree which contained the possum Old Bob had cornered and polish him off for the family pot.

As a practicing healer, I'd match my grandmother against many of the medical men I've since known, although roots, barks, herbs, and other backwoods specifics comprised her total dispensatory. One night a storm glutted the creek, and next morning I dashed down to see the damage. I drove a sharp ash prong through my big toe. I came howling in agony to the house. Infection of wounds killed many a backwoodsman, but Grandma neatly removed the prong, cleansed the hole with a homemade antispetic and soaked it in buttermilk. She fed me something she'd brewed and I fell straight to sleep. The hole healed without infection or scar.

Tearing into her cornpone and home-cured meat, I ate myself into a twelve-year-old stupor, after which, to quote a philosopher: "To eat is human; to digest, divine." But I didn't feel divine. My plumbing was stopped up totally.

Grandma spread my eye with her thumb and finger.

"Tyrus," she diagnosed, "you have a torpid liver. Come with me."

Carrying a hatchet, she marched me into the woods until we located a young black walnut tree. Grandma scalped it down to the sap, chopped off pieces and back at the house placed them in a saucepan. She brewed the sap, adding mysterious potions, until she had a tea as black as ink. All the time, I was edging for the door.

"Drink this!"

She poured it down me—despite my yells at the taste of the awful stuff.

A little bit later, I was sitting on the front porch, reading the latest sporting news in the Atlanta *Journal* as reported by my favorite author, named Grantland Rice. Suddenly, I knew I'd never make it to the Chic Sale located on the far side of the house. I lit out for the orchard on the dead run and just got under the wire. And I spent the rest of the day there.

Toward sundown, when I returned, limply, to the house, Grandma was busy canning. She smiled at me. "Feel better, Tyrus?" she said.

Any time Grandma mixed medicine, she got results that made the Castoria Company and Lydia Pinkham look like bush leaguers.

Some days, my Aunt Norah, who'd studied piano at a Cincinnati conservatory, would drive me by buggy into the villages of Andrews and Murphy, so I could find myself a ball game. My grandparents had nothing against my ballplaying. My father wasn't so agreeable.

His academic mind searched for—but found nothing useful—in whacking a string ball around a cow pasture and then chasing madly about the bases while an opponent tried to retrieve said pill and sock you with it. That was one of the rules of town ball, the first bat-and-glove game I played. If the defensive fielder could hit the base-runner with the ball, the latter was out. Also, a home run entitled the hitter to another turn at bat. If you kept on homering, you could swing all day. In Carnesville, Georgia, first, and, later, when we moved to Royston, I hungered for competition. It wasn't that I gave baseball a second thought as a career—skinny ninety-pounder that I was. My overwhelming need was to prove myself a real man. In the classroom, I was merely adequate—except for a flair for oratory, which brought me a few prizes. I couldn't hope to match my celebrated father for brains. In town ball—pitted against older boys and men at the age of fourteen—was the chance to become more than another schoolboy and the son of Professor Cobb.

The professor's attitude was "Quit fooling around and settle down to some serious work." At fourteen, he felt I should have formed a definite lifetime plan. To encourage scholarliness, he let me write an editorial for the Royston *Record*, of which newspaper he was editor.

I thought, He's my father and of course he's right. I felt guilty that some great, vaulting ambition hadn't seized me beyond handling hard hoppers and line drives. Wracking my mind, I decided that by becoming a doctor might satisfy the situation. Doc Moss, the local sawbones, liked me, and even let me assist in an operation.

It came about when a white boy of Royston shot a Negro. Late one night, Doc and a colleague drove out to the shanty where the wounded lad lay, with me tagging along. They set up surgical operations on a dirty kitchen table. Water was boiled in a food-flecked kitchen vessel. Oil lamp was the only illumination.

The bullet had entered the boy at the belly. He was thrashing about in terrible pain. Doc Moss didn't bother to ask how I re-acted to the sight of blood. He just handed me a dousing mask and a bottle of chloroform and said, "You're the anesthetist, Tyrus."

Well, I put the boy under without much trouble, and the two docs opened him up and after failing to locate the bullet, began searching for a perforation of the intestine. Both being elderly gentlemen, their eyes grew tired under the oil lamp.

"You look, Ty," said Doc Moss. "Damn' blasted if I can find any puncture."

I discovered that blood and exposed matter didn't make me shudder, and I went over the intestine until I found a bruise. But no hole. "Aha," said Doc Moss, "the bullet slanted off somewhere into his side. He's lucky."

They sewed him up and the boy recovered.

Somehow I didn't feel the call, deeply, to become a physician, although at around fourteen or fifteen I needed one myself. We were butchering hogs and I foolishly left my .22 rifle loaded and cocked leaning against a fence. When I reached for it, a branch under the rifle sprung back. And *crack!*

The bullet entered at my collarbone and knocked me kicking. After determining that I wasn't dead, my father rushed me to Atlanta. At the turn of the century, X ray was on the crude side. The doctors never did find the bullet in my clavicle area. For years afterward, I had a burning sensation in the shoulder—that bullet is still in there.

What fascinated me more than medicine was making my own bats with my sidekick, Joe Cunningham, whose father constructed water wheels and coffins in a Royston shed. Joe's father had plenty of tools. The woods were full of prime ash. When I could escape school, plowing chores, and Baptist Sunday School, I put those homemade bats to work by trying out for the Royston Reds—composed mostly of husky eighteen- to twenty-five-year-olds. I wasn't yet fifteen and I was spindly. I guess I swung a bat with my hands spread a few inches apart from the very beginning. I wasn't strong enough to get around on the ball any other way. That grip was to arouse considerable curiosity later and answer many a major league hitting problem for me. But it began not from any acute deduction on my part that a spaced handhold was ideally suited for punching the ball for singles and doubles, but from necessity.

I can't say that the Reds were overwhelmed at my arrival. I had sent away for "How to Sprint" books advertised in the *Police Gazette* and spent hours practicing fast starts and pumping my knees high. Although I had plenty of speed, I looked like a horsefly by comparison with those full-grown ball hawks who played for the "First Nine" of Royston. But they couldn't shoo me away. I was determined to earn one of those cardinal-red uniforms they so splendidly dashed about in.

My first position on the diamond was catcher. A pitch glanced off a bat and caught me in the eye. End of catching. I went out to shortstop, and got in the way of the first hard clod-cutter—off the bat of a grown man—I'd ever tried to handle. It was smashed straight at me. I couldn't duck without dishonor . . . something kept me from pulling my head . . . some instinct told me on what bounce to scoop the ball.

I made the play and threw out the runner.

"Not bad, kid," one of the big guys said. "Let's see what you can do with the stick."

Swinging on the first pitch by a raw-boned right-hander, I shot it over the infield for a clean single.

That bat literally tingled in my hand. It gave off an electric impulse that traveled through my body and told me I'd found the one endeavor that I could do well. I hadn't felt this way when my father lectured on the wonders of the universe, or when I entered, and won, an elocution contest or when I'd helped Doc Moss perform surgery. Instinctively, I knew I was in the right place.

But my glove was a disgrace. It was just a tattered piece of leather I'd sewn together. Down at the dry-goods store was a model I couldn't live without. But I didn't dare ask my father to buy it.

Slipping into my father's library, I selected two of his more-expensive books, traded them for the glove and complimented myself on a deal well made. It wasn't stealing, the way I saw it. The library contained books by the score. I had no glove. The exchange was merited. Anyway, who'd notice the volumes were missing?

Professor Cobb did. And he took another view of it when he discovered that empty space on his shelves. As I've said, he was a big man and a stern one.

"Tyrus," he said in his quietly ominous way, "I want to talk to you." He led me into the library and shut the door.

This was going to be worse than Grandma's black walnut tea.

3

Moment of Decision—
How I Almost Quit

Let us draw the curtain of mercy over the scene that took place in father's study. I wasn't able to forget what happened there for many, many months. The upshot was that when Royston's Reds played in such adjacent towns as Elberton and Harmony Grove. I stayed at home—inhaling clay dust behind a plow attached to the family mule.

The professor's purpose was to curb my terrific desire to play ball because he felt it was leading me straight into the devil's arms. Town ball games often ended in a Donnybrook. When the town mathematician had added up the score, arguments would explode and both sides would use fists and rocks to decide what hadn't been settled on the diamond. It was as gentlemanly as a kick in the crotch.

"Tyrus," said father, "I want you to consider a career in the Army. A West Point appointment isn't impossible for you."

"I don't think I want to become an officer," I said.

"Then *what?*"

I didn't know, and it was back to the plow. I'd work a good part of the day, forbidden to play ball, then I'd bribe a hired hand to take my place, rush home and change into a uniform, and get into the game for a few innings. Uncle Ezra covered up for me. But when Professor Cobb learned I was truant, his words were strong and discouraging.

It was the catcher for the Reds—Bob McCreary, who worked in

the town bank and also managed the team—who finally cracked the ice a bit with father. He assured my parent that I had talent, that baseball had its healthful, muscle-building aspects. On the promise that McCreary, a brother Mason of my father's, would keep a sharp eye on my welfare and conduct, I was allowed to make a road trip with the team to Elberton, Georgia.

The Elbertons were a pretty catty bunch, and we had trouble matching base hits and put-outs with them. Their pitcher was a lanky fireballer with good control for an amateur. I managed a couple of singles, then we came into the final inning with the score tied, and a Royston runner on base.

Being the batter on the spot, I was faintly surprised that my knees didn't knock. I felt comfortable despite the pressure of the hollering Elberton fans. I just felt that I'd get enough wood on the ball to do some damage.

No poet, however great, could describe my sensation when I cowtailed a pitch for my third single of the day—the game-breaking hit. We'd won, and I returned to Royston the boy hero. Once an athlete feels the peculiar thrill that goes with victory and public praise, he's bewitched. He can never get away from it.

Shortly after that, I was made the regular shortstop and occasional outfielder of the Reds. I didn't know it, but my father had been making secret inquiries as to whether I had any real ability, and the reports were flattering. Still he strongly felt I'd be thrown into contact with pool-hall ruffians. After a game with Harmony Grove, I detected a slight change in his viewpoint.

In the eighth inning, when Harmony Grove had three men on base and two out, a towering drive was lifted to left-center. It looked like a potential two-bagger. Something told me that our left-fielder was going to miss it, and I ran behind him at top speed. He backed up on the ball and just managed to fingertip it. At full tilt, and by adding a dive, I managed to scoop the ball one-handed off his glove with the catch that saved the game. In all my life, I never made a stop I thrilled to more.

The crowd whooped and threw coins—I must have picked up $11 in small change, the first money I ever made from baseball. The Royston *Record*, of which my father was editor, had no sporting page. All the same, a full account of the game was carried . . . and

I suspected that the author was a mathematics professor temporarily turned baseball writer.

In paternal-filial relationship, until I was almost seventeen, my father held me down, withholding acceptance of me as the man I yearned to be. He was critical, very strict, and I couldn't reach him. One turning point may have been my new willingness to work at cultivating the crops. What had been a meaningless chore took on new significance when the first plants I'd sowed showed above ground. I saw farming in new light. My handiwork had become a live thing, a growing, breathing reward for my labors. After that, I pitched in with vigor and wasn't ashamed of my overalls and grimy face—passing girls or not.

It was the sweetest thing in the world to be fully accepted by my father. All at once, he was willing to hear my ideas, discuss them, and even exchange opinions. We'd talk about crop production, English import of cotton which competed with our Georgia output, and I never felt closer to him than when he said "Do you think we should sell now, or hold on for a better price?" To learn more about cotton, I landed a job with a local factor, or commission agent. Already I was well-versed in pulverizing the seed bed, drop-seeding, chopping and hoeing, the maturing of the bolls and picking of the lint. Under the factor, I learned about ginning, baling, grading, and transport of the product to market. Nearly twenty years later, when post-World War I cotton was short, I used my firsthand knowledge to move into the trading market. The shares I acquired brought me a profit of $155,000 before long . . . and led me into many an intricate speculation in commodities, the automotive industry and other issues.

We went to buy a mule, my father and I. Instead of dismissing my opinion, he welcomed it. We circled the critter and compared notes. "He looks a little long in the barrel to me," I ventured.

My father nodded. "And notice his hock action—it's on the draggy side." We made sudden jumps at the mule to note his steadiness, jabbed our hands at his eyes to test possible blindness. We didn't buy the mule. But Professor Cobb "bought" me as his son in the year 1903—a great year of my life.

For he was not to be with us much longer.

Somewhat reluctantly, I professionalized myself by accepting $2.50 per game for two contests with Anderson, South Carolina, against

Hartwell. I earned my pay. Yet to me it was an ungrateful and greedy thing I'd done, since as a pro I'd be unable to compete in college. And my father's dearest wish was that I attend a Georgia university. If not that, a West Point or Annapolis appointment seemed fairly well assured, since my scholarship had improved and, as a state senator, my father was not without influence.

I vowed I'd never take another quarter for playing ball, and in country games I didn't.

Early in 1904, the South Atlantic Baseball League was in the process of formation and I secretly wrote letters of application to every entry, requesting a tryout. Only one reply returned, from Augusta. It merely said:

"Tyrus Cobb: This will notify you that you are free to join our spring practice, with the understanding that you will pay all your expenses."

I agreed in spades. If that one team hadn't answered, I wonder if I'd ever have made baseball a career, for my ambition hung by a tenuous thread . . . suspended between my duty to my father, and my own desire. An Augusta contract arrived, which I signed without telling Professor Cobb, and calling for a $50 a month salary if I made the team. I did confide the deed to my mother, who patted my hand and said, "If you must—." Faced with the desperate need for railway fare, meal money, hotel upkeep, and whatnot, I stalled furiously until the night before I was to catch the Southern Railroad spur line south. Then I had no choice. I said, "Father, I'd like to speak to you."

He was as austere as ever, but he gave me his complete attention.

I confessed to the contractual agreement, outlined my reasons, and waited for the roof to fall in. He spoke gravely, not heatedly.

"Beyond any advice I can give you is this: if you fail to develop your mind, you will become a mere muscle-worker the rest of your days. You are seventeen and this is the decisive moment for you. In baseball, you can't help but fall into the company of a riffraffish type of men who drink and carouse and lead a pointless life."

Striding up and down the room, hands behind his back, he gave me the full picture of the future I was throwing away—measured, hard-hitting words which bore down on the absolute necessity for an education.

"I just have to go," I kept breaking in.

It was three o'clock in the morning before he began to tire. I think it was because he knew that, if he refused my wish, I'd be out the window during the night and hiking the eight miles to the next rail station. My telescope grip was here, packed and ready, as evidence.

Father walked to his roll-top desk, sat down and began writing checks. He wrote six of them—each for $15. My guess always has been that he feared I'd shoot the bankroll before proving or disproving my highly dubious point if he handed me a lump sum.

"You've chosen. So be it, son," he said. "Go get it out of your system, and let us hear from you."

I left Royston scared. What if I broke a leg or got beaned or rammed into a fence and crippled myself? What if I wasn't good enough to last past the first day? I'd seen little of the caliber of players I was off to vie with. My Aunt Norah's parting words—"Tyrus, you're going straight to hell if you defy your father!"—worried around inside my head all the way to Augusta.

The people of Royston, however, made quite a thing out of the fact that Tyrus was big-city bound, and I arrived loaded with letters of introduction to various Augustans who'd help me over the bumps and shield me from wickedness. The trouble was, no one thought to write a note to my first manager, Con Strouthers. He barely looked at me out at the park. "Get into the clubhouse and get dressed," Strouthers grunted, and walked off. No attendants being around, I had to hunt for ten minutes before I discovered the team quarters.

Emerging in my bright-red Royston uniform, I must have been a laugh to those pros. I was the lone candidate who had paid my own way to camp and who was buying my own steaks and bed. I hustled balls and hung wistfully around the batting box, not invited to take my swings. No one expected anything of me. They saw I could run with good speed and could catch a ball. Nothing unusual about that. The assumption was that I'd be back in Royston a few trains later. Through the exhibition schedule, I didn't get into a game. Then came the grand opening-day contest against Columbia, South Carolina.

Strouthers, with a sour look, sent me to center field. Our first baseman, Harry Bussey, was in contractual difficulties, ineligible to play, which meant shifting McMillin, the center fielder to first.

With only a 17- or 18-man squad, Strouthers had no one else to play in the middle field.

When I batted my second or third time—I'm not sure which—Engle, the Columbia pitcher, fired one into my groove. Lining it into left field and over the fielder's head, I tore around the bases as if my pants were on fire. Before the ball was relayed in, I was sliding into the plate for an inside-the-park homer. This isn't so hard, I thought. When I doubled off Engle next time up, I was positive of it.

Two days later, Strouthers had news for me. In my second game, I managed a base hit and a stolen bag, and felt sure Augusta would keep me on, and then Strouthers said: "Come into my office."

This would be it, I was sure—the proffering of a regular contract. Which meant that my room and meal expense would be picked up by the club.

"Bussey just got a telegram reinstating him," said Strouthers. "You're released."

I was too stunned to understand him for a moment.

"But . . . but I'm hitting for you, Mr. Strouthers," I said, choking up.

"Can't use you," he said shortly. "You're a free agent now and that means you can do business with any club you can hook on with."

I went out of there, angry and sick. Back at the hotel, I ran into Thad Hayes, a young pitcher from Mobile who'd drawn his own pink slip two days earlier. Thad said he had a friend who was managing a semipro team in Anniston, Alabama. "I've talked to him, and he needs a pitcher," said Thad. "He also said that if there's an outfielder around looking for work, he can use him. That's you, kid."

"I don't know, Thad," I replied. "When I left home, my father told me to come down here and get all this baseball out of my system and then come home and go to college. I'll have to talk to him first."

Over the phone, I told Professor Cobb of my dismissal. From my hangdog voice he must have known that I was on the verge of throwing over the whole thing. At which, he gave me the greatest surprise—and lift—of my life.

His voice was as commanding as ever. I fully expected him to order me home, but he demanded, "Well, if that's the case, what are you going to do?"

I fumbled, and then answered, "There's a job open with a team over in Anniston. . . ."

"Go after it," he said. "And I want to tell you one other thing—*don't come home a failure.*"

In giving me his blessing, his sanction of my quest for success in my hour of defeat, my father put more determination in me than even he knew. I had the shivers when I hung up. I hurried back to Thad and told him to count me in.

My $90 having dwindled, Hayes and I crammed ourselves into an upper berth for the train ride to Anniston. We were stiff and sore upon arriving. But we still managed to look like the berries when we joined Anniston, a team that wasn't in Organized Baseball, but was a conglomeration of Southern college boys and semipros competing in what was called the Southeastern League. Thad and I were well up to this caliber of play. In fact, we strutted a bit. After all, we were professionals deigning to associate with lowly bushers. Anniston was impressed enough to pay me $65 a month, throwing in room and board with a family named Darden. Mr. Darden was a well-to-do steel executive who set a table that was most welcome. I began to put pounds on my slight 150-pound frame.

It was little trouble to make the starting line-up and before long I was in the running for the league batting championship. It struck me that *someone* in Augusta or Atlanta must have heard of my feats. I began haunting the public library, checking each issue of the Georgia metropolitan papers for some mention of my name that would let my family know I was doing well. Earlier, I'd sent home a few one- and two-line squibs which mentioned some play or other I'd made, knowing that Mother would relay them to Father. But it wasn't the same as getting a break in, say, the Atlanta *Journal*, to which Father religiously subscribed.

Wondering how to bring this about, I remembered that the best-read columnist in my state was Grant Rice, the *Journal*'s sporting editor. Presently, Rice began to receive letters and postcards from "interested fans," such as:

"Tyrus Raymond Cobb, the dashing young star with Anniston,

Ala., is going great guns. He is as fast as a deer and undoubtedly a phenom."

A "Mr. Jones" signed that one.

Another Alabaman named "Jackson" went even further and forecast a sure big-league career for Cobb, suggesting that Rice should be the first sportswriter to proclaim it. There followed more letters —"Cobb had three hits yesterday, made two sensational catches"— signed by Smith, Brown, McIntyre, and Kelly.

In sending these to Rice, I used every type of handwriting I could manage—round hand, slanting hand, Spencerian, Palmer method, and even a scrawly left-handed script. Rice ignored them for a long time. Then, one day at the library, a box on the sports page leaped out at me.

Grant Rice had run a short feature in self-defense against the barrage of Cobb mail. He wrote that "rumors had reached Atlanta from numerous sources that over in Alabama there's a young fellow named Cobb who seems to be showing an unusual lot of talent."

I was happy. I hoped my father would see it, and he did. But not until years later did I learn that he carried the clipping in his wallet and showed it to his state senate friends. For he never let me know that he prized my writeups.

Wonderful Granny Rice, my great friend of later years, didn't awaken to the fact that he'd been flim-flammed by a mere babe until a long time afterward, when we shared the speaker's platform at a General Electric Company banquet. Now that we were both grizzled veterans, I decided the time had come to confess all. When I was finished, Grant just looked at me and shook his massive head. "Why did you do it?" he asked.

"I was in a hurry," I told him.

The Anniston interlude didn't last long. I was leading the Southeastern League with a .370 average when the Augusta club decided it could use me, after all. For one thing, my nemesis, Con Strouthers, had been dropped as manager. Returning to Augusta, I managed a modest .237 for my on-again-off-again season's work there. My bat work may have been light, but the fans liked my peppery attitude. When Strouthers released me earlier that season, the fans had made it hot for him. That red Royston uniform of mine seemed to stick in their memory. So I finished my first go-round as a pro and wondered what would happen next.

With so many fine ballplayers in Dixie, would I be forgotten over the winter?

Andy Roth, the new Augusta manager, seemed to think I could cut the mustard in the Sally League, even though some Dixie papers were so unaware of me that they printed my name as "Cyrus Cobb" and "Cy Cobb." That winter, Roth sent me a "feeler" for the 1905 campaign.

While I talked contract with them, my father was observing me closely for signs of a swelled head. I came home from Anniston and showed him where I'd saved $200 and had opened my first bank account. "Very impressive," he said.

There was no liquor on my breath, either, but still he wanted to know more.

One of his fields—corn, wheat, and cotton—had been cultivated for planting, but was not yet sowed. And there were predictions of snow. "I'm worried, Tyrus," said Father.

"Why?" I asked.

"Well, we must get the grain in the ground before it gets too wet. I'm short of hands and don't know what I'm going to do."

I had the answer. Without bothering to change from dress-up shoes to farm boots, I hurried out there, and found a team of horses waiting, fully hitched to a wheat-sower. Uncle Ezra, our main workman, was nowhere in sight. I went to work and toiled until night fell. Next day, same thing. I was all aglow at my ability to help out, never suspecting that Uncle Ezra was in hiding, that there was no labor shortage, that the hitched team was a premeditated trick and that Father was hoping with everything he had that I'd roll up my sleeves as I did. I think that when I sowed that field, he felt successful as a parent—more so by far than when my name made the newspapers.

A Spanish sage has written "What costs little is valued less." I stuck with that thought through a lifetime of baseball contract negotiations—some of them so stormy that I was called all sorts of money-grubber and egotist—and I began with the Augusta salary dickering for 1905. First, I had to be assured that Con Strouthers was nowhere in the picture. I wanted no part of the man who'd released me without a fair trial. Then I demanded $125 a month— quite a salary for an eighteen-year-old with 37 games of Organized Ball behind him. Augusta finally agreed.

Andy Roth, the new manager, ran what was termed a "joy club." That is, the players blithely went through the motions and had nighttime fun. But we were a team long on talent. Nap Rucker, one of our pitchers, went up to Brooklyn in 1907 and won 15 to 22 games a season. We had Eddie Cicotte, later a 29-game winner with the Chicago Americans. Clyde Engle, a catcher, and Ducky Holmes, a pitcher, also made the big league. But Roth held too loose a rein, and as an impressionable kid I fell into the spirit of things. I was fast losing all ambition to go higher in the game. The Augusta surroundings satisfied me pretty well. I had no desire to reach the far-off big league. But in midsummer of 1906, a fateful thing happened to me. Roth was released as manager. George Leidy, an outfielder, succeeded him. Leidy was a sore-armed veteran, but the type who tore into every play with all he had—a team man to the bone.

One night, playing Savannah, I strolled to the outfield with a bag of popcorn in my hand. Alibi Ike, the Ring Lardner character, never was more nonchalant about earning his salary.

We had a 2–0 shutout going when my ex-manager, Roth, hit a fly ball my way. My dilemma was—how to handle the fly without losing my popcorn? I did neither. The popcorn flew one way while the ball bounced off my glove. It was a gross thing to do, and a run scored. We just managed to pull out the game, 2–1. On the bench, the boys joshed me about it, while Leidy stared at me reflectively.

That night, he dropped by my room. Leidy was an old-time minor league star, quiet, fatherly, and big-hearted, with a remarkable understanding of psychology and a way with words which dug deep. He was well aware that I was not yet eighteen and thought playing the clown made me a real joy-team member. The weather was steaming hot, and in those little Georgian towns, riding a trolley car out to an amusement park at night was the thing to do. No one could sleep much before midnight, when it cooled off slightly.

"Let's go for a ride, Ty," George said.

We rode, and he began to talk. Not angrily, but as he said, in disappointment. "Kid, you don't know what you've got. What you did today was most unbecoming any player. But in your case, it's even worse. Baseball is serious work and you have natural ability. Sell yourself that short, and others will, too. You're in a great game, son, and just think of the opportunity awaiting you if you'll study and practice and make the most of what nature gave you. Do you know what you can have?"

George Leidy drew castles in the air. Why, he said, I'd see towns that would make Augusta look like a whistle stop, become famous, earn a fortune, honor my parents, hobnob with great men and, best of all, I'd be true to myself. His hand on my knee, he said, "Ty, I think you can go down in the history books. I honestly believe that you can go on and have every boy in America idolizing you.

"But not unless you stop fooling around and keep your eye on the ball every instant."

Nothing ever affected me much more than those firm, fatherly words. "I'll do what you say," I told him emotionally. Better yet, George showed me what he meant. He knew many of the big-time, inside maneuvers—the hit-and-run, chopping the ball to the opposite field, the double steal, bunting. Out at the park, each morning, just the two of us, George would spread a sweater down the first base line and then step into the pitcher's box. The sweater was on the exact spot where a bunted ball was almost impossible for the defense to field and make the play. "Place it there now, Ty," he said.

For hours, day after day, with an arm long since dead, he threw to me and I bunted. I bunted until I was worn out. Bit by bit, I got the knack of applying the bat squarely but with a withdrawing movement of the arms which softly placed the ball on or near the target. Next, George showed me how to poke a hit-run ball through the hole left by infielders while covering second base. We worked on luring the third baseman in on a faked bunt, then slashing the ball past him. At night, Leidy and I would see a theatrical show or take in an amusement park . . . but always his theme was self-improvement and a firing of my imagination.

Roth had called me a harum-scarum base-runner and held me down. Leidy, after becoming playing manager in mid-1906, turned me loose. He let me hit ahead of him in the line-up and pick my spots. Before long we were working the hit-and-run—and what a thrill it was the first time we succeeded on the play. My first help inside baseball came from Leidy—the reason I later made good in the majors was Leidy. And he never asked to earn a nickel from Ty

Cobb. The time came when I was able to arrange a scouting position for George with the Detroit Tigers—small repayment for the boost he had given me.

I had to improve and concentrate. Leidy would have it no other way. From a .260 hitter that season, I climbed to a .326 mark, which put me in the lead by August for the Sally League batting title. Maybe this story tells something about my new spark:

On a train one day, I met a roly-poly lad from Milledgeville, Georgia, who said his name was Hardy.

"Mine's Cobb," I said. "Tyrus Cobb."

"What's your dodge?" the fat boy inquired.

"I play ball for Augusta," said I.

"What are you, anyway," said Hardy, sizing up my slight frame and unripe features, "the bat boy?"

"Bat boy!" I hollered. "Come out to the game tomorrow and I'll show you what I am!"

Fat boy came and with my pride stung I got a homer, triple, double, and a single, and stole two bases.

My plump acquaintance later became Babe Hardy of the comedy team of Stan Laurel and Oliver Hardy and he never tired of telling the story.

In Macon, Georgia, in August, I had my first hunch that something exceptional was up. After singling, I was edging off first base for a possible steal when the opposition first baseman said to me, "Hey, Cobb, I hear you're going up."

"Going up where?" I asked.

I knew that scouts from Cleveland, Detroit, and other major teams had been following Augusta, but it hadn't crossed my mind that they were interested in me. Not long later, I hurt my thumb while head-first sliding and was recuperating on the bench. Heinie Youngman, a Detroit scout, sat by me, and asked a lot of questions. When I returned to action, I raised my bat mark several points and my stolen bases to 40. August 9 arrived, the blackest of days. A message arrived that my father had been killed. A gun accident in Royston had taken him away from me forever.

In my grief, it didn't matter much when George Leidy told me that I now belonged to the Detroit Tigers of the American Baseball League. I only thought, Father won't know it.

52

Just to correct a badly warped record on my transfer to the majors, it happened this way: Detroit had held spring training in Augusta in '05 and had left behind pitcher Eddie Cicotte, in lieu of certain training expenses, and with the understanding that the Tigers were entitled to the pick of the Augusta team for the additional sum of $500. The man they wanted was Clyde Engle, who could play almost any infield spot plus the outfield—not Kid Cobb. Engle, however, had slowed down in the dog days of August. And Detroit needed outfield help fast. So I was picked up by the scruff of the neck and tossed into the Big Show—for $500 and an added $250 for immediate delivery.

The father I'd loved and respected so much never knew that his six $15 checks set me on the road to a whole new life.

On my last day in Augusta, I was ready to take my turn at bat when I saw a delegation approaching the plate. The mayor of the city was in the lead, followed by others, including a pretty girl. They announced that the fans had taken up a collection and wished to present me with a gold watch.

I was unable to speak. But I had to say something.

Stammering and red-faced, I managed to blurt my thanks, and then I turned to face the pitcher.

Under the circumstances, a hit *had* to be forthcoming. Even a one-base blooper would get me off the spot.

The pitcher wound and I swung from the heels.

He wound again and I swung even harder.

He wound a third time . . . and I couldn't have hit that ball with a six-by-eight if he'd rolled it up to the plate, I was so excited and tightened up.

Ingloriously, I struck out.

The crowd let out a collective sigh of disappointment while I sheepishly walked away. It was one of those moments a ballplayer would like to forget, but never can.

One leather-lunged fan wasn't just disappointed.

"Let Detroit have him!" he roared.

4

Pennant Madness—
And a Boy Grows Up

Soon after the long trip up from Georgia to the biggest burg I'd yet seen (Detroit population: about 300,000 in 1905), I began to suspect that I had worse troubles than earning my spurs with manager Bill Armour's collection of hard-nosed athletes.

Like most eighteen-year-olds, I put off doing anything about it. Aside from the usual childhood ailments and the time I shot myself in the collarbone, I'd always been as healthy as a colt in the Bluegrass.

But I hadn't been a Tiger rookie very long when my throat began to pain me like fury. Burly Germany Schaefer, the second baseman, watched me at the dinner table one night.

"Say, kid," he said curiously, "why do you grip the chair seat with both hands after swallowing your soup?"

"Because it hurts so much," I groaned.

I wanted to take my problem to Armour, but didn't dare. I had the well-founded fear that the small toehold I had on the position of right-fielder with the team would be stolen by another player if I reported sick. So I suffered and covered it up and suffered some more.

Finally, when we made an exhibition game stop in Toledo, pausing at the Boodie House, I was running such a fever and in such agony that I hunted up the house doctor—who was neither a surgeon nor equipped for the treatment I needed. Germany came along to lend support.

"Tonsillitis, and an acute case," the doc diagnosed.

He sat me in a chair, tipped it back and went to work, without anesthetic. My tonsils were in such a condition that they had to be removed in sections. Each time a piece of them came out, blood surged into my mouth, choking me, and I had to demand a rest period. Putting a stranglehold on my neck, the doc would probe and cut for 10 or 15 minutes before letting me collapse on a sofa. Stretched out there, I'd wonder how I could ever take another round in that chair.

"Let's go, son," the M.D. would say cheerfully, brandishing his tonsil-chopper.

He cut me seven times before he was finished, after which I was so weak from pain, loss of blood, and shock that Germany had to half-carry me to bed. The Tigers had a game scheduled next day and you can bet I showed up for it—wobbly, but playing seven innings and making sure I was still around when the game was won. I don't remember getting any sympathy.

A few people remarked that the doc must have been crazy to extract the tonsils so informally. I wondered about that, and checked up on him the following season.

Sure enough, during the winter he had been committed to an asylum for the insane.

Let a modern-day player develop a bit of indigestion or a minor bone chip in his arm and he's clamped into a bed at Johns Hopkins, attended by world-noted specialists, fed by dieticians, and generally treated like a maharaja with the gout. His team pays all the bills. In my day, a sick ballplayer was just another liability—unless he got himself well in a hurry, and cheaply. As a new boy who didn't know how to protest, I even paid my own hospital tab on one occasion.

I'd been with the Tigers little more than a year when a "slider"— an abrasion caused by hitting the hard infield dirt too often in base-steals—became inflamed and filled with pus. Did Frank Navin, the Detroit president, offer me any assistance? Not a nickel's worth. At a Fort Street hospital, the wound was lanced and drained and I paid for the privilege, at a time when I was earning $2400 a season. Navin visited me just once while I was invalided, and kept both hands in his pockets, clutching his bankroll, throughout.

Split a finger fifty years ago and you stuck it in the dirt and kept going. It gives me a wry laugh to hear players today complain about the conditions they labor under. They even find certain parks of the 1960s "tough to play in." In 1907, old Bennett Park in Detroit, as well as other arenas, sprouted grass which had been planted at the wrong time of year and was cow-pasture rough and rutted with holes and soft spots. Where the infield grass met the skinned infield area, there were drop-offs that sent balls flying in all directions. Diamonds were given a quick once-over with a rake maybe once a week, where these days they are scientifically planted, cultivated, and manicured, and dragged smooth before, during, and after games. Drainage was crude and on wet days the outer pastures were marshy, if not worse. Danny McGann, who played for the old Baltimore Orioles, was galloping after a fly ball one day when he suddenly disappeared from sight. Then McGann's hand appeared above the turf, waving in distress. Dan had fallen into a long-abandoned sewer outlet over which a few thin boards, dirt, and grass had been placed.

In the old-time clubhouses, we had nothing. Whirlpool baths, electrotherapy, skilled trainers with all their healing apparatus and hot-water showers were luxuries the Wagners, Lajoies, Speakers, Mathewsons, McGinnitys, Radbourns, Planks, and Tinkers never experienced. We put on our uniforms in primitive quarters, waited in line for the single shower to be vacated and dressed next day in damp uniforms.

That's right—damp, if not wet. Uniforms were jammed into containers after a game in their natural sweat-soaked state and seldom saw a laundry. We wore them until they were a grimy disgrace.

Train travel was in non-air-conditioned chair cars and if you compare the jump of 16 to 18 hours from Boston to St. Louis with the modern magic carpet air trip, one wonders how it was that yesterday's baseball regularly produced dozens of hitters in the .350 to .400 class and pitchers who won 30 or more games per season as against today's sprinkling of .300 hitters and handful of 20-game winners. These days the player has everything in the way of comfort, consideration, and scientific assistance. We had no batting cages, motion pictures to record our form, pitching machines, coaching specialists, and multivitamin tablets. The pancake gloves we wore, the washboard fields we played on, the cramped upper berths we climbed into on endless rides over poor roadbeds, the need to wrestle with your own luggage, the four-men-to-one-bathtub system in hotels and the crude equipment should have produced baseball which can't be compared to the modern brand. For instance, bases were left out there until they were spiked apart. They weren't anchored and strapped down firmly, giving you a solid cushion for sliding. Those sawdust bags would shift a foot or more when you tore into them. Pitchers dosed baseballs with licorice, talcum, slippery elm, and saliva flavored with tobacco until they came at the hitter so discolored that he could hardly pick them out of the shadows. If you tore a muscle or broke a bone, a long lay-off was out of the question— some eager rival would have your job in a minute. You played, whether you were lame, sick, or half-blind from pain. The first shin guards and sliding pads were coming into vogue when I was young, but we never heard of flip-down sunglasses, gloves with fantastic webbed extensions, outfield walls with cinder-track borders to save you from crashing the fence, finely clipped infield grass, and specially arranged backdrops to give the hitters a clear view of the ball.

Nevertheless, I'll take for my all-star line-up a group that includes George Sisler, Roger Bresnahan, Eddie Collins, Honus Wagner, Buck Weaver, Joe Jackson, Tris Speaker, Walter Johnson, Eddie Plank, Christy Mathewson, Grover Alexander, Ed Walsh, and Cy Young over any that can be named from a list of stars covering the past 30 years. Every index we have show their superiority over the fat-cat athletes of today. Why is this? I'll explain why it's true in another section of this book, but for now I'll put it in a few words: *The present-day boys lack the fighting dedication to the game that was entirely commonplace in my day.*

In short, we didn't have business agents out soliciting lecture dates, advertising testimonials, special bonuses, TV appearances, and autograph parties for us. We simply tried to hang onto our jobs by playing up to 100 per cent of our ability every inning, without distractions.

The men I jousted with in the early years were a strange breed that the United States of America never will see again—as long gone from the scene as the sodbuster, the hide-skinner, the riverboat gambler, and the map makers of the Old West. To them, baseball was a whole way of life, their reason for existence—not a means to another monetary end. They were poor boys from farms and villages, burning with ambition, who studied, practiced, threw themselves into games without thought of injury and who suffered rigors without complaint that would send a modern pro crying to the Players Association for relief.

If you had glanced down a hotel hallway fifty years ago, you'd have seen "ghosts" moving down those clammy corridors. These were ballplayers. They were wrapped in bedsheets, grimy and sore from the day's battle, and unable to find a bathtub anywhere. Sometimes we had to use public toilets in the second-rate hotels patronized by our nickel-squeezing owners. Detroit was a standout example. Bill Armour and Hughie Jennings, my first managers, rated a private tub in their room. We used to hang around their door in our sheets, hoping for a crack at just five minutes of soaking in hot water.

We dried out in our own sweat, put sticking plaster on open wounds and still managed to produce men like Kid Nichols of the Boston Nationals *who won 30 or more pitching decisions in seven seasons* and 20 or more for ten years successively. How long since baseball has known a one-season 30-game winner? Not for a quarter-century, since Dizzy Dean.

Toughness. The old-timers had it in a measure the moderns don't even begin to understand. In having my tonsils jerked cold-turkey by a hotel M.D., I did nothing extraordinary. "Old Hoss" Radbourn once won 60 games in a season, pitching almost every day when his team ran shy of moundsmen—and did it with a sore arm. Hugh Duffy's leg was slashed open by spikes from ankle to knee, but he played out the season and compiled the highest batting average of all time: .438. So it went, back then.

In the beginning years, I didn't mind the hardships. Starting in 1907, a period of emergence began for me. That was my second full year with the Tigers and my third as a major leaguer, and it seemed to me that the concentrated, organized attempt of a certain clique of Detroit veterans to run me back to the minors was tapering off, if not ended. As I've already described, the clique had waged bitter war with me all through '06. I had been harassed to the point of hating to even show up at the park. Gradually, though, the antagonisms were fading . . . as a player I was progressing in skill . . . the formation of friendships with various Tigers was becoming a solid and warming thing.

But there remained Sam Crawford, our big outfielder-first baseman. Wahoo Sam, who'd trained to be a barber, chose to continue the feud. Sam had been the slugging star of the Tigers before my arrival, the fan's darling, after having earlier led the National League in homers while with Cincinnati. As 1907 rolled along, my bat average rose above .330. For the first time, Crawford was running second on his own club.

Just then some more of my bats turned up mysteriously broken. The vandalism infuriated me. It didn't take Sherlock Holmes to know that Sam was sicking the boys on me. He made no overt moves himself, preferring to agitate in the background.

At batting practice one day, I couldn't take another minute of it. I marched up to Crawford.

"You big ——," I said. "You've been making trouble for me long enough. Now, put up your hands."

Crawford blinked and looked uncomfortable.

"Go ahead," I barked. "I'm calling you."

Sam muttered something about me having him all wrong, and edged away from there.

The one and only way I could see to settle the clique's hash was to outhustle and, if possible, outplay all members of the anti-Cobb faction, and this I bore down on with everything I had. By July, the Chicago White Sox had won 53 and lost 33 and led the American League over Detroit, with 49–33. In Boston, we knocked off the Red Sox in a nip-tuck game, aided by my eleventh-inning double off Charley Pruitt. Moving to New York, I was in right field when Frank LaPorte of the Highlanders sliced a drive that looked absolutely good for three bases. With two out, a pair of New Yorkers were on base and they went dashing for home. Tearing after the ball, I ran out of my shoes, but saw I wasn't going to make it, so I took off in a headlong dive and stabbed out barehandedly. Somehow the ball smacked my palm and stuck there long enough for me to clench it. Landing on my chest, I plowed up grass for half a dozen feet, somersaulted twice and held up the ball to the umpire.

It sounded like a gas bag had exploded. A vast *whoosh* of disappointment came from the crowd. Hughie Jennings, our new manager, did an Indian war dance on the sideline, uncorked his favorite yell of "*Eee-yah!*" and generally went crazy.

Two New York runs had crossed the plate while I was pursuing LaPorte's drive, but the catch ended the inning and the runs did not count. We went on to win a crucial game and move closer to the league lead.

About this time, I gashed my thumb and whenever I had to hit the dirt in a slide, the wound broke open and bled freely. It hurt, but I kept sliding. My bloody thumb became a sort of a symbol of the clawing, scrapping, determined Tigers and drew more newspaper space than my base hits. Charlie Schmidt, the 215-pound catcher who'd once broken my nose with a sneak punch, gave out an interview praising my "game" play. "Why," he told the newsboys, "Cobb loses a good pint of blood every time he slides!"

It was more like a thimbleful. But it helped break the ice with my teammates, and Schmidt, who'd been a tool of the clique that hated me, began to act like my press agent. He was even cheering for me to win the league batting championship. Hughie Jennings gave me *carte blanche* to run the bases as freely as I liked. Smiles replaced snarls, now that I was helping the Tigers toward that pennant money. In this happy atmosphere, I became a ballplayer.

When 1907 opened, no one suspected that I was up to any heroics and, in fact, that spring the Tigers came close to trading me away. A deal which would have sent me to Clark Griffith in New York in exchange for Billy Hogg, a 14-game-winning pitcher, was discussed. Also, Jennings had a dicker cooking with Cleveland—me for Elmer Flick, a .311 hitting outfielder.

"How come you want to get rid of Cobb?" the other clubs are said to have asked Jennings.

"Too many fights," Jennings replied. "We need harmony on this team, not brawling."

Well, I hadn't inspired the brawls, and I've often wondered what would have happened to my career if I'd been traded to New York as a youngster. I can think of two benefits over those I enjoyed in Detroit:

1) I'd have been free of a money-pinching owner, Frank Navin, with whom I had contract trouble for many years and who used many a cheap trick—such as appropriating and reading my personal telegrams—to hold my salary down. In New York, I'd have worked

under owners Frank Farrell and Big Bill Devery, famed for their fair dealing and liberality with players.

2) As a New York Yankee, I'd have been exposed to a much larger and therefore better press than in Detroit. Over the years, my sharpest critics have been New York sportswriters. If I'd joined their club, kisses would have replaced brickbats.

On the other hand, I would have missed out on the many fine friendships and beneficial business connections I made among leading Detroiters. And the Tigers of my youth were a scrapping, indomitable crew who outdid New York in finishing in the money. Between 1907–16, we won three pennants, placed second twice, were third twice and once fourth. All in all, I'm glad I wore those Tiger stripes for 22 seasons.

That 1907 fight for the World Series money was one of the wildest I ever saw. Jennings had us thinking every minute, driving the opposition daffy with our gambling tactics. By early August, we were swapping first place every few days with either the Philadelphia A's, Chicago, or Cleveland. The country was in a lather of excitement over the four-way race. Typical of our hotspur attitude was a game in Washington. Wild Bill Donovan, our workhorse pitcher, had gone 17 innings three days earlier. George Mullin, another dependable, had worked 15 innings two days before. Both of them were sagging with fatigue, but they pleaded with Hughie Jennings:

"Let me work today. I'll win for you."

Hughie looked at their limp and drooping arms and, with the rest of his staff worn down to the nub, picked Donovan.

Well, you couldn't let a battler like Wild Bill down. During the game, played in 90-degree temperature, I stole second and wrenched my knee, sliding. Then I stole third and was shaken up on the play. Up came Rowdy Bill Coughlin for our side and hit sharply to Billy Shipke, at third base for the Nats. Feeling pretty groggy, nevertheless, I smelled opportunity. I dashed in and then up and down the line between home and third. The whole Washington infield was after me as I ducked back and forth in the hotbox. Finally, Jim Delahanty chased me toward the plate, caught me and slammed the ball into the small of my back.

The force of the blow on top of my exertions on top of the terrific heat knocked me all but out as I sprawled forward. In tagging me, Delahanty dropped the ball. It rolled away.

Flat on my face, I could see the plate just three feet away. I tried with everything I had to crawl that remaining distance. I looked like a wounded crab, they said, as I scrabbled painfully along, using my fingernails and elbows to inch forward. Every fan in the house was up screaming.

Delahanty retrieved the ball and dived at me for the tag-out an instant before I touched the plate and collapsed. They half-carried me to the bench and the trainer shot something into me that brought a little life back into my limp frame. I was out—but Coughlin was safe at first, another Tiger was safe at second and the Nats were all jittered up. They were wondering what hare-brained play we might make next. And they made a couple of fatal errors while thinking about it.

Donovan went the distance for his 24th win of the season and we had gained another notch in the race.

Just about then, at the age of twenty, I made a wonderful discovery. I learned the value of playing on an opponent's nerves and forcing miscues. We went into New York, needing 14 out of the remaining 16 games to grab the "peanut"—as the pennant was called. Paul Bruske, a Detroit baseball writer, opened his story next day with the lines:

> Listen, my children, and I will sob
> Of the desperate stunt of Tyrus Cobb. . . .

The situation was a tense, ninth-inning 0–0 pitching duel between Judd (Slow Joe) Doyle of the Highlanders and Twilight Ed Killian for our side. As the runner on first base, I got the hit-run sign. Claude Rossman, our lanky first baseman, was at bat. Rossman, with his long arms, that could reach anything around the plate, was one of the most dependable hit-run men and the best sacrifice bunter I ever saw. But this time Claude missed the ball, and Red Kleinow, the Highlander catcher, fired to second to catch me on the slide. The ball was a bit wide and bounced off Danny Hoffman's glove into shallow right field. To everybody's amazement, I popped right up and tore for third. It looked like sure-enough suicide.

Hoffman's recovery throw easily had me beat, except that I watched Third Baseman LaPorte's eyes and swerved my body into the way of the ball. As it bounced off my hip, I was in safe. "——" said La-Porte.

But there were two out and Germany Schaefer, at bat, was in a slump. I watched the duel between Pitcher Doyle and Germany for a while and then began to cut capers. When Doyle wound up, I dashed in almost halfway to the plate and then hastily retreated. My motive seemed to be to unsettle Doyle, which was only partially true. Each dash down the base path was an experiment aimed to show whether or not I could go all the way and beat the ball.

Doyle wound again, and this time I kept going. Germany was so startled to see me coming that he half-swung, and topped the ball toward third, enabling me to cross the plate without bothering to slide. But Schaefer still had to beat the throw to first to make my run count.

As I'd hoped, my unorthodox tactics had Doyle so unstrung and ridden with tension that he grabbed Germany's topper, couldn't find the handle, fumbled it an instant, threw low and missed getting Schaefer by a step. The game was over—by a score of 1–0.

It filled me with delight to find that you could arrange for the other gents to beat themselves by applying pressure at the psychological moment—even great players. In that same New York series, I walked and Rossman sacrificed. The bunt was handled slick as a whistle and fired to Hal Chase, the "Prince" of first basemen. Rossman was out. The play was routine enough, and Chase, assuming I'd stop at second, gloved the ball and then dropped his meat hand.

To his disbelief, I was already bearing down on third base. Both mortified and momentarily paralyzed, Chase fired hastily. The throw pulled the third baseman, George Moriarty, a right-hander, toward left field, for a reaching stop. Being safe at third, by all odds I should have stopped there. But to throw home, Moriarty now had to recover from his awkward position, cross his legs and turn clear around, while transferring the ball from glove to hand, and that was all the edge I needed. From first base, on a cleanly handled bunt, I slid in under Moriarty's throw to the plate and scored.

Some who saw it said it was impossible. Clark Griffith, the New York manager, didn't like it, possible or not. After the game, stopping at a water cooler outside the Highlander clubhouse, I could hear voices floating over the transom. Griff was giving Chase and Moriarty a scorching.

"Dumb clucks!" roared Griff. "Why didn't you keep your eyes on him?"

Chase and Moriarty came right back, defending themselves.

"How was I to know that that Georgia —— was going to do a fool thing like that?" demanded Chase.

"The —— won't get away with it again! We'll take care of the ——!" promised Moriarty.

Maybe my Southern blood did boil, as it's been claimed by witnesses of the affair. I certainly didn't appreciate the epithets tossed my way. Strong language never did appeal to me as a ballplayer, and there were times when I wouldn't invite friends into the Detroit clubhouse, because of the cursing and general blasphemy tossed around.

That night I told Claude Rossman, "Every time I get on first tomorrow, you bunt." Claude agreed.

The next day, with the Highlanders laying for any trick I might pull, we came into the seventh inning, and up to now I'd played strictly by the book. The New Yorkers perhaps were overanxious for what should have come, but hadn't. Rossman bunted and they fumbled and I went the whole 180 feet from first to third, slipping in just under Moriarty's tag. Moriarty was so mad about it that he jumped up and down, then slammed the ball on the ground and caught it on the bounce.

He shouldn't have done that. By the time the ball came down, I was over the plate again with a run.

I'd have hated to have been Moriarty, or any other New York infielder, that night.

They were saying now that Tyrus the Speed Boy maybe was the fastest thing in flannel, but it wasn't true. There were faster men around, then and later—Harry Niles of St. Louis, for instance, an ex-sprinter; Pat Dougherty of New York and Chicago; Harry (Deerfoot) Bay of Cleveland, a 10-second man at 100 yards; Bill Maloney of Brooklyn and others. A few discerning observers saw through my plan of attack. They realized that my speed was linked to a "new style" of running bases, based on observation of pitchers, catchers, infielders, and outfielders, the forcing of errors by doing the totally unexpected, a variety of slides and the demand that basemen give me my proper right to the base path, rather than on any great swiftness of foot. All the newspaper debates about Speed Kings didn't matter to me. All I cared about was helping Detroit lock up that pennant.

On August 2, 1907, with the race virtually tied among three teams, I encountered the most threatening sight I ever saw on a ball field.

He was only a rookie, and we licked our lips as we warmed up for the first game of a doubleheader in Washington. Evidently, manager Pongo Joe Cantillon of the Nats had picked a rube out of the corn fields of the deepest bushes to pitch against us. The new boy was making his big league debut that day. All we knew about him was that he'd gone 75 straight innings in the Idaho State League without giving up a run—and what we could see. He was a tall, shambling galoot of about 20 with arms so long they hung far out of his sleeves and with a side-arm delivery that looked unimpressive at first glance. We began to ride him as the game opened.

One of the Tigers imitated a cow mooing and we hollered at Cantillon: "Get the pitchfork ready, Joe—your hayseed's on his way back to the barn!"

The sandy-haired youngster paid no attention at all. The first time I faced him, I watched him take that easy wind-up—and then something went past me that made me flinch. The ball came in so fast that I wondered if he had a concealed gun on his person. I hardly saw the pitch, but I heard it. The thing just hissed with danger. We couldn't touch him, and so we waited, expecting the kid to turn wild and start issuing walks. But after four innings, he hadn't thrown more than a dozen balls.

We were most respectful now—in fact, awed—and there was only one answer left to his incredible, overpowering speed. We bunted. Sure enough, the boy hadn't handled many bunts, and I beat one out, then advanced to third on his wild throw, following another bunt, and scored a moment later.

Scrambling all the way, we finally beat him, 3–2, but every one of us knew we'd met the most powerful arm ever turned loose in a ball park. Several of us went to Detroit club officials and urged them to buy the boy. "Even if he costs you $25,000 get him," I told Frank Navin, our club owner. Navin just stared at me and did nothing about it.

And so Walter Perry Johnson stayed with Washington for twenty-one years and won more games—416—than any American League pitcher in history, struck out the most batters of any pitcher—3497—and once pitched a record 56 straight scoreless innings. He was called the Big Train, and he was the greatest of them all, in my book. Of Johnson, and my duels with him, I'll have more to say in its proper place—but here's a sidelight.

All over the baseball map are fans who like to boast, "*I saw Walter Johnson pitch his first game.*" In the 1940s, the Senators invited all those who witnessed the historic debut to sit in a special section at the park. More than 8000 people declared themselves eye-witnesses, overflowing the reserved seats.

I can tell you—since I was there—that the attendance that August 2, 1907, day was exactly 2841.

Meanwhile, Detroit was blowing its top with pennant fever as we entered the stretch run of the season. In twenty years in Organized Baseball, the city hadn't produced a flag winner, and the boys and girls were parading the streets with torches. A Hughie Jennings Club was organized, buttons were struck off for all to wear and banners decorated the streets. Extra newspaper editions heralded every game. Everyone in town seemed to own a tin whistle, using them to imitate Jennings' piercing sound effects from the coaching box.

Caught up in this, I did desperate things that got me a reputation as a "fool" base-runner who'd take such wild chances "that it was a wonder Jennings didn't bench him." Sometimes, I'd gamble and lose. I'd be thrown out with feet to spare. Jennings understood, though, my strategy—that I was establishing a threat that would come in handy later, when in a tight moment the opposition might become the victim of their own nerves with "that crazy Cobb" on base.

In one game, I was cut down twice in three innings while running wild. But that game already had been won by a wide margin—we could afford losing a run if it planted the seed of fear and un-certainty in the other side.

On the other hand, against Cleveland on June 27, 1907, I scored four runs for the first time in one game—most of them coming on gay base-running. On July 18, against Washington, I stole three bases for the first time in the big league. On October 2, playing the Nats again, I got away with four steals for the first time in my life. We were staying up there in the championship race not because of potent hitting. Germany Schaefer averaged .258 that season, Davey Jones .273, Claude Rossman .277, Bill Coughlin .243, Charlie Schmidt .244, Charley O'Leary .241, and Red Downs .219 —with Wahoo Sam Crawford, of course, coming through with a fine .323—and to overcome our moderate batwork, we needed every scheme ever hatched by mortals.

It all came down to a three-game series with the Philadelphia White Elephants at Columbia Park in Philadelphia in late September. The second of those two games has been called the most exciting and craziest ever to happen in the majors. For sure, it was my all-time thrill game among the 3033 season games I played.

The Elephants, or A's, of Connie Mack, led us by three percentage points when we reached town, which we took care of by a 5–4 margin in the opener. Now we were all but tied. Rain washed out the second contest, requiring a doubleheader on Monday, September 30. But only one of those two scheduled games were played. Had there been a second, we'd have had to fight it out by moonlight.

People trampled one another down for the privilege of a seat— at 1:30 the gates were locked with 25,000 in the park and with another 5000 milling outside, cursing the coppers. At 2 P.M., Jimmy Dygert of the A's pitched the first ball and the fur began to fly.

The A's simply murdered us for six innings. They hammered Wild Bill Donovan for a 7–1 lead and the Philadelphia crowd gloated over a championship only three innings away. We were frantic, as we watched our golden dream slipping away.

Davey Jones, our lead-off man, caught the brunt of our passion. Davey was a ripper on the bases, but he was known to shy away from balls driven near the fence or into any standing-room-only outfield-fringing crowd. Bravery, after all, is relative. And Davey let a ball escape him that scored an Athletic run.

As the inning ended, Davey was met by a delegation of his fellow Tigers near third base. They grabbed him, hauled him around, and roared, "If we lose this one, what we'll do to you!" Jones was threatened with dismemberment of every portion of his body.

In the seventh, we got to Rube Waddell for four runs to make the score 7–5. Dygert had been replaced by Waddell back in the second inning, when Dygert filled the bases. Rube had started out as a reliever like a roaring lion. He'd struck out Davey Jones and Schaefer to end our second-inning rally, and he strutted around out there, lapping up the applause. Waddell was out of Bradford, Pennsylvania, and had the greatest combination of speed and a quick-breaking curve you'd want to see. He stood almost 6-2, weighed 196, has his bust in the Hall of Fame at Cooperstown, New York, and owned a mocking bird which drove his teammates wild by constantly imitating a peanut vendor's whistle. Someone finally strangled the poor bird.

Rube liked a feminine audience. One day he showed up at the park with a sweetie on either arm and stashed the girls in a box back of home plate. Every now and then he blew them a kiss as he left-handed his way to a 1–0 lead in the ninth inning. Then Cleveland filled the bases on Rube, due to the fact that he was distracted.

The Rube left everyone speechless by walking in from the box to the seats occupied by his ladies, bowing gallantly and announcing, "Girls, I'll be with you in just a minute."

Then, on nine pitches, he struck out Larry Lajoie, Elmer Flick, and Bill Bradley, three of the league's greatest hitters.

But in the big showdown game of 1907 against Detroit, Rube suddenly stopped strutting. As I said, we began pasting his deliveries and, with an error here and there helping out, narrowed the gap until we were trailing the A's by 8–6 in the ninth inning.

Sam Crawford opened for us with a single. I came next, and Waddell threw a fast ball past me for a strike. Then came his big curve.

With only five home runs that season, I wasn't known as a fence-buster, but the timing was right and at the impact of bat on ball, I knew I'd tagged one. It was high up there and climbing. I was past first base when I glimpsed the ball disappearing over the right-field fence into Twenty-ninth Street. By any number of accounts, Connie Mack slid right off the Athletics' bench and went sprawling among a pile of bats.

That home run was as sweet as any I ever got, and it tied it at 8–8.

Waddell was removed in favor of Eddie Plank and I'm sorry to say that this was the Rube's swan song in Philadelphia. He appeared in only one more A's game after that, then was sent to St. Louis.

Now things became deadly serious. Each team scored a run in

the tenth. Then we stymied each other with shutout pitching by Donovan and Plank, and struggled on into the fourteenth inning still tied up. The shades of night were falling, but there was no thought of abandoning the epic struggle. In the fourteenth, Harry Davis slugged a long fly into the center field crowd for what seemed a ground-rule double. Sam Crawford angled for the ball, but just then up jumped a Philadelphia policeman to cross before Sam's path.

"Interference!" we yelled, rushing the umpires.

Umpire Silk O'Loughlin stalled around, and finally asked his colleague, Tommy Connolly, "Was there interference?" Connolly said there certainly was. The A's didn't take it laying down when Silk called Davis out. One of their infielders, Monte Cross, rushed out with his fists doubled. Rube Waddell—having showered, and now in street clothes—joined the scene. Cross and Claude Rossman of our side traded punches, then others got to swinging and the field became tangled with policemen and players. Our pitcher, Bill Donovan, was trying to restrain Waddell, but found himself placed under arrest.

"You can't arrest Donovan," Germany Schaefer informed the coppers. "Why, he comes from Philadelphia, and the stands are filled with his Irish relatives. Pinch him, and they'll tear you apart."

Donovan was quickly de-arrested. Instead, the bluecoats took Rossman into custody.

Eventually, we obtained Rossman's release, and the game staggered on into the seventeenth inning, with neither side able to score, and the field so dark that we were all guess-swinging. Nearly four hours after we started, the game was called with both sides exhausted and the score 9–9.

That tie made the pennant difference. We went on to win four straight games over Washington, with the A's matching our pace, and finally took the championship by a final hairbreadth margin of .613 to .607.

Detroiters didn't go to bed for two nights running—it was the biggest event in the city's history since the 1813 Battle of Lake Erie when Oliver Hazard Perry's men defeated the British.

The rewards of being with a winner began to pour in on me, leaving me fairly dizzy. That gold watch I'd admired in the store window the year before was mine. With a .350 batting mark, I took my first American League title and tied Honus Wagner, also with .350 in the National League, for the over-all championship. My 212 hits and 116 runs batted in also led the league, as did my 49 stolen bases.

Detroiters gave me a beautiful $500 gold medal. Fans in the South and elsewhere contributed dimes and dollars and when I returned home, I was called on stage at the Orpheum Theater in Atlanta for a presentation by Major Joyner. He handed me another gold watch.

And I was offered $200 a week for a vaudeville tour—declined with thanks—plus various other inducements.

Modern players who spend the wintertime hitting the endorsement and banquet circuit might take note that I avoided all money entanglements, oiled up my rifle, and with a couple of dogs hit the hunting trail. I logged 20 to 30 miles a day, a practice I never deviated from over the years to come. Later, I tacked lead weights into the insteps of my hunting boots to make the going tougher.

In other words, boys, I was keeping my legs in shape—a thought that seems not to occur to too many of you in the off season. At any spring training camp today, a lot of you turn up soft, fat-bellied, and out of wind from a winter of loafing.

You can't be a part-time athlete—it's contrary to all the laws of nature. However, just try to tell that to ballplayers nowadays. They laugh off the warning, and in less than ten years the average playing career is over.

As 1907 ended, I had another reason for hitting the roadwork. After beating the A's for the pennant, we Tigers had fallen on our faces in the World Series against the Chicago Cubs—especially yours truly.

My pride was stung when the Chicago writers called me "a bust."

"A bust, huh?" I told myself, down in the Georgia pine woods. "I'm going back next spring and make those umpha-umphas eat those words."

5

"Bugs"—That First Bitter Series— $5000 or Bust

A World Series of fifty-odd years ago was something wonderfully special. You'll see nothing like it today. The players hadn't built a high wall of publicity men, business agents and indifference between them and Josephus Fan, who pays the bill, and even though sometimes the "bugs" used fists and beer bottles on us, we had a rooting section unparalleled in sporting history.

One evening, for instance, Germany Schaefer was loafing in a hotel lobby when fifty Detroit fans marched in to make a citizens' arrest. Some of the bugs were dressed as policemen and Schaefer squawked long and loud that he hadn't done anything.

"The hell you didn't," the posse told him. "You slugged one of our leading citizens in a bar last night, and you'll pay to the full limit of the law."

Germany was frog-marched to the front door and began to beg, "Don't put me in jail . . . we've got a game tomorrow!"

At the door, everyone stopped, broke out in roars of laughter and handed the German a letter—from the man he'd tangled with in the saloon. It read:

Dear Mr. Schaefer:
Just a line to thank you for the beautiful black eye and busted jaw you gave me yesterday—it is worth while looking at it today and I am proud of it. Hope there are no bad feelings between us over this

matter, as I now understand I had a few too many and it was my fault.

Your pal and admirer,
MURRAY TIARKS

When the Detroit team was riding a bus or tallyho to the park, Germany would mount the rear steps and engage in conversation with passers-by.

"My, what a pretty infant!" he'd holler to a mother pushing a perambulator. "What's his name?"

Ladies were too refined to respond to total strangers in those days, yet—noticing Schaefer's honest and beaming face—the mother would be lulled into answering.

"*Augustus!*" she would shout back.

"*Boy or girl?*" Germany would yell.

"*Why . . . Boy.*"

"*And how old is the little darling?*" Germany would inquire at the top of his lungs, as the bus drew ahead.

"*Ten months . . . !*"

"*Is he an only child?*"

By now, all street traffic would have stopped to listen open-mouthed to the dialogue and Germany never considered the stunt a complete success unless he still had the mother screeching answers when we were half a block away. In a few miles' ride, the droll infielder could pry more personal information out of strange females than any man I ever saw.

As a World Series neared, there was little sophisticated scalping of tickets or music played by canned recording artists, but a fierce fervor composed of marching bands, torchlight parades, and all-night debates in the watering holes of Detroit that kept the Black Marias clanging and the bluecoats busy separating partisans. From City Hall, flew the handsome silk flag which had adorned the cruiser U.S.S. *Detroit* in the Spanish-American War. It was our battle flag—for we were facing the hated Chicago Cubs of Frank Chance, the "Peerless Leader," who had cakewalked to the National League pennant by a 17-game margin behind the great catching of Johnny Kling, the immortal infield trio of Tinker-to-Evers-to-Chance and the pitching of Mordecai (Three Finger) Brown, Big Ed Reulbach, and Orvie Overall. We were the 8–5 underdogs, with something

72

like $1,000,000 bet on the Series. From the Metropole Hotel cigar stand to the Light Guard Armory to Buckenberger's Cafe, business stopped and no one in Detroit discussed anything but the Tigers' chances.

We opened the 1907 classic—my first Series—in Chicago, where all hell was popping. Bill Phelon, the Chicago *Daily Journal* scribe, turned out a story which got top play over the news that the *Lusitania* had just crossed the Atlantic in a record time.

"A wild day!"

"Early this morning, the camp stirred in the big lot alongside West Side Ball Park. A bugle call awakened those thousands who slept upon the field and they sprang to their feet with shrill shouts of 'Is the box-office open?' In a twinkling, coffee was cooking on 2000 fires, bacon was frying and the pop of the aged egg mingled with the howls of the gent who'd found a cockroach in his biscuit.

"By 8 o'clock the troops began to form in a solid column and echeloned upon the fortress. The ball park-fort was garrisoned under Maj. Charles Williams, a veteran of 500 bottles—pardon me, battles. All through the morning, the major's men held their own under the onslaught of the bugs. The public tried to swarm the walls sans a ticket and was hurled back. Now and then some light infantry scaled a parapet, heedless of the barbed-wire entanglements, and dropped safely inside. These invaders fought tooth and nail, but were captured and hurled forth. Maj. Williams lost his pants in the course of combat, and finished the engagement wearing a horse-blanket."

With only 22,000 seats available, close to 35,000 tried to crowd in and the cries of the wounded were everywhere.

Having been forced to the wire to win our league, we Tigers were a weary bunch, but I pepped up when the Cubs elected me—in advance—as the coming "lemon" of the Series and boasted that I'd steal no bases on Kling's mighty throwing arm, nor be much of a problem for their pitchers.

But I can't say they were too far wrong.

Experience is the only teacher, and despite my .350 season's average, I was still just a kid trying to cope with one of the most amazing teams of all time. Chance's veterans won a record 116 league games in 1906 (never since surpassed), 107 in 1907, 104 in 1909, and 104 in 1910, and led the Senior League four times in

73

five seasons. They taught me as much baseball in a short, painful time as any opponent I ever met. In the first Series game, we fought to a twelve-inning 3–3 tie called by darkness—maybe the most spectacular title game of all time. We'd have won it if catcher Charlie Schmidt hadn't muffed a third strike with two out in the ninth. On the passed ball, Kling scored the tie run for the Cubs. Poor Schmidt was raked over in the clubhouse later.

"Damn you, why didn't you hang onto that pitch, you dumb Dutch so-and-so!" the Tigers raged at him.

I couldn't berate Schmidt. In five times up, I'd gone hitless. I just sat and hated myself.

In game No. 2, I managed a single in three times up, got smacked in the ribs by Cub pitcher Jack Pfeister and pulled a dubious fielding play. As the runner at first, I moved down the line when Rossman lofted a short fly to Wildfire Schulte in right field for Chicago. It seemed to me that Schulte would catch it, forcing me back to the bag. But at the last instant he fiendishly let it bounce, trapped the ball, and sizzled it to Joe Tinker at second base.

"Cobb hit second so hard he tore the bag from its moorings and knocked it into left field," wrote Sy Sanborn of the *Daily Tribune*, "but he was out by a foot—the victim of Wildfire's lightning thinking."

At any rate, I was learning. In game No. 3, Eddie Siever pitched for us and his "Lady Godiva ball" (nothing on it) was hammered for a 5–1 Chicago win. After three games, I was batting a magnificent .167.

Big Ed Reulbach showed me some control twirling in that third match. He threw me a fast sidearm inshoot straight across the outside corner, which I let go for a strike one. He broke a fast drop curve on the inside corner of the plate at my belt, which I swung on and missed. He dropped another six inches lower and inside which I swung on and missed. Reulbach had placed three straight pitches precisely where he wanted them.

We moved to Detroit for the fourth game, where I finally ended my famine and hit a triple off Orvie Overall. But the Cubs beat us again, 6–1. Frank Chance broke a finger, had it taped and stole a base on the next play with his injured hand tearing up dirt. He was a Peerless Leader, all right—one of a breed of wildcat ballplayers they have few of nowadays.

Mordecai Brown with his three-fingered forkball shut us out 2–0 to end the Series on a dismal note, my contribution being a single. So I finished with a .200 average and was called a "bust" by some of the writers. In terms of experience gained, though, I'd profited handsomely, which I think showed up in the World Series of the following fall when I stole second and third on the almost steal-proof Johnny Kling and averaged .368 off pretty much the same Chicago pitching that baffled me in '07.

Under the new 60–40 winner-loser split introduced to the Series in 1907, each Tiger picked up a check for $1945.96. It was within $500 of my season's salary, the largest chunk of cash I'd yet seen. Becoming a man of substance meant a great deal. That summer before the Series, my mother and sister had come North and shared an apartment with me on the outskirts of Detroit. I was able to afford a player piano, a few snappy suits, an elegant derby, and my first automobile, a two-seat Chalmers with racy lines.

And I felt strongly that Frank Navin, the operator of the Detroit Baseball & Amusement Company, owed me a good-sized salary hike for 1908. Having led the league at nineteen, I reasoned, "If I don't ask for and get recognition now, I'll have shown myself a poor businessman and Navin will have me over a barrel in our future dealings."

So, down South, that winter, it reached the newspapers that I'd asked for $5000 and a three-year contract for 1908. It also was publicized that I didn't like Navin's contractual power to release me within ten days after giving notice—if, for instance, I fell ill or was badly injured. This was a condition right on peonage and all ball-players were forced to live under it. We players had no equal right to abrogate the agreement—which, under all law, made it no contract at all. I demanded this clause be stricken from my contract.

But Navin bridled and acted as if I'd put a gun in his ribs. "Who does Cobb think he is?" he announced. "Our other stars, Sam Crawford and Bill Donovan, have signed their contracts at reasonable figures without a murmur, but Cobb seems to think he deserves special treatment. Well the creation cannot be greater than the creator—Cobb is not bigger than baseball."

Pretty grandiloquent stuff—and Navin's remarks put the fat in the fire. After two years of working for Detroit at $1800 and $2400, I intended to be pushed around no longer.

If $5000 seems a measly sum by modern standards to quibble over, keep in mind that Christy Mathewson was paid $6000 the year he won 37 games for the New York Giants, Cy Young never drew more than $3500 as the winningest pitcher of all time, Eddie Plank and Chief Bender worked for $4000 at their peak and Honus Wagner had to win five National League batting crowns before pushing his salary to $9000. Old-time ownership held you in a condition of bondage; those who challenged the front office were waived out of the game or dropped so fast it'd singe your hair to watch.

I came right back at Navin—retorting that a .350 average and the fact that I'd established myself at low pay made it obvious that I wasn't acting in a fractious matter. I made no threats. But Navin was full of them.

He bent the ear of the Associated Press with: "We have offered Cobb $3000 and a one-year contract, and to allow him to bluff us would be to court a hold-up by every other player. It would disorganize our club in the future far more than Cobb's absence for a season could do. It puts a premium on being a crab and a penalty on a man who treats the club with honor and respect.

"Cobb can have his contract back any time he wants it. We have the best outfield in baseball, as I figure it, with Crawford, Matty McIntyre and Davey Jones, and if Cobb doesn't get the point, let it be on his head. He surely won't be foolish enough to let us go to training camp in the spring without him."

No one has known it, until now, but Navin not only failed to pressure me into abandoning my hold-out, he came within a hair of causing me to quit baseball permanently.

"Forget it, Tyrus," my family advised me. "Navin has called you a fathead, a bluffer, a crab, dishonorable and a lot of other things. No Cobb has to take that from anyone. Give up all this and do as your father wanted you to do."

My people were college-bred, they looked down on baseball as a low-life occupation and pleaded with me to chuck it all and enroll at a Southern university in medicine or law. And for many weeks, while Navin pulled one nefarious trick after another, I seriously thought about taking their advice.

I've been called one of the hardest bargainers who ever held out, and I'm proud of it. One Navin had no regard for a mere boy, and resorted to every trickery he could think of to befuddle me. For what it's worth to players today who must fight over seven battlefields to gain a decent paycheck, notice that he used three stratagems:

First, he circulated his conviction that Detroit's outfield and hitting would be plenty strong enough if Cobb sat on the sideline in 1908. "Let him go roll his little top," challenged Frank J.

This was to plant seeds of doubt and right in me—to lower my evaluation of myself. The belittling process scares many a man into capitulating.

Next, he arranged for friends of mine in and out of baseball to write and phone me, urging that I sign on his terms. Knowing I was a babe in years and impressionable, he didn't hesitate to use men of influence to pressure me. I've always considered that a despicable move. Navin was trying to make me think *If these men believe I'm wrong in asking $5000, perhaps I am.*

As his foxiest gambit, Navin coached a Detroit sportswriter to wire me: NAVIN SAYS IF SICK AND ACCIDENT CLAUSE ELIMINATED QUESTION OF SALARY WILL COUNT LITTLE. SAYS COME ON TO DETROIT AND TALK BUSINESS. WHAT DO YOU SAY? SEND REPLY COLLECT.

Willing to compromise to the extent of dropping the ten-day sick-or-hurt waiver I'd made, I took this to mean that the Tigers were acceding to my request on pay. Happily, I pulled my bats out of storage and began boning them. I wired back: I ACCEPT YOUR PROPOSITION. SHALL I REPORT TO SPRING TRAINING CAMP?

Navin now slugged me with this reply: "HAVE MADE NO PROPOSITION. TO WHAT DO YOU REFER?"

The thing soon became a nightmare of telegrams, rumor, threats, and intrigue, with the whole country choosing up sides pro and con. When I left Georgia for Detroit to see if I couldn't force a few straight cards to be dealt, sporting editor Tom Hamilton of the Augusta *Herald* brought the truth into the open:

WILL COBB BE VICTIM OF DOUBLE-CROSS? headlined Hamilton.

He said: "Navin intends to fake a contract out of Tyrus by luring him to Detroit with false promises, where he will be able to bring big guns to bear. Of course, most of the fans in America are hoping that Cobb wins out. But it's a 40-to-1 shot that the majority of his friends would have advised him to steer clear of the Navin lair and stay home until he had an iron-clad offer from Detroit's attorneys. The Lord help him up North."

In Detroit, I was given the treatment Hamilton expected—ex-Mayor George Codd, Fielding (Hurry-Up) Yost, the famed football coach of the University of Michigan, and other impressive names did some brainwashing before I entered Navin's sumptuous office to reach one of two decisions: quit baseball or stay with it under respectable salary terms. "You're a fool if you continue to hold out," they assured me.

A word about Navin, the man. We players called him "The Chinaman" for his cold, implacable expression. He'd begun as a bookkeeper in the office of Sam Angus, a Detroit insurance man and railroad contractor who owned the Tigers prior to my arrival in 1905. Angus sold out for $50,000 to William Hoover Yawkey, a grand fellow, but to whom a baseball club was but a plaything. Yawkey gave Navin $5000 worth of stock and jumped him to club secretary-treasurer.

As a clue to Navin, the jolly, generous Bill Yawkey would slip a $100 bill to some Tiger or other who'd helped win a game. Navin turned blue when that happened. "It'll spoil them," he'd protest.

Yawkey was a delight to play for. He hired ex-middleweight champ Tommy Ryan to travel and box with him and one night at the Hollenden Hotel, high in his cups, he bet Billy Lamb, a rugged customer, $10,000 that he could pin Lamb in a wrestling match. Lamb said he didn't have $10,000.

"Hell, then if I win, you owe me nothing!" boomed Yawkey. "If I lose, I owe you $10,000."

They stripped and in a minute, Lamb had Bill's shoulders pinned. Yawkey paid off, Lamb refused the money, and Bill became so affronted at his pal's refusal to help him discharge an honorable debt that Lamb finally had to accept the 10,000 simoleons.

After our 1907 pennant, Yawkey moved to New York and handed co-ownership of the Detroit Ball Club to Navin, even lending him $40,000 with which to purchase half the stock. And now, in full control, he intended to box young Tyrus Cobb's ears publicly.

He had quite an edge on me. I wasn't yet old enough to vote; Navin was thirty-seven, a graduate of the Detroit College of Law, and backed by years of immutable baseball tradition wherein Slave served Master.

In earlier days, Navin also had been a croupier in a gambling hall and he followed the horses avidly, thinking nothing of dropping $1000 on a race. But paying a ballplayer his worth pained Old Stone Face deeply. In his office that day, he puffed his cheeks and gave me an intimidating glower.

"What's this about you going outlaw?" he demanded.

"I've had offers," I replied. Navin knew damned well that I had, for they'd made coast-to-coast headlines. The president of the up-start new Union League, A. W. Lawson, had tendered me a $10,000 start-per-season contract—said to be the highest offer ever made to a ballplayer—and Jimmy Callahan, of a Chicago semipro league, had made a similar tempting bid. Neither being in Organized Baseball, I'd be branded an "outlaw"—beyond the pale forever, probably—if I accepted.

"Lawson is full of hot air. His league is on paper only, and noth-ing'll come of it," barked Navin.

"Maybe not," I said. "But to get to the point, I am willing to waive all other clauses in my contract and take a straight-out $5000 a sea-son. It isn't a question of principle with me, Mr. Navin. I want the money because I've earned it. It's the only way my earning capacity can be satisfied for this year."

"Can't pay it," he said. "Impossible. I'll come up $1000 from $3000, and that's the absolute limit. Look at Sam Crawford—he doesn't get more than $4000 and he's been a star for seven years."

"What you do with Crawford is your business and his," I retorted, getting hot under the collar at Navin's latest diversion. "All I know is that a ballplayer starts out at small pay, gets old in a hurry in the service of the team and finishes his career making peanuts. I want mine while I'm producing for you."

Navin wouldn't budge and I walked out, caught a train back to Dixie and sat tight while the Tigers left for spring training in Hot Springs, Arkansas. Days dragged by and training was almost finished. It rained buckets in Arkansas. The Tigers looked bedraggled, rather than like defending league champions. Hughie Jennings had some blunt things to say to Navin about the loss of my services. And out of Cleveland—a story that's always tickled me—came this yarn, published in the *Press* under the bannerline:

79

The piece said, in part:

"Cobb, so far as the records go, has never attacked his manager, quarreled with him when forced to sacrifice, or explained after a lost game how it might have been won but for his swell-headed teammates.

"Careless in Cobb. A direct violation of a popular players' bylaw.

"The usual thing for a recruit in the ranks of first magnitude stars to do is to whine about the injustice of his upper train berth, the requirement to stay sober and to hustle for a beggarly $15 or $20 a day.

"Cobb has utterly failed to do this.

"It is customary for a player lately become a national hero to perch himself on the top seat of a $500 carriage enroute to the park and tell the driver to go to the devil when the poor employee of the transfer company protests against the costly vehicle being marred by the player's spikes.

"Cobb blatantly overlooked this ancient and popular custom.

"The usual thing is to swagger about the hotel, snarl at being quizzed by reporters, bark at waitresses who fetch him better food than he ever ate before and knife his owner behind his back as a cheap crook and tax-dodger.

"Cobb has been woefully negligent in these particulars.

"In brief, this young man from Georgia has preached treason in mysteriously believing that he was hired to play ball and isn't being toted around the circuit because his name is Cobb. Somehow, too, Cobb appears to hold the opinion that it isn't his duty to wreak vengeance on his critics, or to play off sick every time he loses a chunk of skin or to pick flaws in the Tigers' itinerary of hotels or railroad routes or to complain of Navin's penuriousness or Jennings' arbitrary ways. Somehow Cobb has drifted into the forbidden way of thinking that a player owes a whole lot, not only to the public, but to his employer.

"The question is: what does the Detroit Ball Club owe the strange Ty Cobb?

"It owes him $5,000 and had better wake up to that fact before the wrath of all fair-minded people descends upon it!"

With that sort of press going for me, it came about, at length, that

Navin capitulated and offered a $4000 season's contract, plus an $800 bonus if I averaged .300 or better and fielded .900. I had no fear about qualifying for the bonus, and signed. I'd come within $200 of my demand, which was victory enough.

When we bowed in the season at Chicago on April 13, the Windy City audience of 20,000 climbed on my back with cries of, "Here comes the World Series lemon!" and "That's the bird who wanted an accident clause in his contract!" The bugs sang a ditty, "In that dear old Georgia home, he is sleeping. . . ."

I tried to stay awake in *that* game.

After touching up the White Sox's opening pitcher, Doc White, for a double, scoring three runs, I faced a new hurler, Nick Altrock, in the ninth inning. As Altrock strutted out, the band burst into "For He's a Jolly Good Fellow" and "Budweiser's a Friend of Mine."

Altrock wound up and confidently hummed his first pitch of the season in there and the last seen of the ball it was vanishing over the right-field bleachers.

"I always was unlucky early in the year," Altrock told the newspaper boys—one of the best lines that great diamond clown ever unlimbered.

With a home run, single, and double on Opening Day, I was well satisfied. The Chicago bleachers became silent and "lemon" no longer was associated with my name. In fact, I believe it was in 1908 that Grantland Rice first coined the nickname "Georgia Peach" for me, a tag that was both flattering and profitable to my career. However, I couldn't suspect as the new season started that all manner of explosive events awaited me up the line.

Before long, I'd fear that I was going blind as my inability to judge fast balls faltered and both eyes became mysteriously out of focus. Up ahead, I'd crash into a Tiger teammate and tear all the ligaments of my right knee. In a few years, I'd be engaged in my most bitter salary battle of all with Frank Navin—a contest that reached the floor of the United States Senate.

And if anyone had told me I'd barnstorm around the country dressed as a football hero and play-acting in a comedy by George Ade called *The College Widow*, I'd have laughed them away.

A ball bat is a wondrous weapon.

6

In Which Many Things Came True

An eager young Tiger named Cobb
Exclaimed, "I am hep to this job,"
Then he missed three wide shoots
While magnificent hoots
Were emitted by all of the mob

A Chicago versifier pinned that one on me, and it was poetry that hurt. Too much truth in that blankety-blank ditty when I was in the White Sox park facing Eddie Cicotte.

Cicotte had everyone mystified. He'd kicked around the league quite a while with only medium success, and suddenly came up with the strangest pitch I've ever seen. Knuckles Eddie began to win 18 to 29 games a season with a ball that looked softy-boiled when it reached the plate. But, oh brother! No matter how closely you focused on it, you never could see the thing break. It looked like Cicotte had nothing—then you were swinging at a phantom. Even when he threw it letter-high, where I liked a pitch, I'd cut under the ball. He kept winging that devil ball in there until 1920—when the Black Sox scandal threw Cicotte out of baseball—and even then the mystery hadn't been solved.

Maybe it was a reverse spitter. I always had a hunch that Cicotte applied dampness to the ball in such a way to get an extra amount of spin from his first two fingers, causing the apple to hop upward instead of falling away like a spitball sinker. Or it could have been a take-off on the "shine" ball, as Cicotte once hinted. Old-time pitchers kept a little cache of transparent paraffin on the side of one pants leg, or used talcum powder, to slick up one side of the ball. It did pretty tricks, take my word.

All I'm sure of is that Cicotte had me drawing some "magnificent hoots." From 1915–20, Babe Ruth never touched Cicotte for more than a double. Earlier, I was his pigeon.

Not forever, though. Some applied study gave me an idea of how to neutralize Cicotte somewhat.

It began in the ninth inning of a tight game when I was batting lead-off. When I stepped into the box, I paid absolutely no attention to the Chicago ace. I half-turned and began a conversation with Sam Crawford, who was swinging two bats and waiting his turn at the plate. My eyes were on Sam. "Get any good duck-hunting last winter, Sam?" I asked.

"Fair," said Crawford, catching on. "But there was more grouse than anything else down home."

"Some time you've got to join me in a shoot down around New Orleans, Sam."

"Swell, Ty."

It was as if Cicotte didn't exist. My bat wasn't even raised. And yet I was in the box, legally placed, and he was required to pitch. He'd never seen anything like it—a batter who wouldn't look at the ball about to come speeding toward him.

He was so rattled that on four straight pitched balls he didn't find the plate, and I walked. The base on balls to a man who had his back turned made Cicotte so mad he blew up and had to be removed.

Ways and means—you had to look for them. Cicotte was also vulnerable to razzing, and I didn't spare him. "So your middle name is Vivian, eh?" I'd tell him, scornfully. "My, what a pretty name. And how's your brother, Montmorency?" Despite his trick pitch, the record shows my lifetime mark against Cicotte to be:

Games	At-bat	Hits	Extra-base-hits	Pct.
27	99	34	9	.344

What with no rules to stop them, as we have these days, the old-time mound tricksters wrote a whole new book on cunning. Not one of the freak deliveries we had to face remains today: all were outlawed when the magnates greedily sold out to home runs. Allen Sothoron of the Browns used a razor blade on the little bits of leather which occur between the stitches of a baseball. He'd cut a couple of them on the bias, smooth down the surface with saliva and the ball would present an absolutely even surface. On the mound, he'd rub the slits the wrong way and have himself a ball with two of the prettiest little wings on it you ever saw. Fluttered like a butterfly, or sailed. Dave Danforth of the A's and White Sox was an ex-dentist with thick, rough calluses on his palm. He used a pickling substance until he had two horny pads on which to rough up the ball. Considering that the pitcher also was allowed to rub the ball in the dirt, splatter it with licorice and tobacco and pound it against his cleats, Danforth was only gilding the lily. We often went five or six innings using the same black old ball. In the late innings, in the shadows, you had to hit at a dark streak that almost defied detection.

Any small smudge on the ball today, and out it goes for a shiny new one. In contrast, one day at Cleveland, we had swung against a tired old tomato until nobody could hit it out of the infield. Big Larry Lajoie of the Indians protested to umpire Tommy Connolly, demanding a new ball. "You'll hit against the same ball as the Tigers did," answered Connolly, in his County Kerry brogue. "Now stand in there and give me no more of your tongue."

"Why, you Irish immigrant!" yelled Lajoie. "I remember you when you couldn't say 'ball.' You just said 'B-r-r' and we had to guess what you meant."

"You French chowderhead!" roared Connolly. "I remember you when you carried everything you owned in a paper suitcase!"

Lajoie and Connolly now were wrestling for the ball.

"Out it goes!"

"It stays in!"

With a sudden wrench, Lajoie got possession, rared back and heaved with all his might. Over the grandstand into the gloom sailed the horsehide—so discolored you could hardly follow its flight.

"*Now* it's out!" cried Lajoie triumphantly.

"And so are you!" said Connolly, jerking his thumb.

But we got a new ball out of it.

Then there was the home team's device of storing balls in an ice chest to deaden them and inserting BB shot into one seam of the ball and pounding it down with a mallet. The home pitcher would know just where the ball had been weighted with shot. The shot unbalanced the ball and imparted a pull or sail, especially on its downward break. The visiting pitcher would go crazy wondering why his shoots were going wild.

In the clubhouse, you'd think you were watching a meeting of a ladies' sewing circle. Players sat around with jaws bulging with chaws of tobacco and employing needle and thread. Baseball talk would be punctuated now and then with a loud curse as a needle bored through a leather wrist strap and drew blood. Pitchers and infielders of my day sewed emery paper onto their gloves. When a new ball was thrown in, the catcher's throw to the pitcher was allowed to roll out to the second baseman or shortstop. The infielder would give the ball a good working over against the emery, before tossing it to the pitcher, who'd then use the sharp point of his belt buckle on the seams, or run his hands through his hair and apply slickum, or employ a small piece of nutmeg grater secreted in his pocket. Players didn't leave their "loaded" gloves on the field when they came in to bat. If you did, the opposition would rip off the emery paper.

Despite all the liberal rules, piercing the skin of the ball was illegal, but it didn't slow up the freak-delivery boys. Sandpaper and emery paper was popularized by Russ Ford in 1909. Earlier, Ford was pitching in the minors with Atlanta when, during a warm-up, the ball got away and struck the concrete base of the grandstand. Right away, it began to dip and swerve when he threw it. Ford and his catcher were puzzled, but finally figured out that a scuffed "wing" on the ball was making it perform dipsy-doodles.

The New York Highlanders bought Ford when he suddenly became a big winner at Atlanta. He told no one of his discovery. Ford insisted that New York use his Atlanta catcher, named Ed Sweeney, so that he could protect the secret. Sweeney hit from .146 to .268 and didn't belong in the big league, but he was kept around because he was vital to Ford's scheme. Came an afternoon when the ever-alert Eddie Collins of the A's became curious. He noticed that Ford always carried his glove back to the bench instead of tossing it near the base line.

"Let's have a look at that glove," said Collins, meeting Ford near the third base line.

"Go take a flying dive off the Flatiron Building," replied Ford.

But Collins waited, got ahold of the glove and found a hole at the bottom of one finger, under which was a patch of emery paper.

With the secret out, every pitcher in both leagues began to run in every grade of abrasive paper that was manufactured. Umpires checked them over closely, to detect "foreign agents." But by then the catchers were doing the dirty work. They'd pry up a metal eyelet on their mitt and give the ball a good scoring. And after the catchers were suspected and fell under surveillance, the job was passed to the first basemen, who could do the foul deed while the ball was being tossed around the infield. The thing could go on endlessly, a whodunit that the Bill Burns Detective Agency and the Pinkertons couldn't have solved.

Notice I didn't say that Ford invented the emery ball. That goes back to the 1890s and Clark Griffith and other ancients who had various ways of roughing the ball. They found that one half of the leather used to wrap a ball generally is softer than the other and sharp fingernails could work wonders. The spitball often is credited to Jack Chesbro and Ed Walsh of the 1900-and-on era. But Walsh learned about salivating the ball from Elmer Stricklett, who in turn got it from a Chicago Nationals pitcher named Fiddler Corridon —who got it where? Nobody knows.

Of the clever dodges I grew up with, I always admired as much as any the sign-flashing technique of the Philadelphia A's when they were world champions. Eddie Collins had a crackproof code he could use with a teammate at bat when he was on base. He used the deaf-and-dumb signs.

And the old Philly Nationals went a step further than my own Tigers. We used a movable slot in a sign on the outfield fence, behind which hid a spotter, to signal fast balls or curves to the batter. But the Phils had a buzzer buried in the third base coaching box. Their coach kept his toe on the apparatus and waited for the signal from a spotter in center field, who was stealing the rival catcher's signs through high-powered field glasses. The spotter would push a button, activating a device which gave off one buzz for a fast ball, two for a curve. At which the coach would hand-flash the information to the batter.

Coach-to-batter signals evolved from this, and from various desires to steal a march on the opposition. I may have had something to do with the development of signs. Around 1906, when we found our signs were being intercepted, the Tigers began to use the "rub" system. I would be at bat, with runners aboard, and would wish them to know that the hit-and-run was on, or perhaps the double steal. So I'd hitch up my pants, rub my arm and come back to my shirt again. Thus I ended on an uneven rub-number—three. We switched from odd to even numbers to frustrate the smart counterespionage boys on the other side. We used the cloth-flesh-cloth-flesh system, among others. We devised code words—shouted by a coach or player. We never stopped inventing anything that would help us to win.

Incidentally, the electronic age might be thought of as modern, yet that buzzer in the Philadelphia coaching box was working around the turn of the century. It came to terrible grief one day when a rival third baseman happened to hear the sound and ripped the whole apparatus, wires and all, out of the dirt.

Pulling fast ones never appealed to me. I liked far more the sort of trickery perpetrated by Germany Schaefer, our fun-loving second baseman. Schaefer was the runner at first base one day, with Davey Jones, our brilliant little lead-off man, the runner at third. The sign was flashed for a double steal. Schaef was an uncanny base runner. He was on his way as the pitch left the Cleveland moundsman's hand and arrived at second without drawing a throw from catcher Nig Clarke. That delighted Schaef.

But Jones stood anchored at third, not daring to try for home and be tagged out by the waiting Clarke.

"Let's try it again!" yelled Schaef—and he dashed *back to first, a reverse steal.* The rookie pitcher for Cleveland stood with his mouth open. So did all the fans, the umpires, and the Detroit and Cleveland ball clubs. It was so crazy that when Schaef darted for second again, the kid pitcher held the ball too long, and Davey Jones sprinted across the plate with the winning run.

All the rest of that season, Schaef argued with the official scorer that he was entitled to three stolen bases on the play—second, first, and then second again.

They soon introduced a new rule to prevent such tactics, but not before Schaef had pulled it a few more times.

Upset the enemy! Confuse him, throw him into shock, make him worry constantly! That was the Detroit brand of ball that made the Tigers the tail-twisters of the league for season after season. Too bad it's all but vanished and fans of today can't enjoy the battle of wits that was everyday stuff in my youth.

87

I thrived on such a team, once I'd overcome the problems I've earlier related. As 1908 moved along, I felt for the first time the positive conviction that baseball was the career for me. I'd been filled with apprehension for almost two years. It vanished now as events took a fast turn. The Tigers gave me a few days off late in August to rush to Georgia and marry a young lady I'd been courting, Charlotte Marion Lombard. It had to be a speedy wedding. The date was August 6, the Tigers were in the running for the pennant and I was needed. I arrived by train in Augusta late at night, to avoid well-wishers. At noon the next day, at the Lombard family's country home, "The Oaks," the Reverend George Walker performed the ceremony. My hazel-eyed bride and I rushed back to Detroit the same day, and I joined the Tigers on a 14-game road trip to Boston, New York, Washington, and Philadelphia. Not much of a honeymoon. But the Tigers were locked in one of the tightest flag races in history.

On the final day of the season, Cleveland's Indians had the championship won if they could sweep a pair and a final single game from the Browns. But they split the two games, to leave the standings at:

Cleveland	90 won, 64 lost
Detroit	89 won, 63 lost
Chicago	88 won, 63 lost

And we had one game left—against the third-place White Sox of Chicago at their South Side grounds.

A most freakish situation, any way you look at it. Cleveland, although holding the most wins, was eliminated. Chicago, although in third place, could win the pennant by defeating us. We, on the other hand, could take the bunting with a victory.

Checking into the Lexington Hotel in Chicago, we found the White Sox "bugs" in their usual good voice. For half the night, they stood in the street and serenaded us with yowls, horns, sirens, songs, the banging of dishpans and garbage can lids. Anything to assure us of no sleep that night.

"Beat it, you bums!" yelled down Bill Coughlin and Charlie Schmidt. When the rooters didn't desist, Bill and Charlie found an all-night delicatessen and bought several bagfuls of tomatoes. Back at the hotel, they exercised their throwing arms on the mob below. The boys were accurate. They splattered many a Sox fan. But it didn't shut them up.

Pulling a pillow over my head, I finally managed to drop off around 4 A.M.

Sore as boiled owls over this treatment, we made the all-deciding game a walkaway. Wild Bill Donovan pitched a masterly two-hitter against Chicago's Doc White and Ed Walsh, who'd won 40 games that season while working in a superhuman 464 innings. We walloped them like they were sand-lotters. Manager Fielder Jones ran in Piano Legs Frank Smith and we walloped him harder. Sam Crawford had a double and three singles for our side. My contribution was a triple and two singles. By a 7–0 score, we breezed home with our second straight championship—by a margin of .004 percentage points over Cleveland.

Nope, I'll never forget 1908. I was run out of my first big league game earlier that season. Up to then, I'd never had a cross word with an umpire, but against these same White Sox I socked a long one over John Anderson's head in right field. Looking for an inside-the-park homer, I tried for the plate. Anderson fired to relayman Jakie Atz who fired to catcher Billy Sullivan. If I ever had a ball beat, it was that one. I'm every bit as sure right now as I was then that I hooked that plate an instant before Sullivan tagged me.

Ump Silk O'Loughlin had the gall to call me out.

I was all over him in an instant, shouting, "No! No! No!"

"Ah," replied O'Loughlin, "but yes."

In the heat of the moment, I grabbed his arm. In the National League in those days, you could spit in an umpire's eye and often get away with it, but in our circuit, the boys in blue were sacred. Silk tossed me off the lot.

And I still say he missed that call.

About this time, I had the thrill of receiving my first commercial endorsement offer. No doubt it came my way because I'd led the league in hitting again, although with a reduced average of .324. I'd also topped the field in doubles (36), triples (20), runs-batted-in (101), assists (23), and total hits (188). From J. F. Hillerich & Son, makers of the famed Louisville Slugger bat, came an offer of $75 for the use of my signature on the company's product. Hans Wagner, in 1905, had been the first big leaguer so singled out. Larry Lajoie had been second. I was to be third.

I thought about it, and while $75 was a chunk of real money, I made a counterproposition.

"I'll give you my name for nothing," I said, "if you'll provide me with selected bats. I want you to agree to set aside the best wood that comes into your plant. I want my own bin right at the factory. I'd like the privilege of specifying the kind of lumber to be used."

J. Frederick Hillerich and his son "Bud" were surprised at the offer, but accepted.

Having studied the problem pretty closely, I knew that the finest ash came from Tennessee and Kentucky and that ash was stronger than hackberry and hickory, also popular woods. I wanted my bats to weigh 36 ounces and up—graduated in weight so that I could go from a 40-ouncer in the spring to a lighter stick in the dog days of September. I also specified that the woodturner give me a rather thin handle. To get the best grip, and do away with using resin, I taped the handle and then lapped the tape, producing an uneven surface. As to the grain of the wood, I was most finicky.

"Give me a straight and fine grain, not a heavy grain," I told the Louisville Slugger people. "And try to find wood with small whirly knots in it." This is indicative of trees that have had a long, slow growth, producing the most resilient and stoutest timber.

A "Ty Cobb bin" was set up at the Louisville, Kentucky, factory and it was never disturbed over the years while special billets were aged there. I made many a pilgrimage to the Slugger plant, to test my freshly turned equipment. I'd give each finished bat a hard smack on hard ground. If it rang tenor, I'd put that one aside to keep. If I got a dull "thump," that one I discarded.

I made a fetish of caring for my delivered bats, as did most of the old-timers. Moisture would get into the wood during damp spring days and crack a lovely model. I'd fasten my bats in a clubhouse vise and rub them for hours with a large bone hollowed out from the thigh of a steer. Last time I was in the Detroit clubhouse, that bone still was in use. We also soaked our sticks in neat's-foot oil or tobacco juice to "set" the seams. My own favorite prescription was a chewing tobacco called Navy Nerve-Cut, the juiciest kind I ever discovered. Using the steer bone, I rubbed in Navy by the hour.

One day when I'd broken some of my bats and was exasperated, a fan sidled up to me. "I work in a plant that turns out hammer handles," he said. "You want a tip?"

I said that I sure did.

"Well, we've got some special machinery for treating wood with oil under pressure. Give me your bats and I'll put them through the process."

The whole thing sounded highly dubious to me, but I turned over some old culls that I hadn't planned to use. When the fan returned them, they were so heavy with oil that I could hardly swing them. I thanked my stars I hadn't let him take my good wood.

That winter, I hung them next to the furnace down in Augusta and in spring training, to my surprise, I had the finest batch of bats that ever came my way. I looked all over for my benefactor when we reached Detroit, but he had disappeared. I never saw him again.

I'll never forget my original woodturner at the Louisville Slugger plant—John Morrow. He was a hand lathe operator in 1908. Many years later, on a visit, I found that John had risen to one of the top executive posts in the now huge and prosperous Hillerich organization.

Hearing I was on hand, Morrow bustled out of his office, grabbed an apron and personally turned a new batch of bats for me. As always, they were perfect.

"Haven't lost my touch," he chuckled. "Just don't lose yours, Ty."

Back in 1908, I didn't think I'd ever lose it. It was one wonderful year.

Incidentally, I could never swing one of those ridiculously skinny witch's broomsticks of 30 ounces that 1960-era players employ. They might as well be playing stickball and trying to hit for six sewers on the streets of New York.

7

Beanballs Were the Least of It

Life in the big league was a lot more hazardous then than now. We were wide open to sneak attacks from overwrought fans, transportation could be downright dangerous and ball teams didn't supply legal batteries to bail you out of any extracurricular trouble that might come along.

In the spring of 1911, when I was holding out for a $15,000 salary, I organized a club of semipros down South. We barnstormed through Dixie, drawing pretty well. My idea wasn't to make money, but to stay in shape while waiting for that Shylock of the front office—owner Frank Navin of Detroit—to meet my demand. By then I'd led the league four years running with .350, .324, .377, and .385 averages. From 23 stolen bases in 1906, I'd advanced to 76 in 1909 and twice topped the circuit in that department. At the age of twenty-three, I had three Triple Crowns to my credit—which meant I'd put together three seasons in which my total hits, runs-batted-in and batting average were No. 1 in the league. (Home runs were not a factor of Baseball's Triple Crown until 1913–14, when Baker and Cravath popularized them.) Yet Navin was trying to hold me as close to my $9000 pay of previous years as his wily ways would allow.

So I ignored him, put together my own little nine, and away we went, playing whistle stops and big cities. At one stop, a wild-eyed youth came out of the stands and rushed at me, shouting curses. I fended him off and advised him to apologize.

"Cobb, you're a dirty ——!" he screamed.

Next thing I knew he'd pulled a pistol from his pocket and had it centered on my gizzard.

He was just hysterical enough—about what I didn't know—to pull the trigger. That pistol muzzle looked as large as a cannon. In the next instant, I reached his chin with a punch that floored the boy, and sent the gun sailing.

But it had been close . . . and now that I think of it, there were other escapes that helped thin my hair at a young age. In Philadelphia, in 1909, there was a hairline scrape with a streetcar. I was returning by taxicab to our hotel with Charley O'Leary, our second baseman and erstwhile shortstop, and trainer Harry Tuthill. Seated up front with the driver, I saw the trolley car rolling full speed out of a side street. "Turn!" I told the driver.

Although we were moving at a good clip, too, and a collision was certain, the hackie seemed dazed and unable to spin the wheel. When we were almost upon the car, I seized the wheel and threw the car sideways. We hit with a terrific crash. Our rear wheels were caught and ripped off and we went catapulting on past by a margin so close that several onlookers fainted. The four of us came within a second or so of being caught and mangled under those trolley wheels.

Every season the high pressure under which we played caught up with some of the boys. And usually, it was in the springtime that tragedy struck. Johnny Evers, the great Cub, had a nervous breakdown before the 1911 season. That same spring, Addie Joss, a wonderful pitcher with Cleveland, died of tubercular meningitis at the age of thirty-one. In 1906, the Senators lost two fine youngsters, Joe Cassidy and Punch Knoll, to physical ailments. Joe was twenty-three, Punch twenty-four when they died. Chick Stahl resigned as Red Sox manager during spring training at West Baden, Indiana, in 1907 and then killed himself by swallowing carbolic acid. Big Ed Delahanty, an all-time hitting great, either fell or jumped from a train crossing a bridge near Niagara Falls—the mystery never has been solved. There were wild and incredible characters in the game in those days, but while they lasted they lived life to the hilt.

One day I was leaving the Hotel Ponchartrain in Detroit for the ball park and stepped into Woodward Avenue. Hearing a roar behind me, I made an instinctive sideways leap to avoid being run down by a motorist whose new gas buggy evidently had gone to his head. In leaping, I landed in some freshly poured asphalt.

"What the —— are you doing there?" demanded a workman, who had been smoothing the stuff. He was belligerent and insulting. Being imbedded in the sticky stuff hardly could have been a purposeful act. But I replied that a car had just missed me. Again, I was insulted.

So I let the workman join me in the asphalt by bopping him on the chin. He made a nice splash. Unfortunately, he was a Negro.

When he learned my identity, the workman, named Collins, made a big hoo-raw in the papers about it. As a Southerner, he claimed, I was a black-hater. My true feeling was that of anyone who'd had a Negro "mammy" as a child, which I did, and who had lived most peaceably with colored folk for years. Collins demanded $100, or court action. I was inclined to let it go to court, since Collins had started it, but finally paid $75 to be rid of the nuisance.

While ducking pistols, trolleys, and legal threats, I learned that you couldn't gain prominence as a ballplayer without making blood enemies of players I had no grudge against—except when they decided to play beanbag with my slender 168-pound body. American League catchers were out to stop my base-running. The St. Louis receiver, Paul Krichell, had a vicious habit of hooking my leg when I slid into the plate and flipping me over so that I scraped up dirt with my face. The second or third time it happened, I advised him, "Don't ever do that again."

Krichell gave me the hook once more, and this time I scissored my legs, caught him under an arm and almost detached it from his body. The arm was forced back and badly torn at the shoulder. Krichell's career ended right there, after only two major league seasons.

"I'm sorry about it," I told the St. Louis players, "but I warned him."

The belief that I tore up basemen with my spikes never was tempered with any understanding of what I faced—such as Jack Warner, who'd been a teammate of mine, but had been traded to Washington in 1906. Warner's stunt—when he saw me coming in from third—was to drop his heavy catcher's mask squarely before the plate. Since a proper slide is *on the ground*, I had to risk a broken or lacerated foot or ankle if I tried plowing through that mask. Behind the mask waited Warner, grinning at my predicament.

Solution: I could only slide in *over* the mask, and if either Warner or I was hurt in the collision, it hadn't been something I'd arranged. Warner forced me to leave the ground and, quite true, my spikes were high on such occasions. But protests thundered from all sides. From New York to Chicago, I was painted as a deep-dyed villain, a threat to humanity. John I. Taylor, the Boston club owner, threatened to ban me from his park. Some of my supporters retorted that Taylor had good reason, inasmuch as in this general period I was averaging around .370 against Red Sox pitchers Joe Wood, Cy Young, Ray Collins, and Eddie Cicotte. Taylor took care not to mention Rube Foster, one of a number of beanballing Boston pitchers who'd stuck one in my ribs, breaking two of them.

All this animosity came to a head in 1910, the year the Chalmers Motor Car Company offered its most expensive model of touring car as a prize to the batting champion of the major leagues.

As the season moved into the final weeks, a two-man race shaped up between myself, at a .371 mark, and Larry Lajoie of Cleveland, at .375. The Chalmers contest became a more vital issue than the political rift between President Taft and Teddy Roosevelt or the crackdown on trusts by the Supreme Court. It was so hot, in fact, that a Detroit fan named Tim Carrigan dropped dead of a heart attack at the Century Club while shouting down a Lajoie backer.

Just as it looked as if I might catch up with Lajoie, an eye ailment that had been bothering me grew serious and I had to leave the line-up briefly. One eye became inflamed to the point that I couldn't see the ball well in its flight. The headline—*IS COBB GOING BLIND IN ONE EYE?*—was spread over sport pages after a confidential letter I sent to a Cleveland friend became public. In it, I said:

". . . my eyes are not very good now and I have to use one eye to write.

I feel greatly disappointed to go all season so well and then have something bob up the last month to throw me out of the running for the auto. I realize my eyes may not be right when I go in again, and if I'm forced out again, Lajoie surely will beat my present

95

average. However, I am taking treatment from eye specialists and tomorrow am going to consult a stomach specialist, as this may be the answer to the trouble. The blur in front of the right eye causes it not to focus and I can only see well from the left eye; the other is smoky. I am very worried.

But if I am not to win, no better, cleaner contestant could win than Lajoie. He is the one I wish to win it, if I can't.

T.R.C.

While I was benched, Lajoie went on a tremendous spree, getting 23 hits in 10 games, and pushed past the .380 mark. My eyes did not respond to treatment, but I had no choice. Returning to action, I had a badly needed big day against New York. In four times up, I walked and beat out three infield smashes to as many fielders, Jimmy Austin, Hal Chase, and Schoolboy Knight. Over the course of that 4-game New York series, I had a double, two triples, a homer, and three singles in 13 at-bats for a .534 figure. By the last two days of the season, I'd forged to a .384 percentage. And then the eye trouble flared up worse than ever, and I had to drop out of the final two games of the year.

Now the edge was mine—slightly. Lajoie had two games in which to take the Chalmers away from me.

Since I wasn't present to see what happened when Lajoie and the Indians played St. Louis in the final double-header, let the following copyrighted report from the Detroit *Free Press* tell the tale of the biggest Brannigan of 1910:

ST. LOUIS TEAM "LAYS DOWN" TO LET LAJOIE WIN

Gets Eight Hits in Race with Cobb When Opponents Refuse to Field "Gift" Bunts

ST. LOUIS, Oct. 9—A palpable case of "lay down" on the part of members of the St. Louis club occurred here today, enabling Nap Lajoie to make eight hits and either come very close or go ahead of Ty Cobb in the race for the Chalmers 30 automobile and batting championship.

After today's farce—a hippodrome which should be investigated by the highest authorities—the winner probably will not be known until the official averages are made public weeks from now.

HERE'S AN excellent study of Frank (Home
Run) Baker after he left the Philadelphia
White Elephants to play with the New York
Americans. My life was threatened and the
park was placed under police protection after
I was accused of maliciously spiking Baker.
The true story? Read it here.

ALTHOUGH I stole bases many ways, the
proper way to slide is illustrated here—down
on the ground, hooking the bag with a toe
placed as far away from the baseman as possible. I left the ground, with spikes high,
only when illegally forced to take such action.
Baker was just one more player who knew
that I didn't play dirty.

WIDE WORLD PHOTO

MANY A TIME Babe Ruth would have liked to teed off with that bat on my skull. We were rabid rivals—I could get Babe's goat almost every time I tried. Here he is, the season after hitting 60 home runs.

YEARS AFTER we retired, Babe hooked up with me in a knock-down—drag-out golf battle. This was taken on the fifth green of the first of our three matches. In golf, Babe showed me a different temperament and I took full advantage of it.

MY BATTING STYLE didn't change much once I had it established. Note that as an eighteen-year-old rookie in 1905, I was already choking up on the stick. Photo No. 2 and 3 show me in my late twenties and toward the end of the line, when I was past forty.

KID GLEASON, a grand man and [ ]
master-mind—who should have suc[ ]
Hughie Jennings as manager of the [ ]
Instead, it was forced upon me. Afte[ ]
I suffered torture.

As a MANAGER, I had many criti[ ]
they couldn't complain about th[ ]
did with Harry Heilmann. I take[ ]
for making Harry a hitter who [ ]
.393, .398, and .403 averages and [ ]
league no less than four times.

Closeup of Ty Cobb, manager of the Detroit Tigers, in his new goggles.

'D JUST removed a growth from my eyes when these shots were taken. Between
nd managing under Frank Navin's ownership, baseball no longer was fun for
was thinking: "Will my eyes respond fast enough to get me out of the way of
alls?"

A VILE PLOT to ruin Tris Speaker (shown here with me when we were 1928
mates on the Athletics) and me had recently backfired when this was taken.
my bow-out season in the game.

Lajoie got one hit even halfway legitimate today—a fly to centre his first time up. It went for a triple, although any kind of fielding by Northen of St. Louis could have converted it into an easy out.

The hate-Ty-Cobb-campaign never was so miserably evident as today.

The other seven hits by Lajoie were the product of bunts laid down toward third base and shortstop and which the St. Louis men allowed to roll, without any sort of fielding effort. Six of them went to Red Corriden, playing third, and one to Wallace, at short. In each instance, while the ball was fielded perfectly, it was not thrown to first.

According to local figures, Lajoie had to make eight hits out of as many times at bat to catch and go ahead of Cobb. Lajoie seldom uses the bunt. Today he did—through connivance that has made a mockery of American baseball.

Even St. Louis newspapers were enraged at the play of their team, as this *Post* excerpt shows:

All St. Louis is up in arms over the deplorable spectacle, conceived in stupidity and executed in jealousy. The obvious frame-up to beat Cobb out of the title surely will place a period upon the career of whatever officials of the home team ordered this gross affair.

St. Louis people should subscribe to a fund to buy Ty Cobb a Chalmers auto, should it prove that he has lost one he legitimately won. At Sportsman's Park (ironic is the name) last Sunday, Corriden played far back on the grass, in short left field, and made no try for the ball. Corriden is a mere boy, new to the major leagues. He must have had orders from someone higher up. The man higher up should be reached and punished.

We should hate to think that Manager Jack O'Connor of the Brownies, who has long been a close personal friend, had anything to do with this monstrous fraud. But O'Connor was present, in command of the team, and even if he did not conceive and have executed the affair, it seems that he could at least have stopped it. We hope Mr. O'Connor will be able to clear his skirts to the fullest. If not, friend or no friend, let justice and right take its fullest course.

In New York, then writing sports, Heywood Broun, had a few pithy remarks:

As the world knows now, Tyrus Raymond Cobb is less popular than Napoleon Lajoie. Perhaps Cobb is the least popular player who ever lived. And why? Whether you like or dislike this young fellow, you must concede him one virtue: what he has won, he has taken by might of his own play. He asks no quarter and gives none. Pistareen ball players whom he has "shown up" dislike him. Third basemen with bum arms, second basemen with tender shins, catchers who cannot throw out a talented slider—all despise Cobb. And their attitude has infected the stands. Why do they so resent Cobb when he plays the game at every point on the field, giving his best at every moment, and makes life miserable for those less willing?

Ahhh—one wonders. Here is the best man in all the world at his game, without the shade of doubt; the best of any time. Is it because he is swell-headed? But Cobb is not—he is, indeed, not spoiled at all. He is a gentle, well-mannered youth off the field, full of boyish life and spirits. On the field, he is full of the ebullience of his 24 years and of power and success. Hated why? What player gives the fans so much value for their money?

Yet it seems he is fated to move across the field as did Bobby Burns' gallant scapegrace, who danced beneath the noose—"Sae wantonly, sae dauntingly, sae rantingly gaied he."

He played a spring and danced it 'round the gallows tree. If Cobb sticks his cap on three hairs, as the Irish say, laughs in the faces of his opponents and steals bases while they stand with the ball in their hands, is he to be damned by the populace?

With the curious crassity which always leads the mob to rend that hand that feeds it and to lick that which whips it, spectators at baseball games do not like this boy who gives them more for their hard-earned ticket than any man alive or dead ever gave them. When humanity put to death its Greatest Servant, all that he could say in condonation was "Father, forgive them, for they know not what they do."

That was the biggest and truest thing He ever said. Humanity, the mob, never knows what it is doing. It always prefers guile and gaud to honesty and worth. No man who ever did anything for it ever got anything but its worst.

Humanity is asinine.

Broun really pulled out all stops for me. So did many others. After such an outpouring of disapproval, Ban Johnson, president of the American League, dug into the St. Louis affair, and quickly absolved Red Corriden of any complicity, on the grounds that he was only a rookie who had to do as he was ordered. "What instructions did you have?" Johnson asked Corriden.

"My orders were to play Lajoie back on the edge of the grass," said Corriden.

"Who gave you those orders?"

Corriden had to admit that Manager O'Connor had been the brain behind the plot.

Further investigation turned up that various Browns, including pitcher-coach Harry Howell, were determined to see Lajoie win the Chalmers. Ban Johnson announced that an anonymous note had been passed to the St. Louis official scorer, promising him a suit of clothes if he gave Lajoie the benefit of the doubt on any close plays. Howell had visited the press box several times during the game to inquire whether the Lajoie bunts were being scored as hits.

Right has always triumphed in baseball, more than in any other sport. Both O'Connor and Howell were dropped by the Browns. They were all through as major leaguers. Lajoie, it goes without saying, knew nothing of the scheme. That marvelous hitter, who according to the Official Encyclopedia of Baseball had a lifetime 3242 safeties, didn't need anyone's help to rank right at the top.

And then the newspaper battle began again—who had copped the Chalmers? The Chicago *Tribune* statisticians gave it to Larry by three points, .385 to .382. The Cleveland *Leader* gave it to Larry by .382 to .381. The *Sporting News*, the authoritative voice of baseball, however, calculated that Cobb had a gnat's eyebrow margin of .38415 to .38411. Everyone held his breath until the official figures were released, which were:

Cobb—.3848

Lajoie—.3841

You can't win by a much smaller margin then seven ten-thousandths of a percentage point, but I settled for it gladly. It was so close that when I drove off to Georgia in the Chalmers, my good friend, Larry Lajoie, departed for his home in Woonsocket, Rhode Island, also in a Chalmers. The motor company decided we both deserved an auto.

All the fussing and feuding had been for nothing—as it so usually is in life.

What concerned me far more than winning a car was the condition of my eyes, the threat they posed to my future. During the 1909 World Series, of the season before the Lajoie incident, I'd wondered why my batting average had dipped. One explanation, of course, was that I was young. Entering into the Series so early in my career has always been one of my regrets. If the Tigers had won pennants after 1909, I'm sure I could have performed better. We put together three straight flags in '07, '08, and '09, and I'm not especially proud of my performance in any of the world title matches that followed. Against the Chicago Cubs in '08, I managed a .368 average and had one game—the third—when a double, three singles, and two bases stolen off catcher Johnny Kling made me feel good. But in 1909, against Pittsburgh in the Series, I was off form. When I did meet the ball solidly, some Pirate would make a circus catch. In 26 trips to bat, I had but six hits for a .231 mark. A steal of home in the second game, a long running catch of Dots Miller's short fly and a two-run double in the third game were the only efforts I could comfort myself with that winter.

I'll take time out for a moment from the matter of my eyes.

I've often been asked about that steal, since pilfering home base in a World Series falls on the unusual side. It happened this way:

By the third inning, Detroit had reached Howard Camnitz, the Pirate pitcher, for six hits and five runs, and manager Fred Clarke of Pittsburgh called from the bull pen Vic Willis. I was the runner at third base. The moment I saw Willis coming in, I decided to try for a steal of home. My reasoning was that Willis, facing a lot of hot Tiger bats, would have his mind far more on stopping our attack than on me. First, however, I needed to experiment. Willis was a twelve-year veteran. So far I was only *guessing* that he'd neglect to be watchful of Cobb.

As soon as Willis took his pose on the rubber, I walked some distance off third to see if he was watching me closely. His eyes were fixed on the signal of his catcher, Gibson. It was a thrilling moment—Willis had left an opening. I turned back toward third, in order to disarm Willis, Gibson and third baseman Bob Byrne. Then —just as Willis raised his arm to go into his wind-up—I broke for the plate with everything I had.

Since a right-handed hitter was at bat for Detroit, I had some protection—namely, the screening effect of his body—part way down the line. Gibson didn't see me coming at first. Meanwhile,

Willis was reacting violently on the mound: checking his wind-up and stance in order to fire the ball home.

It was another of those harrowing moments, those close escapes. I ripped up dirt for 30 inches with my spikes, twisted my body away from the plate and hooked it with one toe, which Gibson pounced upon. If I'd been called out, I suppose I'd have been termed an all-time goat. But the ump yelled "Safe!"

I'm still happy about that steal. Because it wasn't based on luck, but on seeing a psychological opportunity, setting the stage, taking advantage of our right-handed hitter at bat and timing it just right.

At bat against Pittsburgh, I was less happy. I was annoyed to find myself missing pitches I should have hit. By 1910, the problem hadn't improved. By then, I was involved with Lajoie and the batting championship race, and I found myself called out on pitches I was sure were not strikes. At first, I squawked to the umpires. I thought the umps were missing them. Finally, Bill Dinneen, an umpire I respected, said to me, "Ty, we're not missing these calls. There must be something wrong with your vision."

Alarmed, I went to Dr. William Wilmer, later founder of the Wilmer Clinic at Johns Hopkins Hospital, a specialist who had treated kings and presidents. He peered long and hard into my eyes. "Yes, this could be serious," he said.

His examination showed that an inflammation had attacked the focusing folds of the eyes, where the optical organ functions like the shutter of a camera. Any fast ball I had to follow couldn't be picked up with real certainty while I was in this condition. Dr. Wilmer had me use an eyecup many times a day, bathing the afflicted part in a healing solution. "You see," he told me, "the nerves, too, are affected, and can't accommodate quickly to what your job requires."

After long and tedious treatment, I began to improve. Gradually, my sight became normal again.

That wasn't my last scare . . . some years later, a growth called pterygium appeared in both my eyes, and I went under Dr. Wilmer's knife at Johns Hopkins. There was speculation that I'd never be able to see well enough to hit big league pitching again.

Oh, I went on hitting, all right. I went on so long that people began to wonder whether I had some alchemist down in Georgia mixing me a magic elixir that staved off old age. Not long ago, a fan asked me, "Ty, with all the things that happened to you—fights and feuds and beanballs and guns and trolley cars and eye trouble and all—how in the world did you stick around so long?"

Doggoned if I know. But, at this writing, I'm still breathing and following those box scores.

8

The Case of the Purloined Telegrams

Someone in the Detroit front office was intercepting and reading my private telegrams. The invasion of my privacy made me quite unhappy. Someone would pay for it.

That someone, as I had definite evidence at hand, was Frank Navin, the majority owner of the Tiger club stock and my boss, as such.

Club president or not, Navin had no business sticking his nose into my personal messages. That slippery gentleman had taken advantage of me many times before, and now I determined to make him a good boy, once and for all.

This was in the season of 1913, but the immediate background to the telegram-espionage went back a few seasons. Until then, about 1910, I'd been earning the magnificent sum of $4500 per 154 games. After my fourth consecutive batting championship and that .385 average in '10, I told Navin that nothing less than $10,000 would satisfy me. A $15,000 salary would have been more appropriate, but the sum was unheard of in those days. To get the raise, I had to hold out again, refusing to report for 14 days of the 1911 season. Navin had his neck bowed and Hughie Jennings was forced to play Oscar Vitt in my outfield spot. Vitt was an infielder. The Tigers began to blow games left and right. The fans complained and then grew angry. They demanded my return, and Navin reluctantly surrendered.

To polish apples with his public, he set the stage rather neatly.

My Great Benefactor went into an act when I appeared in his offices for the contract-signing ceremony.

Looking around, I found most of the baseball writers of Detroit—Harry Salsinger, Joe Jackson, Paul Bruske, Malcolm Bingay, E. A. Batchelor, Bill Comfort, and others—assembled. Navin took me aside and confidentially whispered a request.

"As a favor, Ty, I want you to announce to the boys that you are allowing me to name your salary and write in the figure," said he. "It'll be like a vote of confidence in me from you. Of course, you and I know what the figure will be, but the writers don't."

Well, I was still a bit of a trusting kid, and I said, "Okay, I'll do it."

When I'd obliged him and it came time for the signing, on a hunch that everything wasn't kosher, I walked over and stood by Navin at his desk. And I saw him put down $9000 as my new salary.

Furiously, I whispered to him, "You've just put yourself over a nice barrel. That is not the figure."

Taking another look, I saw where Navin originally had written in $10,000, but now he was penning in $9000 over it.

Navin fiddled around with his pen and harrumphed a few times and finally restored the $10,000 sum, but I told him, "I won't accept this contract. I want one that is properly executed and not defaced." And that's the contract I finally got. I still have it, as a matter of fact.

I could have unmasked Navin and created a scene in his office that would have made headlines, but held back through a desire not to blow the lid off the delicate situation between us. Navin was widely reputed to be "canny." I'd called it something else ever since my second season as a Tiger, when he let me pay my own hospital bill after an injury put me on my back. Not knowing that the club was liable, I'd innocently let Frank J. get away with avoiding the bill.

But I can assure you that by 1913, I had learned a great deal about Navin, and was able to handle my financial affairs in a little better shape. With 1913–14 came the showdown between us.

My batting titles now stood at seven in a row, one less than Honus Wagner's record of eight in the National League. But the Dutchman's hadn't been consecutive. After putting up .385, .420, and .410 marks, I'd expressed a keen desire to Navin to be raised from $10,000 to $12,000. As usual, he saw fit to sling mud and blacken my name.

"Cobb is becoming a real threat," said Navin. "He may or may not belong on our team. Does he want to wind up owning it?"

My reply was, "Navin has my proposition. There are no petty or big desires on my part to be more than a ballplayer. It begins to look as if he doesn't want me in his clubhouse, and I've about concluded that it would be best for all concerned if I was traded to another organization. It's Navin's move."

We remained stymied for weeks. Hugh McKinnon, a prominent baseball man, came out with a statement that aroused wide attention. "My belief is," said McKinnon, "that Cobb is the victim of a plot to run him out of baseball because he is becoming too expensive. Ban Johnson, president of the American League, has threatened to suspend him if he continues these every-season hold-outs. Now, Cobb is well aware of this plan to make him knuckle under, and rob him of his prestige.

"But the salary future of every player in baseball is at stake here. Cobb is out to create new pay standards, for not only himself, but every other underpaid man in the profession. Baseball has become a major big business. In Detroit, Navin is doing such a box-office that he upped Bennett Field from 11,000 to 14,000 capacity and currently is ripping out the old wooden stands and building a concrete single-decker seating 23,000. Since 1910, we have seen a great stadium-building spree. Comiskey Park has risen in Chicago, Griffith Stadium has been opened in Washington and a new Polo Grounds has been erected in New York. Fenway Park has just opened in Boston, Ebbets Field in Brooklyn will be inaugurated soon and Wrigley Field in Chicago is in the design stages.

"Hard times for the magnates? Phaugh!"

As the '13 season opened, Navin was still moaning that $12,000 for Cobb would bankrupt him, and then United States Senator Hoke Smith of Georgia entered the scene. On April 19, I received a wire from Senator Smith which read:

WASHINGTON, D.C.—SEND ME A COPY OF YOUR CONTRACT WITH DETROIT INCLUDING RESERVE CLAUSE. WISH TO INVESTIGATE IT TO SEE IF ILLEGAL CONTRACT VIOLATING FEDERAL STATUTES HAS BEEN MADE. HOKE SMITH, U.S. SENATE.

When that message hit the fan, Navin and baseball owners in general ducked all over the map. Senator Smith and Representative Thomas W. Hardwick of Georgia quoted the Sherman Anti-Trust

Act on the floor of Congress for the first time. Federal peonage laws were involved and Hoke Smith wanted to know whether a "baseball trust" was conspiring to keep me from earning a living. The reserve clause, as it is today, was the bone of contention. Did baseball, unlike any other money-making enterprise, have the right to inflexibly reserve a player's services for another season, although he might be poorly paid or otherwise misused, and by what equity was he unable to deal with another employer on threat of instant banishment from Organized Baseball?

Secondly, how could Detroit hold the right to release me within any 10-day period, when I had no equal right to abrogate our agreement?

Navin gave me the $12,000 with no further argument, but on a one-season basis only. If he hadn't capitulated, I'd have sued the Detroit club and Organized Ball. With Hoke Smith's Senatorial friends behind me, I couldn't have lost.

Well, I wasn't satisfied, only temporarily mollified. I could see $30,000 or $40,000 a season up the line, and sensed that big-money era for ballplayers was dawning, if we only fought for every inch of progress and cultivated the right friends in political circles.

At this point, the Federal League came into being as the single most powerful threat to baseball monopoly that ever has been posed.

The Feds, even though they picked a poor time to launch operations and were too late in starting, gave the country the first and only third major league that ever came close to succeeding. Behind it was a mintful of money, supplied by such men as Jim Gilmore (a coal-and-paper magnate), Charlie Weeghman (a Chicago restaurateur), Phil DeCatesby Ball (St. Louis ice king), Bob Ward (bakeries), and Harry Sinclair (the oil Croesus). They were determined to move in on some of the profits the game was earning and from which they were excluded by the National Agreement, profits which kept the game virtually a closed private club. The Feds, meeting in secret with name players, began to sign a few real stars. Joe Tinker was the first to jump, signing as player-manager of the Chicago Whales in the Federal League. Then Hal Chase jumped the White Sox to the Buffalo Federals. Mordecai Brown, Russ Ford, Chief Bender, Jack Quinn, and Eddie Plank deserted the "legitimate" ranks to turn "outlaw." Walter Johnson agreed to Federal terms, but backed off at the last minute when Washington increased his stipend to top the Fed offer.

I saw no chance for the upstart league to last. But I won't say I neglected the opportunity it presented. I did talk to the leaders of the circuit.

We met privately in the summer of 1913 in the Commodore Hotel in New York, to which I was invited by President Gilmore of the Feds and Harry Sinclair.

"Would you consider leaving Detroit to join us?" they said, after the preliminary palaver.

"No," I replied, "and for several reasons."

"What are they?" asked Gilmore.

"My feeling is," I said, "that you gentlemen have missed your play. You have started too late to be ready for 1914 operations. You can't plan substantial parks at this late date and you'll find it almost impossible to gather enough players of major league ability."

I didn't go into all the angles with them, but the fact was that the Feds could have salivated the American and National Leagues had they only realized the advantage they held. Players by the score were anxious to jump. The Feds could have picked off almost every star in the game—we were that sore at our bosses and the contracts they bonded us to. The Feds didn't even have to raise the ante in salary, but only guarantee two- and three-year contracts, to raid the AL and NL from top to bottom. But they failed to see what they had and acted in too opportunistic a way. They talked too big, too wildly, without hard-headed planning, to convince the more thoughtful ballplayers.

"What other reason have you for not joining us?" Sinclair wanted to know.

"Simply that I've signed a $12,000 contract with Detroit. And it happens that I honor my contracts."

Sinclair, who won the Kentucky Derby with Zev later on and reputedly controlled $60,000,000 at the time the Teapot Dome scandal of the 1920s sent him to jail, studied me keenly.

"We'll give you $100,000 and a three-year contract," he said, very calmly. "Furthermore, we will put the money in escrow. Furthermore, we will see that you don't lose by it if the league should fail."

I'll remember as long as I live Sinclair's next statement. "If we should fail, you will be the highest-priced oil lease man in the history of the Sinclair company. You can quit baseball and sign up oil lands for us and name your own price."

One hundred thousand against $12,000. . . .

"Thank you," I said, "but I think not. The American League is where I made my name and there I'll stay."

They seemed mightily surprised, but some of the surprise disappeared when they learned all the facts of a new-type contract the American and National Leagues were rushing into print. The Feds had sued in the U. S. District Court in Chicago under the Sherman Anti-Trust Act, charging that the National Agreement was an illegal instrument and based in peonage. Now an option contract was issued by the AL and NL by which the player reserved his *own* services to his team for the following season, and paid for the reservation out of his salary. By signing, the player tacitly agreed to put himself on option (the club's option, not his), and so rendered the courts unable to act. As smooth as goose grease was this agreement, and few players understood the number of rights they signed away.

For the 1914 season, when I wanted another raise from Detroit, I played the waiting game and did not sign. Which is when Frank Navin began to become interested in my private telegrams.

He was convinced I was on the verge of jumping to the Federal League. To learn more, he arranged to see my wires, even before Western Union delivered them to me.

I got hep to this when I noticed that Navin's private home telephone number appeared penciled on the back of the telegrams. What was it doing there? I discovered to my shock that all wires to Tyrus Cobb were first routed to Navin. But Western Union was duty-bound to record the place and time of delivery, and, unknown to Navin, the information showed up where I couldn't miss it. Even a wire from my wife and children sent from Cincinnati, saying they were arriving in Detroit in a few days, was among those intercepted.

To establish proof positive, to catch Navin redhanded, I worked out a little scheme.

At the time, I was writing syndicated stories for Bell Newspaper Syndicate, headed up by the highly respected John N. Wheeler. Among the Federal League bigwigs was one John M. Ward. The similarity of the initials—J.N.W. and J.M.W.—was most fortunate. Wheeler was urging me to sign to do more World Series reportage. So I asked him to wire me as follows: DO NOTHING UNTIL YOU SEE ME ON NEXT TRIP EAST. J.N.W.

Wheeler obliged me, and sure enough, when the wire reached my hands, it was marked with Navin's home address and somewhat wrinkled. I was sure he'd mistaken Wheeler for Ward.

When we returned to Detroit from an eastern road trip, I was burning mad and ready for Act Three of the drama. Here I'd turned down the Federal offer, remained loyal and had honored my contract, and yet was being treated like a viper in Navin's bosom. *I'll make him pay for this*, I vowed.

Word arrived in our clubhouse, "Mr. Navin would like to see Ty Cobb in his office."

I knew why he wanted me—to talk me into signing the new form of contract which self-reserved my services and vitiated the 10-day release clause. I simply ignored the message. Next day came another more urgent message. Would I please hustle upstairs right away? I showered after the game and left without seeing Navin. On the third call, when I had him softened up, I deigned to drop into his sanctum.

"Well, Ty, you've been going great," said Navin, affably, "and I thought we'd just get things fixed up for 1914. Meanwhile, if you'll just sign this new form of contract, it'll make it conform to those the other players have signed. In this agreement, we strike the 10-day release clause from the agreement. All the boys are in favor of that."

"Why should I sign it?" I replied. "I've been operating under this 10-day clause and the reserve agreement for a long time. My signature is on the old contract. It's perfectly good, as you should know. Why change the arrangement now?"

Navin began to grow nervous. "Well, it's important you go along on this. Ban Johnson has ordered us to have all players sign the new form. Ban feels that maybe the contract isn't binding just as it is, with that clause written in."

"It seems to me you are pretty much concerned about this thing," I said. "And isn't it a rather late day to find this out? I've been operating over a trap door for nine years. You could drop me in 10 days any time you liked if I was injured or sick. I haven't asked you to take that clause out of my contract—since you turned down the request long ago—and I see no reason to remove it now. I'll just finish out the season with the deal we have."

Well, Navin became highly nervous now. He paced up and down and I could read his mind. *This is just an excuse* he was thinking. *Cobb must be all set to jump to the Federals.*

Although I was only telling him the simple truth when I said, "Navin, I see no rush about this. You have my pledge to play for Detroit"—he couldn't believe it. He was sure I was lying. His own self-built suspicions were in the way. Because he'd been reading my telegrams, such as the one signed "J.N.W."

Navin began to plead. "Ty, if you'll sign this new form, we'll increase your contract by $2500."

"Ohhhhh, Mr. Navin," I replied, "does it mean *that* much to you? My goodness alive, this puts a new construction on it. I'll have to do some thinking. A lot of thinking."

Navin was almost trotting around the room, puffing with exertion, and he gasped, "What are we going to do?"

I let him suffer a while longer, then said, "Well, you've given me an opening and I'll take it. If it means that much to you, let me have your best offer for next year's salary."

"Why, I can't come up more than $2500 on $12,000 for one year," he said. "That's the absolute limit."

"As a matter of fact," I said, shooting the words at him, hard and angrily, "the invasion of certain rights of mine has been made. I have seen your home telephone number on my private telegrams. That's quite an imposition, and I want you to know I resent it.

"Now you want me to sign this contract. I'll tell you what it will cost you to get my signature—$15,000 a season and for a three-year period, or $45,000 guaranteed."

I'm not a doctor, but Navin's breath almost failed. His policy never was to give a player security for more than one season, and he always kept an escape hatch in case of injury. But when I hit him with the telegrams, he floundered for words.

"That's it," I said. "Forty-five thousand guaranteed and no ifs-and-or-buts."

The reader can figure out what it cost Navin to read my telegrams. We signed, then and there, for the largest sum yet tendered a baseball player, and it was only the beginning. The next time we talked contract, Navin paid me $20,000 per annum, then $35,000 and, finally, $50,000. From 1913 on, I was in the catbird's seat when it came to money.

The $100,000 I rejected from the Federal League? I didn't make such a bad guess. After completing seasons in 1914–15, the inexperience of the Fed leaders and the imminence of World War I brought their downfall, and their properties were absorbed by the existing major leagues at a cost of almost $400,000.

I'll say one thing for the short-lived Federals, however. I never heard of anyone in that organization pilfering a man's personal telegrams.

9

"Beware of Entrance to a Quarrel"

I have been roughed up in print possibly more than any man who ever played at sport. The smaller slanders I've chosen to ignore. But in my personal files and clipping books are hundreds of stories that dishonor my name—wildcat junk that fans still mistake for the truth.

Why have I saved all this claptrap? Perhaps because some day I intended to write this book.

It was Bugs Baer (among many writers) who convinced the country that I sat by the Detroit bench, whetting my spikes razor-sharp with a file, and then putting them to bloody use on the base paths.

One of the South's most celebrated editors, Ralph McGill, of the Atlanta *Constitution*, once wrote that I kicked and brutalized a bird dog of mine because he broke on point and lost a field trail.

Modern ball fans may not remember the 1909 Hans Wagner hoax. But they know the Ted Williams story. In the former, I'm described as standing on first base in the World Series, and yelling to Wagner, playing shortstop for the Pirates: "Look out, Krauthead, I'm coming down!" In variously circulated accounts, when I arrived, Wagner slammed the ball into my teeth and split my lip for three stitches. With Williams, I'm supposed to have handed him some tips on how to hit to left field. The location varies—sometimes we're at Santa Anita race track, in other versions at Boston, Yankee Stadium, and Chicago. The punch line, when I'm finished, is that Williams snorts, "Oh, nuts," and walks away.

Once upon a time, in 1912, baseball experienced its one and only walk-out strike by an entire team, the Detroit Tigers. Why? Because, as it's told, Cobb flew into one of his terrible rages, attacked a paying customer in the stands, was suspended by League president Ban Johnson and incited the Tigers to pull a disgraceful revolt. The story has become so garbled that today almost no one knows the facts.

I'm the ballplayer who "hated" an umpire so much that I fist-whipped and tromped Billy Evans under the stands until little of poor Evans was left to carry away. Or so grandfathers read forty-seven years back. And so passed on to their sons, and they to the generation of the sixties.

A Philadelphia sportswriter was the author of a barefaced fraud that set a local mob—and a good part of the nation—against me fifty-two years ago. His fantasy never has died. It still fills many a rainy-day sports column. In this one, I maliciously spiked Frank (Home Run) Baker and crippled the great third baseman of the Philadelphia A's. Youngsters I meet nowadays look at me wide-eyed, expecting to see me wearing horns. "Sure, I know you," innocent little kids will say. "You spiked Home Run Baker."

This is not a book of alibi. I would not profane it with anything untrue or a build-up for Cobb. But I'll confess to a weak point in my armor. It hurts me deeply to be wrongly accused in matters involving honor, fair play, and decent deportment on and off the field, and that record must be set straight.

I was eighteen years old, a Tiger rookie, when my philosopher father warned me against any act "degrading your dignity or belittling your manhood." He put it in the form of a letter—I still cherish it—which ends with:

"Starve and drive out the evil demon that lurks in all human blood and ready to arise and reign. Be under the perpetual guidance of the better angel of your nature. Be good."

I claim that I lived up to his creed. I *know* that I did. In my 3033 games, I always went into action with every ounce of fight I had—"ferocious" is an adjective I won't quarrel with—but I want all young Americans to know that never in twenty-four years did I do anything low or underhanded.

In legend, I am a sadistic, slashing, swashbuckling despot, a Draco of the diamond, who waged war in the guise of sport. The men I went against didn't call me a "dirty" player. That charge has come from those anointed with the critical powers developed only through carrying a press card. The truth is that I believe, and always have believed, that no man, in any walk of life, can attain success who holds in his heart malice, spite, or littleness toward his opponents. The competitor who comes armed with right in his heart and mind has nothing whatever to fear. The honorable way is the only way.

But I *did* retaliate. That I freely admit. If any player took unfair advantage of me, my one thought was to strike back as quickly and effectively as I could and put the fear of God into him. Let the other fellow fire the first shot, and he needed to be on the *qui vive* from then on in. For I went looking for him. And when I found him, he usually regretted his act—and rarely repeated it. I commend this procedure to all young players who are of the aggressive type. The results are most satisfactory.

Along with the counsel of my father, I fell back on Polonius, when in *Hamlet* he advises Laertes: "Beware of entrance to a quarrel; but being in, bear't, that the opposed may beware of thee." No better guide for a ballplayer ever was written.

Of the scurvier stories marketed and remarketed about me, the one that hurts as much as any, concerns Frank Baker. Baker was a clever third baseman and a lifetime .308 hitter, but better known as the original popularizer of the home run. On August 24, 25, and 26 of 1909, the Tigers met the Athletics at Bennett Park, Detroit, in a critical three-game series—the A's of Mr. Connie Mack holding a two-game lead over our side in the flag race, after the Bengals had topped the league almost from Opening Day. George Mullin (who won 29 games that year) slammed the door for our side with a four-hit shutout. Wild Bill Donovan and Kickapoo Ed Summers won the other two games. Detroit went wild. We swept back into first place, headed for our third straight pennant.

In the opening match of the series, while sprinting for third, I found Baker planted in a direct line between third base and second as he fielded the throw. He was in a strictly *offensive* attitude. The base path was mine by all the rules. Baker's two arms were extended to tag me. A photograph of the play exists today which clearly shows that the bag is to his right side, that he is *on the attack* and that I am pulling away from him in order to hook that bag. In fact, I am risking a broken leg to evade him. The photo shows

114

that, as in any forward slide, I'm using my left leg as a sliding frame, coming over with my right foot, and that my foot has passed by Baker's right forearm.

The fable-makers will have you believe that I knocked Baker's arm clear behind his back, *yet it was not even knocked out of line.* They paint Baker as sprawled flat in the dirt and blood-smeared. *He was not injured enough to lose an inning of play,* then, or for the remainder of the season.

There was no scene at third base, no protesting crowd of A's rushed in. Baker was merely scratched, just below the elbow, and he went strolling to the bench, where the trainer slapped a little plaster on it. The next inning, Baker was back at his position—although maybe not so eager now to appropriate the base line.

The small scrimmage would have been forgotten on the spot but for a Philadelphia writer who visioned lurid headlines in the play. His story said that I had cold-bloodedly butchered, maimed, and probably marred the hero of the A's for life. My hunch today is that the sportswriter was working toward a big boost in the gate when the Tigers played in Philly three weeks later. He succeeded. When we arrived, the town was seething with anti-Cobb and anti-Detroit feeling. The local bugs were just spoiling for an excuse to explode.

And the two clubs drew, for a four-game series, an all-time record turnout (until then) of 120,000 fans.

Maybe I was the angriest of all concerned. I held a deep respect for Mr. Mack, which grew into reverence in later years, but before the series in Detroit ended, I walked straight to his bench.

"*You* know, Mr. Mack," I said, "that there's no truth to this spiking. I challenge you to take off that little plaster on Baker's arm. Let's have a look at it right now."

Now I want to say here that Cornelius Alexander McGillicuddy, who was Connie Mack to all men, was forty-seven years old at the time, and already showing the ethereal qualities—the great depth of character—which set him apart from others in baseball. He played his first major league game the year I was born. He was built on the robust lines of a toothpick and as gentle a human as I ever knew. In time, I was to play under his management, and take his directions with the greatest pleasure I've ever known in baseball. The oath or the uncharitable act were unknown to Mr. Mack. Only unlimited patience, tolerance and love for the youth who strives to perform great deeds—and often fails—entered his make up.

But I had been grossly put in the wrong. I spoke flat out to Mr. Mack.

"I see that you won't take the bandage off Baker," I went on. "Naturally not. He isn't hurt, and you know it.

"Somebody will be very sorry for this, because they've done me an injury that is absolutely out of line.

"These wild stories in the papers could have been stopped. And, Mr. Mack, I'm awfully sorry to see *you* sanctioning this stuff."

Our eyes remained locked, but he said nothing.

"If the position had been reversed," I told him, "and I'd been playing third, I would have told the press that it was an accident and that the runner slid in properly. But this has not been done."

"Now, Ty, now, Ty," said Mr. Mack.

"From now on, I'm going to show you some real baseball," I promised him. I stalked away, my piece said.

The fat was in the fire. The race with the A's stayed hot, and in mid-September we rolled into a Philadelphia eager for revenge. "A caldron of Cobb hatred," Grantland Rice described it. By now, I had received 13 Black Hand letters promising to shoot me dead, and with the specifics included. I was going to be picked off by a sniper from the roof of a house outside Shibe Park, or elsewhere. Standing in right field, even an average rifleman couldn't miss me. Also, I was going to be knifed in the melee that was planned for after the game. Hughie Jennings, our manager, was convinced it could happen.

"We've got to get every cop and special officer in Philly out there," Hughie said. "These birds mean business."

I was breezy about the whole thing. Foolish youth.

"It's all bluff," I assured Jennings. "We'll have an overflow crowd, no doubt. That means a mob standing on the grass all around the outfield. I just hope the A's hit one out past me, where I can run and jump for the ball and make the catch falling into that crowd . . . let's find out how tough they'll get."

As I said, foolish youth. I had that spirit then where I wouldn't have noticed the crack of doom from 50 feet away.

Jennings just stared at me and went to Mr. Mack for help. The Tigers rode to the park with two safety police to a taxicab, with a motorcycle escort for me. We went from cabs to clubhouse through a cordon of bodyguards. Inside Shibe Park, something like 300 armed officers prowled the stands for anyone out to pot-shoot me and formed a blue wall between me and the outfield ropes restraining 12,000 ladies and gents of the City of Brotherly Love who were standing jammed against the fences.

It was widely expected that I'd take a run-out powder. A roar of hate from 30,000 voices greeted me when I trotted from the dugout. Jennings would have had to rope me to keep me from playing in this particular ball game.

I had two reasons. One was contained in a Black Hand letter—printed in the local papers—reading: "We know you're yellow because you showed it when you spiked Baker. Now let's see if you've guts enough to show up here for the series. If you do, you are done." Secondly, we held a 3½ game pennant lead entering Philadelphia, which the Athletics could wipe out by sweeping the series. And the A's were a great bunch—Eddie Collins, who hit .346 that year, scrappy Jack Barry at short, Danny Murphy and Rube Oldring in the garden, pitchers Chief Bender, Eddie Plank, Lefty Krause, and Jack Coombs. A World Series winning share then was worth around $2000. Comparatively, my entire season's salary was $4500. I didn't intend that we should blow it.

Well, it was an exciting afternoon. Right field at Shibe Park was of short dimensions and three or four balls were driven my way which required some running activity on my part, and on one of them, I had to half-dive over the barrier between me and the wolves to spear the ball. As I dove, I tumbled right in among them. In the tangle of bodies, I fell on a fan's straw hat and partially crushed it.

Now, a strange thing happened. That mob didn't lay a hand on me, with all the chance available. Maybe they even admired the catch I made. Going back to the bench, I thought it over. It seemed to me a gesture in return was indicated on my part.

So I went into the clubhouse, got a $5 bill from my purse and tucked it into my uniform pocket. When I took the field again, I identified the fellow whose skimmer I'd damaged and said, "Here, I want to reimburse you for your hat."

He had his mouth open, but he accepted the money. In those days, $5 bought a top-flight straw hat.

Well, you can guess the rest. At least in my area of the park, the customers became less hostile, and although I was wide open to a bullet or knife in the back, nothing happened to me. It was a rough ball game. Eddie Collins and Jack Barry of the A's both were hurt. The A's beat us behind Plank, 2–1. Fans rushed the field, overrunning the safety police after the last out.

I suppose I should have run for the dugout. But here is a true fact. *I never ran off a diamond in my life.* Never, at any time, no matter how chancy the situation. And I didn't take to my heels this time. I walked at my own pace toward our bench.

The crowd, snarling and threatening, was all around me, but especially close were six or seven men who seemed trying to box me in. "Just a minute," I said. "What's the idea here? Just give me a little bit of elbow room."

One of the men leaned close to tell me, "Ty, we know you're a Mason, and we're Masons, too. And that's why we're here around you."

Later that night, frustrated toughs gathered outside our midtown hotel. By an estimate that Jim Delahanty, our second-sacker, later gave Westbrook Pegler, some 3000 of them were waiting for me to emerge after dinner. I don't think the crowd was that large. But it did a good job of overflowing the sidewalk and street. And I fully intended to take my usual after-dinner stroll up that street.

The Tigers tried to talk me out of it, and some of them even offered to step out there with me.

"No, boys, I'm going alone," I told them.

On the hotel steps, with one hand in my pocket, I swept an arm around at the reception committee.

"Now, I'm going for a walk," I said, just loud enough for all to hear, "and I just want to say that the first rotten, cowardly hound that tries to stop me is going to drop dead right where he is. Now get out of my way."

My hand stayed in my pocket, and what it might be holding the Philadelphians didn't know. They got out of my way. I took my walk. Right through them and back to the hotel again.

We escaped Philadelphia the losers of three of the four games, but still in front, and we held on to win the pennant with a .645 mark to the A's .621. But the Baker hoax never cooled off. My running feud with the city continued and reached a climax in mid-

118

season of 1912. We were down in sixth place, and out of it. Boston, Philadelphia, and Washington were locked in a dogfight for first place. Up in Boston, where we gave the Red Stockings a tanning, it struck everyone that Cobb might be able to help win the pennant for the Beantown boys. "Do us a favor," said the Boston players. "Give it everything you've got against the A's."

I didn't need to be urged. My fondest wish was to knock my accusers out of the World Series. And Detroit had three consecutive double-headers scheduled in Philadelphia.

So I picked up a phone and called Stoney McLinn, sports editor of the Philadelphia *Press*. "Hello, Stoneyard," I said. "I'm calling to warn you that I'm going to do a job of hitting against your team that will make you sick. Tell all your dear public to be there. You people really have me irritated. I'm going to give you the 'teach' not to push an honest ballplayer around."

I may even had added the threat that I'd be gunning for a new record for base hits in a six-game series. I don't recall, for sure. But Stoney spread it in bannerlines. And McLinn was one sportswriter who was accurate.

Of course, my neck was out a mile with a challenge like that. It meant another 300 or 400 safety police sent by the Commissioner of Public Safety to keep the park roof on. On top of that, the A's of 1912 were solid talent, one of the finest teams Mr. Mack ever managed. In the opening twin bill, his starting pitchers were Eddie Plank, who left-handed his way into the Hall of Fame with a lifetime 325 victories, and Chief Bender, with magnificent speed and control. My contribution against Plank was four hits in six times up and against Bender three hits in five trips. Quite a day—but I was determined to do better.

Next afternoon, the Macks used Herb Pennock, a rookie southpaw, and Carroll Brown, a high-balling rightie. I touched Pennock for five hits in five tries and Brown for two in three at-bats. Now I had 14 base hits in 19 attempts, and we had whipped the A's four straight.

Against a Plank-Pennock combination in the final two-game set, I connected safely four times to end the Philadelphia six games with 18-for-28 and a .643 average. Included were four doubles, a triple, and a pair of home runs.

I consider this the best series performance of my life. It was repayment in full for the Frank Baker slander and it put a certain amount of quietus on the Black Hand authors. When we swept that series, we knocked the Athletics out of the pennant, which went to Boston.

And yet, half a century later, I constantly meet youngsters who have been indoctrinated in the Baker legend so well that they look me over as if I was Old Beelzebub, himself. At the time of the commotion, my own children were disturbed by the stories. Down in Georgia, they read that their father was running around the bases, slashing and cutting, and the effect on their tender minds was something I found impossible to forgive.

But now, in my late years, with the thought that I wish to be on the Christian side in all things, I want to say this: I forgive them. They have long since passed on, and there is no anger left in my heart.

As to Home Run Baker, here's a postscript to the "spiking" of 1909:

A few years ago, I was returning to California on the last leg of a trip from the Hall of Fame at Cooperstown, New York. We'd had quite a shindig there. I was bone-tired. Bed never looked so good to me as one night in a Kansas City hotel. Just then in hurried Paul (Big Poison) Waner, the one-time Pittsburgh star hitter.

"Frank wants you," said Paul. "He thinks he's dying."

I hurried to a room down the hall and there, looking up at me from bed with pitiful eyes, was my one-time antagonist, John Franklin Baker. The old home-run swatter groaned, "It's my heart, Ty, I think . . . I can't get my breath."

For a seventy-odd-year-old man, Home Run didn't look so sick to me. "What'd you have for dinner?" I inquired.

"Seafood," moaned Frank.

"Listen, Paul," I said to Waner. "Go to my room and bring me a bottle of Scotch."

While Waner was gone, Frank let me know that he'd be eased in his mind, now that taps was about to blow, to have me remain by his side. Waner came back with the Scotch and I said, "Now take a pull of this, Frank."

"You know I've never touched the stuff," he objected.

"Well you're going to touch it now," I said.

After a swallow or two, Frank said, "Gosh, Ty, that tastes funny."

He had several more husky pulls. Then he looked up at me and said, "You know—I'm beginning to feel *good*."

I replied, with a straight face, "Frank, you don't know what you've been missing. If you'd indulged yourself a bit in the old days, you'd probably have hit 50 points higher."

Frank headed for his Maryland home next day. His indigestion was cured. We had a sentimental farewell, with arms around each other. If ever I hurt Frank Baker, it did not show then.

And this is the player I'm supposed to have venomously slashed open at third base more than fifty years ago.

Truth always will out. That's the overriding reason why I've written my memoirs—after consistently refusing to speak up over the years. I have no use for the alibi. In the past, I have been dead set against telling my story because I feared the public would feel that I was attempting to palliate or whitewash my rather stormy career. But events have been twisted by false reports beyond forbearance. At my present age of seventy-four, I am thinking most seriously of all matters, and my least inclination is to relate anything that is untrue. I was never a swashbuckler or a bully out looking for trouble. Regardless, I seem to have been cast in this role by several generations of sports commentators and *I think I got the worst of it in a great many cases.*

Bugs Baer helped along the tale that I sat by the dugout, sharpening my spikes with a file with intent to strike fear into the enemy. Baer went so far as to state that I went to a barber shop to insure a finer hone on the steel. It has become an article of faith with fans that I tyrannized basemen with vicious use of those spikes —and that I advertised my intentions beforehand.

It is untrue. At no time did I use a file or any other sharpening device. Not in front of the bench, or anywhere else.

In his syndicated column, Baer not only claimed this, but added that I blew up when accused of rowdy play, and couldn't take criticism. So I wrote him this letter:

Dear Bugs:
    May I ask you to furnish me the names of any individuals, even you, who like criticism? I think we all try to attain—with our hearts in the right place—certain goals. What is criticism, may I ask? Criticism is breaking down, a destroying influence.

As to my sharpening my spikes in a barber shop, no, Bugs, I did not. There is no equipment for that operation in a barber shop. It calls for a file—not that I am well-acquainted with the filing process. The story of my spike-sharpening springs from a prank hatched by members of our club, Detroit.

Now that I have unbosomed myself, with every good wish for your health and happiness, I am,

TY COBB

The infamous file story began one day on the Highlander Grounds in New York, long before the local team became known as the Yankees.

A group of Tiger bench-riders, players who were not in the line-up, and who were looking for a way to relieve their boredom, went to the groundskeeper, who kept a stock of files for sharpening his lawn mowers. Four or five of them borrowed files. They planted one man as lookout. The New Yorkers were holding a clubhouse meeting, and to reach their dugout they had to cross through our bench. When the Highlanders, led by manager Clark Griffith, appeared, the watchman hollered, "Here they come!"

The boys were busily rasping away on their spikes when the Highlanders walked by . . . it was a prank, good for laughs . . . pulled by a gang of guys who weren't even going to be on the field.

What was only horseplay sounded like a declaration of war when the newspapers got through with it. Because they named *me* as the villainous spike-sharpener. It wouldn't have been a story for Baer and other writers if they hadn't put me in it.

I was too busy thinking about the game to enter into tomfoolery. What's more, I had a pride and a personal code of honor which would never allow me to lend myself to such a practice. It was O.K. for the boys who were bench-warmers. But I was just a little bit more reserved and careful about my conduct than the jokesters. Nevertheless, I've never been able to shake the story. It still haunts me like a hundred other headlines—the Honus Wagner affair, for instance.

In this one, Wagner gave me a three-stitch split lip after I hurled a braggart's challenge at him in the World Series. Many newspapers carried the story.

When two league batting champions collide in a World Series, you can expect trouble. Especially, if the two form an instant friendship and strike no sparks. You can't fill sport-page space with simple good fellowship. In 1909, Wagner's .339 average and my .377 led our respective leagues. Looking for color, the photographers posed us in Pittsburgh, before the opening Series game, at home plate. Honus stood right-handed, and I faced him, as a left-hander. We were meeting for the first time and we both blinked in surprise.

Because we both gripped our bat in pretty much the same way— lower hand a few inches from the knob and with hands a palm-width or so apart. Only a few players used the style then, and very few have used it since.

We couldn't have been much less alike physically. Wagner—maybe the greatest star ever to take the diamond—was a bow-legged bull of a man at around 205 pounds and well under six feet. I was on the slim, straight-bodied side, 6-1 and about 175 pounds. Yet we'd both adopted the same style with the hickory stick.

"Did you pick that up yourself?" I asked Honus.

"Yep. How about you?"

"I worked it out, too," I said. "Good luck in the Series. I've admired you for a long time."

It was a rough six games we played, the Pirates winning the world championship. Tom Jones, our first baseman, was carried off the field after crashing into the Pirates' Chief Wilson, and so was Bobby Byrne, of the Bucs, when he tangled with George Moriarty at third base. A few times it looked like fists would fly. But Wagner and I never had a cross word—and I certainly didn't stand on first base, hollering, "Look out, Krauthead, I'm coming down!" And then get my lip split when Wagner slammed me with the ball.

That's 100 per cent concoction, and the proof of it is that, at the time it was supposed to have happened, I wasn't even the runner at first base. The press hasn't had to strain much in building the public image of Ty Cobb. But it seems to me they broke all records for manufacturing hokum when they located me on a base I didn't occupy.

Spike Honus Wagner? It would have taken quite a foolhardy man. He wore thick felt pads under his socks to absorb any slider's cleats. And he could block off a base-runner with his huge, bearlike body in a manner that made the boys very careful when they slid in his vicinity.

So much for another exploded bag of journalistic hot air.

I say this: I ran the bases hard at all times, and I'm proud of that. As I've explained in another chapter, I saw no reason why the base-runner should be a hunted thing, a rabbit chased by wolves. When his team was at bat, he was supposed to be on the all-out attack. But it wasn't working that way when I broke into the game —just the contrary. I wanted a clear shot at the bag, under the rules, and I went after it. I have dozens of spike scars, from my ankles to my thighs, to show for that point of view. I also left a few marks of my own around the league. In staking my claim, people were bound to get hurt, but sometime I'd like to see my critics mention a case such as that involving Joe Sewell of the Cleveland Indians.

Sewell was a wonderful all-around infielder who hit over .300 in ten seasons. But there came a day in the 1920s when one of us had to be hurt.

Taking a throw-in from left field at second base, Sewell grabbed the ball, while blindly fishing around with his foot for the base behind him. Meanwhile, I was moving from first at full speed. Joe couldn't find the bag, and he backed right into my path. I was in mid-air with my slide, and had to twist violently to avoid cutting Sewell down. In the process, I sliced a deep gash in my own leg, just above the right knee. The pain, more than the spurting blood, told me it was bad.

They took me off the field, but the Cleveland club doctor didn't have an anesthetic on hand. I was opened up so that you could see the bone and ligaments. "Ty, I can't deaden the pain," the doc told me.

"That's all right. I'll take it," I told him. "You don't have to hold me."

The doc wanted volunteers to hold me down, but I said, "Give me a cigar." Though it had no anesthetic quality, smoking it did give me something to think about. The doc started to stitch.

Well, it's pretty tough down there, and I guess I wept a few tears. It seemed to me his needle was damned dull. But there was nothing for it but to hang on while he sewed through the cut and came out on the other side and kept on stitching. When he was finished, I wasn't sure how soon I could play again, if ever.

But I had the satisfaction of knowing I hadn't ripped an infielder who was in an indefensible position, and was only trying to do his job.

I spoke a while back of retaliation—of going out after the man who fouled you without recourse to complaints to the umpires, your manager or the press. I never could see running to others. That settles nothing. You've got to take care of it yourself, and I won't say that the spikes didn't come in handy *in very special circumstances*. Only twice did I deliberately try to spike a man.

One was a Cleveland catcher, Harry Bemis, who roughed me up both with his tongue and with a ball clenched in his fist when I slid into home. I missed Bemis, as it happened, but by so little that it cured him of the habit. The other fellow played for the Boston Red Sox in the days when throwing at a batter's head was everyday procedure. There were two great pitchers on manager Bill Carrigan's Boston club who didn't throw at you—Ernie Shore and Smokey Joe Wood. They had so much stuff they didn't have to resort to beanballs and risk killing someone.

But a fellow by the name of Hub Leonard would aim bullets at your head, left-handed, to boot.

Leonard did it once too often. So I dragged a bunt down the chalkline, which the first baseman was forced to field. Leonard sprinted for first to take the throw, and saw that I was after him. He didn't stop at the bag. Leonard kept right on going, into the coaching box, which looked like safe territory to him. He wouldn't have been safe that day if he'd scrambled into the top bleachers. I ignored the bag—since I was already out—and drove feet-first right through the coaching box at Leonard with every intent in the world of doing him damage. He managed to duck as I whipped through there, but he knew he was a marked man with me. The escape was close enough medicine for him. He never threw another beanball at me.

For frank unconcern about your health, though, I'd have to name Cy Morgan, also of the Red Sox, as a pitcher apart. Morgan tried to skull me regularly. Eventually, at Boston, I was the runner at second base when he made a wild pitch. The backstop was fairly close to the plate, which meant a fast retrieve, and almost no chance for me to score.

All the same, I rounded third with the throttle tied down. Morgan was at the plate, reaching for the catcher's recovery throw. I guess

I hadn't taken more than three or four strides past third going home when Morgan had the ball in his hands, waiting for me.

I thought, Well, here's where we settle this.

As I came down the line and went whipping at him with my steel showing, Morgan shocked everyone in the park.

He turned and actually ran away from the plate.

I scored and Morgan was released by Boston that night. The Athletics picked him up. Later, Morgan came around to me, saying, "Ty, I want to apologize for the way I threw at you. Can we call it off?"

I had no objection, inasmuch as we both knew exactly how and why the force of right had triumphed in that moment at home plate. Polonius certainly spoke a mouthful of truth to Laertes when he advised him, in effect, "Don't start a Brannigan. But if somebody else does, give 'em hell!"

If the fans of the 1960s—and the truth-twisters—have learned here how much I believe in this, I'm satisfied. For I carry no latter-day grudges against my inexact historians. Now that I have straightened out some of the record, I forgive them, every one.

10

"But Being In—Let Them Beware!"

There's much more to my history of Brannigans than that which I've set down and separated from fiction in the preceding pages. I'm not proud of some of it. There were vulgar scenes I'd far rather forget and animosities aroused that took years to heal. But I have promised that this book will never avoid the record or make an alibi.

For instance, few people know that at this very moment I stand suspended by the American League. In 1913 I was indefinitely suspended by Byron Bancroft Johnson, the league president, and I remain so today.

Nor is it known why I fought with fists in a Dallas hotel room with Buck Herzog, catcher for the New York Giants, and refused to play against that club again.

I was knifed, once, by hoodlums. That is an event I'd like to pass by quickly, but which I won't, even though it isn't related to baseball.

When Carl Mays of the New York Yankees hit and killed Ray Chapman of the Cleveland Indians with a pitch on August 17, 1920, I was quoted on things I never said. It brought more brickbats flying my way than anything short of the Home Run Baker case. I got out of it by falling back, again, on Polonius.

Any time I was placed unfairly in the wrong, I came back as strongly as I could. It was up to the maker of the quarrel to beware of me.

First, to the famous—and much misunderstood—Herzog affair:

The season was 1917 and the Tigers pitched spring training camp in Waxahachie, Texas. We had booked a series of a dozen or so exhibition games with John J. McGraw's Giants. In Dallas, I was invited to play golf by my manager, Hughie Jennings, his wife and a friend. Well, to me, that was more or less of an order. We played the game, went to the ball park and ran into a chorus of rude Giant jeers.

We were *not late* for the game, as has been often written. But the McGraws rode me unmercifully. In particular, I was the butt of jibes from Herzog, the Giant second baseman, and Art Fletcher, the shortstop—whose theme was that Cobb was playing prima donna and had delayed his entrance to take bows.

They kept it up until I strolled over to Herzog and remarked, "Well, sometime in this game, I expect to get on base. And I'll be down to see you, never fear."

"I'll be waiting!" he snarled back.

First time at bat, I reached first, and I didn't bother taking too big a lead on the pitcher. I wanted Herzog to have plenty of time to make the play first and commit himself. When I did go down, catcher Lew McCarty fired him the ball with margin enough to tag me out. But Herzog failed to execute the play properly—instead of tagging me and moving out, he advanced up the line two or three steps as a welcoming committee, and gave me a nice head-on jab with the ball. We both hit the ground. Maybe I took the first crack at him—I'm not positive. When you get into one of these things, you don't remember all the details.

The crash was as violent as I could make it, and in the melee, Herzog might have hit me a few times. Fletcher jumped in and caught me by the arms, pinning them. Other players were piling in to make it a general Brannigan—some claim that Jim Thorpe, the great Indian playing outfield for the Giants, was flattened by a Tiger —but I know I broke loose from Fletcher and reached Herzog's chin with a solid punch.

When the dust settled, the umpires banished both Herzog and Cobb. Both teams were stopping at the Oriental Hotel in Dallas, and as it happened, I dined alone that evening. Herzog was sitting a few tables away. Suddenly, he got up and walked over. I thought he was about to say something like, "Ty, we're going to be barnstorming quite a while together, and these exhibition games don't count, so let's call the whole thing off."

Instead, he growled, "I want to see you."

I said, "All right, Buck." If I'd known what he wanted, I'd certainly not have addressed him with the familiar "Buck," but as "Mr. Herzog."

I didn't get his meaning at all. And I was surprised to hear him say, "I want to see you after dinner, and I want to see you in your room. And without any swords or pistols."

"Oh?" I said. "Is that what you want?" I looked down at my unfinished meal. "Well, in just thirty minutes, I'll be in my room."

So in thirty minutes I was waiting upstairs. I moved the rugs and furniture aside to allow for maneuvering room. Outside, in the hall, and trying to crowd inside, was a bunch of Giant and Tiger players, who couldn't wait to see the excitement coming up. Our team trainer took charge when Herzog arrived. He ran the boys out. "There can be only two men other than Cobb and Herzog in this room when this happens," he decreed. "Herzog, who do you want with you?"

The Giant said, "I want Heinie Zimmerman"—who was a big, husky third baseman.

I looked around and saw my friend, Oscar Stanage, a catcher on our club. "Oscar, will you come in with us?" I said. Now that seconds were appointed, and everything was fairly set up, the door was shut and locked.

Well, Buck had somewhat prepared for the fray. He had been an Army boxing coach and he wore a khaki shirt, old pants with the belt tightly drawn and rubber-soled shoes. I hadn't considered this before, and I thought, "Oho . . . I just might do some slipping in here with my street shoes, and Herzog in those sneakers. . . ."

So I went over and calmly filled the ice-water pitcher and very thoroughly sprinkled the floor. I took plenty of time about it. On a wet surface, leather will grip better than rubber. I didn't exchange shoes, and I didn't do any slipping that evening, either.

I said, "All right—how do you want to fight?"

To my great joy—since I hadn't been trained in scientific fisticuffs and Herzog knew his way around a fight ring—he barked, "Any way suits me!" That's where Buck made his big mistake. He might have kept me away, with his boxing knowledge, and cut me up, but he left the choice wide open, and I said, "The old rough-and-tumble, then. Anything goes."

I said, "All right, square off there." I've always tried to understand the forces of psychology, in my dumb way, and in a second I had a chance to work on Herzog's nerves. He wavered just a bit. "I'm here to fight you," he told me. "I may get licked, but I'll fight you."

"You know damn well you're going to get licked," I assured him.

We went together. It's been tirelessly told by I don't know how many thousand sportswriters that Herzog floored me with his first punch. He did nothing of the sort. Swinging a right hook, I missed, but I pulled back my fist and gave him a full-swinging back-hander. And down *he* went.

No science on my part, I assure you. And then was when I first got mad. I reached down and grabbed a handful of his khaki shirt—Herzog was on his face—and pulled him erect, and tore out a handful of that shirt. Shoving him back, I said, "All right now." And then I clipped him. I'm not proud of it, even to this day. But I did clip him and he catapulted backward and after a while he climbed to his knees.

From a kneeling position, he grabbed my hand and muttered, "I've got enough . . . I've got enough . . . I've got enough. . . ."

That was it. Herzog left the room, with assistance, and I called out into the hall, to the other Giants, "If anyone else feels ambitious, step right in." None did. The next day manager John McGraw of the Giants jumped me in the lobby and, before a mixed group of ladies and gentlemen, became so vituperative that I had to restrain myself from repeating the performance of Room 404. The next afternoon, half of Dallas jammed the park, hoping for a renewal of hostilities. But they didn't see Cobb. I wanted no part of the Giants and their roughhouse stuff during what was supposed to be the conditioning period. McGraw's pop-off was the decider. I packed my bags, and walked out on the tour to do my training with a minor league team many miles away. When the Tigers and Giants split up in Kansas City at the end of their travels, I received a post-card from Little Napoleon McGraw and his boys.

"It's safe to rejoin your club now," it read. *"We've left."*

That was the one way the Giants could have the last word. By mail.

If the thought has crossed your mind that the old-time major leaguers were a crude, liquor-guzzling bunch—and that's another legend Americans are schooled to believe—let me tell you something. We had far fewer brawls on the field in my era than you see today. And much less consumption of drink. From the turn of the century up into the early 1920s, the boys were *not* hard-liquor drinkers. They drank beer. Lots of it, it's true. But we had serious pride in our profession and passed up the whisky and Scotch in the interest of prolonging our careers. Cocktails and highballs didn't become a problem for managers until after the Volstead Act. If ability to endure is any index of a man's sobriety, and it has to be, glance at the meager all-time list of players who came to bat 9000 or more times in their careers. It is almost solidly old-timer in character—names like Larry Lajoie, Sam Crawford, Tris Speaker, Cap Anson, Lave Cross, Hans Wagner, Zack Wheat, Eagle Eye Beckley, and Max Carey. Real durability in a pitcher exists when he lasts 4000 or more innings. Of the 14 names on the 4000-inning list, 10 are from the early days, the others from the 1930s. To cite only a few of many other cases, Eddie Collins infielded for 25 years, Cy Young pitched for 22 years, Jimmy O'Rourke was a big-leaguer past fifty years of age, Fred Clarke lasted 21, and Bobby Wallace for 25 campaigns. You don't see that any more. You do see the old-timers sketched as hooligans with a fancy girl on either arm. That is totally inaccurate, and as low a blow as has been struck since *Uncle Tom's Cabin* came out, pretending to picture the South. I was, and am, very, very proud of the men I played against. They were fighting, dead-game, dedicated athletes who didn't cave in after a mere eight, ten, or a dozen seasons.

On the unhappy side, we had to put up with a breed of fan you seldom find in a modern ball park. One of these involved me in a beauty of a Brannigan.

In May of 1912, the Tigers swung east for the first time that spring, playing the New York Highlanders at their park up at 168th Street and Broadway. Some of the buildings of Columbia-Presbyterian Medical Center now stand where we played. In the third-base bleacher was a character who had ridden me hard in past New York appearances. He wore an alpaca coat and he was crude beyond belief. Right from the start, this day, he began braying at me. I made as if I didn't hear him, which only increased his foul abuse. To avoid him as much as possible, I even left center field at the inning's end and returned to our bench by the long way of the New York side of the field—this mugwump being located not far from the third-base side of our dugout.

By the sixth inning, he was cursing me and reflecting on my mother's color and morals. I walked to the Yankee side and warned manager Harry Wolverton of the Highlanders, "There's going to be trouble if this fellow isn't stopped." I repeated the warning at a box occupied by New York club officials. All I got was shrugs.

Police protection didn't exist for players, short of a riot, which was why women didn't patronize baseball in 1912. And we players were fed up with the unconcern—the stupidity—of owners. You were supposed to take obscenities, but never lay a hand on your attacker.

Well . . . Polonius didn't figure that way. Nor did I.

As the sixth frame ended, I tried to sneak back to our bench. Wahoo Sam Crawford and Jim Delahanty of our team said to me, "If you don't do something about that, you're a gutless no-good."

The man ripped out something else, and I don't know *how* I got up there—really, to this day, I can't tell you how I scaled the barrier and reached him. The next thing I remember, they were pulling me off him. I do know I didn't just slap him around. The statement given by the fan claimed:

"He hit me in the face with his fist, knocked me down, jumped on me, kicked me, spiked me and booted me behind the ear."

Reading that in an old scrapbook, I'm pleased to note that I didn't overlook any important punitive measures.

There was the devil to pay. Umpires Silk O'Loughlin and Fred Westervelt thumbed me out and, without any sort of hearing before American League president Ban Johnson, I was suspended indefinitely. All this happened on a Wednesday, May 15. Thursday was an open date, after which we were slated against the Athletics at Philadelphia. With no agitation whatever on my part, the Tiger players called a secret meeting. All 18 of them signed an ultimatum and wired it to Johnson:

FEELING MR. COBB IS BEING DONE AN INJUSTICE BY YOUR ACTION IN SUSPENDING HIM, WE, THE UNDERSIGNED, REFUSE TO PLAY IN ANOTHER GAME UNTIL SUCH ACTION IS ADJUSTED TO OUR SATISFACTION. HE WAS FULLY JUSTIFIED, AS NO ONE COULD STAND SUCH PERSONAL ABUSE FROM ANY ONE. WE WANT HIM REINSTATED OR THERE WILL BE

NO GAME. IF PLAYERS CANNOT HAVE PROTECTION, WE MUST PROTECT OURSELVES.

(Signed) SAM CRAWFORD, BILL LOUDEN, RALPH WORKS, GEORGE MULLIN, BILL BURNS, JEAN DUBUC, GEORGE MORIARTY, DAVEY JONES, JAMES DELAHANTY, DONIE BUSH, OSCAR STANAGE, EDGAR WILLETT, OSCAR VITT, TEX COVINGTON, HENRY PERRY, EDDIE SUMMERS, HUB PERNOLL, JACK ONSLOW.

That great panjandrum of the American League, Ban Johnson, rushed to Philadelphia from Chicago. He spouted threats against the rebels. Not only would he have my hide, he said, but he'd drum out of baseball every Tiger who refused to suit up. "Maybe for life," he added.

When game time came, we rode out to Shibe Park in taxis, suited up and at 2:30 P.M., Jim Delahanty asked the chief umpire, "Has Cobb's suspension been lifted?" It hadn't. "Then the hell with it!" snapped Delahanty. We got back in the cabs and defiantly rode back to our hotel.

Organized Baseball now had on its hands its first (and last) player strike by an entire team.

Back at the park, 2000 fans queued up and demanded a ticket refund when they learned that the Tigers were to be replaced by a hastily recruited bunch of pick-up, ragtag Philly semipros and St. Joseph's College kids. It was the weirdest assortment of ball-chasers ever to take a big league field. A theology student, later Reverend Albert Joseph Travers, pitched for the subs. They were murdered, 24–2, by the Athletics. The travesty rang around the country and the striking Tigers became the day's sensation. Over at the Bellevue-Stratford Hotel, Ban Johnson issued a bulletin every ten minutes. At the Aldine Hotel, where we stayed, Delahanty, Crawford, and the others shot back retorts that they'd call for a league-wide walk-out, unless Cobb was reinstated and proper police protection afforded.

Frank Navin, the Detroit owner, faced a $5000 fine for every game in which he didn't field a team—or, at least, so went the newspaper report. The players faced a $50-per-game fine for each game missed. You can bet Navin, a good pursestring-pincher, was there, seeking to cajole the boys into surrendering. But the boys had their necks bowed.

Newspapermen from everywhere flocked to the scene, the largest assortment of scribes I've ever seen in one spot. I told them bluntly what I thought of Johnson. "Words can't express what I think of him," I said. "He's the most egotistical, overbearing man in the game. I can get dozens of witnesses to prove that I had every right to attack this miserable mug who abused me. In fact, only two people are against me—Ban Johnson and the fan. One of two things is certain. Johnson is either dead wrong in this thing, or he is an out-and-out —."

Navin buzzed back and forth between Johnson and the team. En masse, the boys would rise up and say, "Bring that big fat slob down here"—meaning Ban Johnson—"and let *him* talk to us!" Johnson didn't budge. Meanwhile, $100 fines had been inflicted on all 18 strikers.

Immensely cheering to our side was a referendum vote conducted by the New York *American*. Fifteen big ballot boxes were set up around Manhattan and the people became the jury on the question: Was Cobb within his rights in walloping the customer, or did fans have an inalienable right to yell whatever they wanted after passing the box office?

The vote was a landslide for me: 3013 votes pro-Cobb, 1167 against.

Mail poured in—I must have received five hundred letters from fans and folks who were sitting nearby and heard the blasphemy heaped upon me. Included was a couple of priests who offered to take the witness stand in my behalf.

The "T.A.R."—Tigers of the American Revolution—now were summoned to a showdown conference with Johnson, Navin, and other league bigwigs. I attended. When the stalemate stayed stuck, I arose and addressed my fellow players. I said, "Boys, the principle of this thing has been entirely open to the public. With the coverage we've had, every detail is on record. The people won't judge this unfairly, especially knowing of your actions, which have brought it to a head. *That much* has been accomplished.

"I'm going to ask you to forget me and go back. I don't want you paying fines and I'll ask you to make the exaction of Johnson that no fine will be enforced on any of you. Eventually, you've got to go, so why not now? I'll be all right. They'll let me back in there sometime pretty soon—so please go back."

The next day, at Washington, George Mullin threw a two-hit 2–0 victory over Walter (Big Train) Johnson. The boys were most unhappy about returning. Yet they felt that definite gains had been forced from the game's dictators, the promise of safety police patrolling stands, dugouts, and players' gates. Johnson kept me suspended for ten days and fined me $50. Most important, from the historic strike stemmed the first unionization movement by big leaguers, who banded together in the winter of 1912–13 in the Ball Players' Fraternity behind Dave Fultz, an attorney and ex-Highlander outfielder. One of the first concessions they wrung from the National Commission was a rule providing that no player should be farmed to a lower minor league until clubs in classifications between his old club and proposed new affiliation were first given a chance to deal for him. Prior to that, down he went, with no chance to seek another job level. The Dark Ages for ballplayers began to end, it's been said, when a fan opened his mouth too wide one day at the Highlander Grounds.

It wasn't long after that—it seems I was always landing in strange situations—when the Tigers billed an exhibition game at Syracuse. My wife and I were driving to the railway station in Detroit. It was early morning, the streets dark and deserted. Suddenly three men popped into sight. They were waving their hands. "They look like they're in trouble," I said, applying the brakes.

I've made better guesses. The three mugs began attacking me through the window. I needed operating room, and also had to draw them away from my wife. So I slid out of the car from the opposite side. I took on one of them, while the other two circled around. I'd knock one down and then another would be on me. While in this desperate box, one of the mugs I'd knocked down got up and slashed at me with a knife. I dodged, but he cut me in the back. I couldn't tell how bad it was. But my arms were still working.

Just about then a streetcar rolled up and the passengers, noticing the excitement, climbed off. It looked like some help might be forthcoming. Then the motorman clanged the bell. And, lo and behold, everyone climbed back on and rattled off! The street was deserted again—except for the four of us.

While I'd been watching the street car, the three hoodlums had taken off and had about a 50-yard lead on me, up the car tracks. I was in good condition. I turned on the speed after them. One of them I caught after a short rundown. Leaving him in worse condition than he'd arrived in, I turned to my right after one of his chums, who'd ducked between two houses. I was hoping the backyard would prove to be a cul-de-sac, and it was. He was trapped in a blind passageway.

I had something in my hand, which I won't describe, but which often came in handy in Detroit in the days when it was a fairly rough town. I used it on him at some length. If he still lives, he has scars to show for it. Leaving him unconscious, I drove on to the depot. Later, a news story datelined Detroit told how the men had appeared at a doctor's office, for repairs. It seemed they had been hanging out in a saloon that night, boasting that they'd stick up the first car that came along.

The toughs didn't belong to any baseball gang out to get me. I'd simply happened along at the wrong moment.

Aboard the train, my roommate, Jean Dubuc, saw that my coat was soaked with blood. The trainer took over and patched up the knife wound, which was more painful than deep. I played next day in Syracuse and managed to get two hits.

The combination of these unsettling events, the strike and the stabbing, didn't affect my playing markedly over the 1912 season. I felt I was fighting on the side of right in all my controversies. George Washington called it "That little spark of celestial fire—conscience." The year before, I'd reached a personal peak of 248 hits, including 47 doubles and 24 triples, for an average of .420. In '12, I averaged .410. It was again good for the league batting title, although Joseph Jefferson (Shoeless Joe) Jackson of Cleveland made me sweat for it.

"What a hell of a league this is," moaned Joe, and I could sympathize with him. "Ah hit .387, .408, and .395 the last three years and Ah ain't won nothin' yet!"

Frequently, I felt that I couldn't win, either, when the typewriter swamis took it into their heads to build a synthetic headline around me. The Tigers were playing in Boston one August day in 1920, and that evening my hotel phone rang.

"This is ——," the caller said, identifying himself as a reporter. "Did you hear what happened in the Yankee-Cleveland game today?"

"No, I didn't," I replied.

"Ray Chapman was hit on the head by Carl Mays, and he may not live. There's a lot of feeling over this. The Washington club has

136

stated that it won't play the Yankees again while Mays is pitching. They claim he throws at batters deliberately. Cleveland says it'll boycott Mays, too. I'd like to ask you—what about Detroit?"

In any situation which was fraught with trouble, I had a rule of long standing. So I asked this man, "Just who are you? Who do you represent?"

He repeated his name and said he was a reporter with United Press Associations. With that, I talked to him.

But I was careful not to climb out onto any limb, and answered, "Well, I'm only a member of the Detroit team, I don't *own* the club, and I don't set the policy."

"What about Mays—what do you think of his beaning Chapman?" he pressed me.

"I'm here in Boston," I said. "I didn't see the accident. I know nothing of how it happened and under no circumstances would I comment on it . . . even if I'd been there, I doubt that I could have commented."

Pulling into New York the following morning, for a series with the Yankees, I was astounded to find the papers filled with an attack by me on Carl Mays. One of the quotes read: "Mays throws knockdown balls, and every player knows it." Another paper had me saying: "If Chapman dies, Mays should be expelled from baseball forever."

During the night, poor Chapman—a brilliant shortstop, hitting .303 at the time—did die of head injuries. The ball had rebounded from his left temple so hard that it had bounded down to Aaron Ward, at third base for the Yanks. Ward, thinking it a bunt, had scooped it up and shot it to first baseman Wally Pipp. It was all the more tragic because players didn't come any more popular than Ray.

I grabbed up some papers and fell into bed at the Commodore Hotel. Some sort of "bug" had me in its grip. I was running a 102 temperature.

It was plain what was coming. It was a Friday, an off day, and with a Yankee game billed Saturday at the Polo Grounds. It was certain we'd have a park jammed with hostiles, for all New York took it for granted that I'd been correctly quoted—that I'd pronounced pompous judgment on Pitcher Mays while 230 miles distant from the event.

I put in a phone call to my close friend, Grantland Rice, who came right over. Grant said, "You're in for big trouble. But the first thing you need is a doctor."

"Never mind the doctor," I said. "I just want to assure you that I never gave out any such interview. I'm also going to be at that game tomorrow, healthy or not, and face those wolves."

Since I was 100 per cent innocent, a ball game like this one was just the baby I wanted most to play in. When I was armed with right, I had all the inspiration I needed. Rice grinned at me. "Feeling better already?" he inquired.

"Plenty good enough."

Long before game time, all 55,000 Polo Grounds seats were filled —that crowd was really looking for me.

So I told Hughie Jennings, our manager, "I'm not going out for batting practice. Let them think I've done a run-out, if they want to."

I waited until near game time and then I stepped out of the Polo Grounds clubhouse entrance, which was in deep center field. All alone. And the place blew up. Old pros say it was the most fearful riding from a crowd they ever heard. I do know I never before or since had such a booing.

With a definite object in mind, I walked straight up the center of the field, ignoring the blasts—right over second base and right through the pitching box. I even pushed the Yankee batting-practice pitcher aside as I headed for the plate. Everything had to stop, since I had pitcher, catcher, and batter blocked. I continued beyond the plate. The press box at the Polo Grounds was located down low, just back of home base.

Now I was looking right into the open mouths of all that jeering, howling grandstand, and what could I do to explain my side of it? Not a chance to talk to the fans. I couldn't tell my story. But I sure had their attention. The best I could do was attempt to convey the fact that I'd been victimized by some of the men in that press coop.

So I gestured with my hand, from the first base side all the way around. Then I turned and gestured across the third base side. And, finally, I took a few steps forward, doffed my cap to the press boys and made a slight—and ironic—bow to them.

That set the wolves to howling with more volume. They'd read it about Cobb—and they believed it implicitly.

As a means of retribution, the ball game, itself, was another matter. The Yankees, Cleveland, and White Sox were in a seesaw pennant struggle. The season was well into August. Manager Miller Huggins of the Yanks needed every game he could win. That day he elected to pitch right-hander Ernie Shore. Mr. Shore wasn't around long.

With all the Tigers resenting my treatment, we ripped up Shore in four innings, then worked over the veteran John Picus Quinn, and two other pitchers, and beat the Yankees in a rousing contest, 11–9.

I've never in my life been so keyed up for a game, nor had much better luck at bat. I was up six times, had five hits, including a double and triple, scored two runs, drove in two more and stole a pair of bases. On my last time at bat, it must have soaked into the crowd that I had a clear conscience about Mays, and was demonstrating it. Because the jeers stopped and I was roundly applauded. Again it was a case of *right will out*.

We weren't quite through, though. The Tigers wanted to exact more punishment. And we did, winning three of the four series games. And at season's end, the Yanks finished just exactly three games back of pennant-winning Cleveland.

Now about the still bitterly argued matter of Chapman's death . . . I will say that Mays and I never got along well. I dodged a lot of them from him which gave me dark suspicions. Yet keep in mind that he was a submariner with a delivery that started around his knees, resulting in curious breaks of the ball and a tendency for it to sail toward a batter's skull. I believe it is for no one to say that there was purposeful intent behind that fatal pitch; there is absolutely no one, then or now, who could prove it.

And certainly it wasn't my province to pop off about so grave a matter. I wasn't that dumb, to begin with. Secondly, it went against all my rules of conduct.

Still and all, to this day you'll read in books and magazines that I pointed the accusing finger at Carl Mays and called myself judge.

It's widely alleged, as well, that I was a demon with the umpires. The case they haul up and cite forever was my "bloody" fight under the stands with Billy Evans.

I did fight with Evans. I'm far from proud of it. But the few blows we exchanged are beside the point, when they speak of my philosophical approach to the game officials. From my rookie days,

I realized that the umps were doing a hard day's work out there. I saw that they had the most difficult job of any man on the field. If two pitchers, for instance, deliver 200 balls in nine innings, the plate umpire makes as many split decisions as either of the two teams. And this doesn't mention plays at the plate, foul line calls and assorted rulings. In my break-in years I also discovered that we had a fine set of gentlemen working games—Tommy Connolly, Silk O'Loughlin, Bill Dinneen, Brick Owens, Tim Hurst, the dean of American League umpires, Jack Sheridan, and many others. In the league's early days, these men had to handle a game singlehanded.

It was my early conception not to jower at them, not to add to their worries. And, above all, not to alibi. I was just a young country-town boy. I had my worries, and wasn't so bumptious out there. I decided that the best policy when I was called out at a base —and felt I was safe—was to dust myself off and walk away without a word. An inning later, when the teams exchanged positions, and when nobody's attention was attracted, I'd walk near the umpire and say, "You know, I think you missed that one"—*and keep right on walking*. It let him know I wasn't satisfied, but I was no rabble-rouser playing to the crowd. And I think it brought me my fair share of favorable decisions. Fans have forgotten about this procedure of mine in those earlier playing days. Later, when I managed the Detroit ball club, I think many people saw it demonstrated that with umpires I was not wild-eyed or out of line.

Here I was in an entirely different position. All ballplayers put on dramatic acts to rouse the crowd and alibi the fact that they've been called out. Naturally, as manager, I had to come into the debate. I had to let my player think I was backing him up. Secondly, I had to temper what was said so my player wouldn't be tossed off the field. So, often, I'd put on a little act with His Umps.

"Where was my man tagged?" I'd begin. "It looked like he might have been safe." Meanwhile, I'd push my protesting player away, get him out of there, and then I'd *tell the umpire the truth.*

"You know," I'd say, speaking low, "I think he was out, myself."

Then I'd trot back to my outfield position.

I don't think that this hurt our ball club, rather I believe that it was good procedure, satisfying everyone. Such tactics are much to be preferred to the spouting and hair-tearing we see today by managers. Baseball would be a much finer exhibition if we had more tactful handling of touchy situations and less of the bunkum that delays games interminably and settles nothing.

In all my big league career, I had only one serious altercation with an umpire—oddly with a man for whom I held the highest regard. It happened in Washington on a steaming hot day. Tempers were drawn tight. Four crucial decisions went against us, and Billy Evans was involved in all four. After the game—the first half of a double-header—I waited for Bill to arrive at his dressing room.

"Those four decisions cost us the ball game," I told Evans. "I've always liked your work. But it smelled today."

Billy had done some boxing and football playing at Cornell University, and he wasn't the type to take much, so he replied rather bluntly.

It wound up under the stands, and it was a vulgar display by both of us. Evans and I had been friendly since he'd broken in as an umpire in 1906. Our fight has been blown up by historians into a gory affair, in which Evans was badly mauled. In fact, it lasted only a minute or two, and no one was injured.

The very next day, Billy and I met on the bench and impulsively shook hands, talked it out and wound up with arms around each other. We stayed friends right up to the finish in 1927, when Bill hung up his mask and whisk broom.

The cockeyed aftermath is one record I hold that you won't find in any of Taylor Spink's statistics books, thorough as they may be.

Immediately after the Evans affair, I was *indefinitely* suspended by the league office and fined $50. The season was about over. All winter passed and came spring, and there was no notification from the American League that my suspension had in any way been lifted. I received no letter or telegram, nor did the Detroit team, that I was eligible to play again. In any indefinite suspension, the league must raise it by official action and notice of that action before the player can climb into a suit again. My notice never arrived, and now it was Opening Day. Thus I was in a most peculiar position.

Not caring to raise the point, I played for years afterward in what you might call a state of suspended animation—illegally on the field, by all the rules of Organized Baseball. And today I *still* stand suspended. I await with only slightly diminished eagerness the telegram that reinstates me.

As to my "gory" fisticuffs with Bill Evans, I class that fable with the yarn that Ted Williams once said, "Oh, nuts," when I advised him on hitting to left field, and boorishly walked away. Ted thanked me, as a matter of fact. We've met in Arizona at spring training for years. And we still have lively discussions on batwork. We relish our moments together.

The same goes for the much-circulated account of how Leo Durocher knocked me sprawling when I rounded second base. As it's peddled, Durocher said, "That'll hold you, you old goat!" —and I was tagged out.

Leo gets all kinds of credit for having slyly slammed a hip into me and put me flat on my face.

He never saw the day he could do it. In 1928, when this play supposedly happened, I knew a few too many tricks to be caught by some skinny infielder's hip. What makes the lie all the more obvious is that the story has me out on the play. Had Durocher clipped me, I'd have been entitled to the next base on interference.

The many seasons have spun by and my one regret is that so many glorious moments have been marred by sensation-seekers who work with whole cloth rather than truth. For years I bred and sent into competition fine hunting dogs. No one can tell me that a dog doesn't have a soul and a conscience. Did you ever notice that the morals of dogs are much better than those of men? Never gainsay their intelligence, either—turn one loose in a roomful of men and he'll unerringly pick out the real men. Dogs are better judges of people than people are judges of dogs. I've loved every one I ever owned.

Imagine, then, how it felt to read in the Atlanta *Constitution* not many years ago that I once kicked and brutalized a field dog of mine for failing to hold a point.

Let the distinguished editor who signed his name to that story deal with his own conscience. My own is at peace.

11

Batting: The Lost Science

No, I didn't once attack Nap Rucker, the pitcher, in the bathroom and try to throw him out of the tub in which he was relaxing.

That phony fable has dogged me for more than half a century and I doubt there are enough fans to fill a broom closet who don't believe it happened—which it never did. I don't know who first concocted that particular piece of Limburger, but it has an odor I seem to associate with certain New York writers—never exactly *simpatico* to me—who've made certain it appeared in every language but the Sanskrit.

Naturally, they have a moral wrapped up in their tidy little tale. The "Rucker incident" is supposed to delineate with journalistic punch my "savage" will-to-win, to let no man nor beast stand against my "terrible" competitive urge. In due time, I will deal at length with the many false accounts built around me to this purpose. A Chinese sage wrote that exaggeration is to paint a snake and add legs. With me, they attached fangs, claws, file-sharpened spikes, and fire snorting out each nostril. I suppose sportswriters have some right to be carried away with their prose. Yet men like Stoney Mc-Linn, Harry Salsinger, Ed Danforth, Gene Fowler, Boze Bulger, E. A. Batchelor, Ed Bang, Joe Jackson, O. B. Keeler, Tommy Laird, and Grant Rice—all top journalists—managed to write about me and others without making us appear abnormal or ridden by demons.

The Rucker story begins with Nap in the tub in the room we shared, and my sudden appearance, dressed in a bath towel. I'm supposed to have said, "Get out of there!" Rucker replies, "I'm not going to do it. I got here first and I'm taking my bath and the tub belongs to me."

At which, I'm supposed to have flown into a rage, grabbed and shook him and yelled, "Get out! Nobody can be first ahead of me!"

It's just another of those stories that make a ballplayer miserable —the same kind of a fix some of our modern boys, such as Ted Williams and Mickey Mantle have been in, and what the cure is, I don't know. Napoleon Rucker was from my home state—from Crabapple, Georgia—and we were very close from the time we roomed together when members of the Augusta team of the Sally League. To act as I'm described as acting in the fable is as far from my true nature and the way I was reared as you can possibly get. Nap and I never quarreled and after I left Augusta for Detroit, I recommended him to the Tigers, urging them to buy him—he was a cinch to be a big league pitcher. Detroit failed to act, and Nap went up to Brooklyn in 1907 and won a flock of games.

The Rucker story is no more true than the report that "a big, red-haired Southern minister named John Yarborough" discovered me in Royston, Georgia, as a kid, and coached me into the big league. That gentleman of the cloth had nothing whatever to do with my development. Yet in every sports book which speaks of me, the Reverend Yarborough is credited with directing my feet toward baseball.

What is true—and this gets me to the point of a section of this book in which I am vitally interested—is the sometimes questioned story that I was the first big leaguer to carry three bats to the plate. Very early in my playing days, I began weighting myself down with two extra bats, after discovering that upon discarding the extra lumber, the remaining bat felt extremely light and controllable. They used to say, "There's Cobb, the show-off" . . . and accuse me of playing to the stands. I can truthfully say that I never had my mind on the stands. Quite the opposite, since my whole objective was to win. Showmanship didn't enter; mainly I was using the principle of contrast: the same theory used on the horse track, when heavy workout horseshoes are replaced by very light plates the day of the race. Today's players usually swing only one extra bat, but it is heavily weighted and serves the purpose.

Here—in this chapter—I want to discuss the art of batting, from

A to Z, as I know it. If the youngsters of the country gain some help from it, I'll be satisfied. Many words have been turned out about hitting, but almost invariably by modern performers whose viewpoint is limited to the big swing, the long ball and runs scored in large clusters, and missing the fine, scientific nuances of what once was an act of skill rather than simple power. Most hitters today seem ridiculous to me. The game has degenerated into a high-scoring slugging match with thin, whippy bats as weapons and the home run the universal objective. Players limp along on one cylinder. With the same approach in the old days, they'd never have been top performers. The jack-rabbit ball, shortened fences and 30-ounce bats may produce 2000 and more home runs per season in the major leagues, but they have brought on a degeneration of the batting art that can be recognized by a glance at the statistics: in an average year, upward of 60 leading players register only one sacrifice hit apiece in 154 games and another 60 to 70 have no sacrifices at all. Only 20 per cent of all major leaguers are capable of averaging .280 over a season and a disgraceful seven per cent reach .300. The sacrifice bunt is one of the most deadly offensive tools in any player's bag. Yet there are so-called "good" hitters today who won't collect three dozen of them in a 10-year career. The all-time, all-star second baseman, Eddie Collins, dropped 30 and 40 sacrifices a season and had 511 in his career.

As to averages, the .400 hitter is extinct. We haven't seen a .400 average in the past 20 years. Between 1901–25 half a dozen men achieved .400 or better 11 times and the .350 man was commonplace. Tris Speaker averaged .383, .388, .380, and .389 in different seasons and didn't lead his league in any of the four. Rogers Hornsby went .397, .401, .384, .424, and .403 in consecutive seasons. Paul Waner, weighing under 160 pounds, called it a bad year when he missed 200 base hits and a .360 mark.

You see nothing like that nowadays, and you won't as long as baseball teachers continue to tell boys to dig in and plant both feet, to grasp the bat at the very end and swing with all their might.

The home run has been cheapened until it leaves me disgusted, along with millions of fans. The time is here for a return to the old game of hit-and-run, the steal and double steal, the bunt in all its wonderful varieties, the squeeze, the ball hit to the opposite field and the ball punched through openings in the defense for a single.

Instructors should begin telling boys another forgotten fact: that you hit more with your feet than with your arms, hands, and shoulders.

Let me illustrate. They called me "an African dodger" at the plate, for I was rarely hit by a pitched ball. I took a balanced stance with feet close together—not more than 14 inches—and I constantly shifted my feet to adapt to the particular man on the mound. I was forever moving forward or backward in the box, in or out, erect or crouching, as the situation required. Seldom did I "dig in" and plant myself irretrievably for the heavyweight swing. My idea was to be highly mobile in that box, able to open or close my stance instantly, or to shift into the bunting position.

A closed stance is simply one in which the front or striding foot is about four inches closer to the inside of the plate than the rear foot. The open stance brings the front foot four inches or so farther away from the plate's inside edge. Why shift from an orthodox parallel stance into one of these? Well, a big secret of high-average hitting is the ability to knock the ball to the field opposite to your natural pulling power. For me, a left-hander, that was to left field. Being "loose" at bat, it was easy to close my stance by dropping my rear foot back a couple of inches, choke on the bat a bit and punch rather than pull the ball into left field—when the opposition was expecting me to hit toward the second-base–first-base side of the diamond. It got me hundreds of safeties because it caught the defense unaware.

Babe Ruth, for instance, was a natural left-handed pull-hitter, but whenever the defense gave him an opening, he could slap the ball into left field with beautiful ease. It may surprise you to know that while Babe had a record 714 home runs in his career, he also hit twice as many singles—1517 of them. More than 52 per cent of Ruth's total safeties were one-baggers—food for thought. For here was a man the most dedicated to power of all batters.

In my own case, 72-plus per cent of my 4191 lifetime hits were singles, obviously the reason I was able to average .367 over an extended period of years. In modern years, a handful of good hitters only—Phil Rizzuto, Nellie Fox, Pete Runnels, Harvey Kuenn, Billy Goodman, and George Kell just about exhaust the list—have concentrated on spraying singles and doubles. The rest of the boys focus on the fence. And what a shame it is—what great potential is lost, even among the Ted Williamses and Joe DiMaggios, by lack of learning the simple art of hitting to all parts of the field.

In coming to the plate, a boy should first of all adopt a comfortable stance. He should imitate *nobody*. He should stand the way in which he feels most relaxed and confident. Normally, though, this will not include a deep or exaggerated crouch. The best hitters have stood fairly erect. If this feels uncomfortable, while awaiting the delivery, it will help to break at the knees—a dip or slight squat. But in actually swinging, you should come back to the position first assumed.

Shoeless Joe Jackson, along with Rogers Hornsby the greatest of right-handed hitters, stood with his feet close together. Joe usually marked a line three inches from home plate and then drew a line at right angles to it. He stayed back of the right-angle line, behind the plate. As the ball approached, he took a slow, even stride, starting his swing in unison with the stride. None of that wide-spread, dug-in stuff for Jackson. And he averaged .356, lifetime, the third-best mark in history.

Balance—ability to shift around in the box—a proper stride—these are basics of sound hitting. The home run should be the last thing the young batter thinks about.

There is no batting secret of mine I'm not willing to impart here. You will find it most profitable to bend from the waist up—as if bowing slightly to the pitcher—for this increases the ability to follow the ball's flight. And with the feet limber and loose under you, balance is maintained.

I seldom took the same stance twice running. I intended that the pitcher never would know whether I'd chop at the ball or swing away. I tried to be all things to all pitchers, keeping them unsettled by my flexibility. It pains me to see boys wound up in a coiled-spring knot, waiting to pickle the ball. They'll be .250 hitters all their life. A Stan Musial or an Al Simmons could get away with a coil or a foot planted in the "bucket"—the rest of us cannot.

As to striding, the fatal error is to over-stride. It causes upper-cutting and fly balls, the upsetting of co-ordination and costs you the freedom to step in or out on the ball. As you stride, the hips and shoulders pivot forward on a level line and the arms come around in synchronization. As the weight shifts from the rear foot to the front foot, your hands automatically are brought forward and in front of the body. If you are able to place a little extra weight on the front foot and still feel balanced to step either way, so much the better. The ability to do this will assure proper stride and, when swinging, will bring the body and arms up to the ball more smoothly and automatically.

On grip of the bat, I am accused of being hopelessly old-fashioned. Yet I see in my mind's eye the one and only Honus Wagner, with his hands spread a palm's breadth apart. He choked that bat and he could push outside pitches to the opposite field with consistent ease. Wagner almost never pulled the ball. He hit line drives that either fell in front of the outfielders or crashed the fences above their heads like a well-hit long-iron shot in golf. Honus held for a long time the National League record for most doubles and triples —for you do not necessarily surrender power by choking the bat. This is a fallacy spread by the power-school-of-thought boys. What you really do is improve your timing.

How many times have you seen one of today's "big" sluggers look foolish when he coiled himself—and found a curve ball cutting the outside corner, beyond his reach? He's too deep in the box, too wound up, to do more than lunge awkwardly at the curve outside.

Ask yourself this: If you held a 12-foot pole in your hands and intended to touch a spot on the wall of a room with it, how could you manage it best? By holding it way down at the end with both hands? Or by placing one hand down the pole and the other near the end to give better leverage? For the boy who lacks size—and most boys do breaking in—this is the ideal grip for getting around on the ball. Yet, at 190 pounds, it remained as effective for me as at 150.

"Loss of power" remains the criticism against spread-hands hitting. The truth is that the mania for killing the ball has replaced common sense. "Power" is not just producing home runs. With a hands-apart grip, I once hit a pitch by Chief Warhop of the New York Highlanders that ripped the glove off Harry Wolter in deep right field and broke his finger. I used to love to choke up and smash them at Hal Chase at first base for New York—the kind that carom off the knees of an infielder and leave him limping for days. You can make the ball ring like a bell off the right-field fence with a choked grip, and never doubt it. Again—timing.

In 1919, I remember watching Roger Peckinpaugh, the Yankee shortstop—a light hitter who usually aimed the ball into left field

—come out with a heavily bandaged hand which forced him to spread his grip. "Watch him start hitting," I predicted.

Peckinpaugh began hitting the Hades out of pitchers to *right* field. For a while, he even had me worried that he might beat me out for the batting title, he was going so good. It was the only season in 17 he played that he topped .300.

Wee Willie Keeler would wait for them to play him a little short in the outfield, then whacked the ball over their heads with his controlled grip. He was under 5 feet 5 and looked like a grinny little kid who couldn't swat a fly hard enough to kill it. But look at his season averages. They range into the phenomenal—from .376 to .392 to .432.

Loss of power through choking up? The statement is laughable. In 1925, when I'd been twenty years in the American League, and was thirty-eight years old, Detroit played a series in St. Louis. The newspapers were saying that Cobb might be all right as a hitter, but he couldn't deliver the king-sized wallop like Babe Ruth. My home-run production never passed a dozen a year, whereas Ruth was in the 40s and 50s.

I'd been hearing this so long that it nettled me.

"Boys," I said to some sportswriters, "the next two days, I'm going to give you a little demonstration. Just to settle a point I think you're missing."

On May 5, I hit three homers against the Browns. The next day, I had two more. Two other shots struck right at top of the stands and fell back for doubles. The five home runs in two consecutive games tied a Cap Anson record going back 41 years, and it silenced most of the critics. Unfortunately, they still missed my point.

I was demonstrating that there was power aplenty in my style of holding a bat. With the choke grip, I merely slid my left hand down the wood as the pitcher delivered and locked it with my right and took a full swing. The grip I recommend has endless adaptiveness, as this incident should prove.

I was content to let Ruth have his homers and stick with scientific hitting. Babe also struck out a record 1330 times, a mark I'd rather not have against my name.

It would be easy to go on for pages, demonstrating the attributes of the spread grip. But I'll name four more and then desist.

One of the most devastating things you can do on the attack is to

149

fake a bunt, lure the third baseman in and then slash it past him. You can't do that holding the bat at the knob end. And today you seldom see this old-time feat on the diamond, because batters lack control of their weapon.

I'll wager that almost no fans today can identify the terms "Baltimore chop" and "Big Bill." The chop was made famous by Ned Hanlon's Baltimore Orioles before the turn of the century and this punch-style of hitting produced slow-hopping ground balls called "Big Bills," which a fast man could beat out. You chopped the ball into the ground deliberately—infielders were forced to charge the lazy bounders and throw on the run, or lose their man. That's another form of baseball offense which is all but extinct.

In meeting the ball the bat must be parallel to the ground. But before the level bat connects, the heavy end of the stick takes over, often producing a dip in the swing. Most hitters are unaware they are dipping, but such is the case. By dividing the hands you gain greater guidance over the stick and reduce dip to a minimum.

Finally, your hands and wrists roll over together during the late stages of the swing. With both hands clamped tightly together, they are bound to cramp to some degree. Apart—no cramp.

All these correct fundamentals must be tirelessly *practiced*. Using improper fundamentals you can improve only to a point, then the wrongs take over to frustrate you. Practice also instills the confidence you need to feel master of the situation when batting.

American boys should realize that with a controlled hold on the bat and the right footwork, they can spray hits in all directions. If you are an all-field hitter, the outfielders are forced to play you straightaway, and this means that they give you the foul lines. Down those lines, many a single and double can be rifled. Never let them stack the defense on you, boys, as they do with so many home-run larrupers today, who can only pull the ball. It's a crime the way these men have let their power be neutralized and an insult to their ability and judgment.

Generally, pulling the ball should be avoided. A left-handed hitter never should try to pull speed against a left-handed pitcher. Why? Because you will be hitting to the long side of the infield. The first and second basemen are back on the grass, needing only a short throw to first base and with all the percentage in their favor if you drive a ball toward them. Usually, that lefty pitcher will be putting the ball on the outside of the plate, fast or curved, to prevent you from pulling. In such a case, how easy it is to step into it and stroke it to left field, not right field. Keep in mind that the third baseman is the infielder closest to you and that a sharply hit ball has more chance of getting through him than any other defender.

I firmly believe in keeping the arms out away from the body, directly opposite to the in-tight method widely favored these days. And I mean well out from the chest, with the forward-arm elbow up and pointed toward the pitcher. You cannot connect with maximum force by hugging the bat—it is exactly the wrong mechanical hold.

Try a simple finger test with a friend, and prove it. Holding one near your chest, have the friend lock onto your little finger with his second finger and pull laterally. He will be able to overcome your resistance. Now move that hand out 14 to 20 inches in front of your body and have him pull. He won't be able to move your hand.

The in-tight boys, out to pull the ball, also give away a vital area of the hitting zone to the pitcher. Cramped as they are, they can't protect the outside of the plate—because they can't reach it. They are off balance when reaching and without power.

Max Carey, once the National League's leading base stealer and a keen batting student, had trouble for years hitting high balls. Every pitcher knew it. Max languished in the .260-.270 class as a batter until he began studying my approach to the high pitch. I got my right (front) elbow up and out there—where the power is located— went into a crouch, and had no trouble cuffing letter-high deliveries. The accentuated elbow worked for Carey, too. He went over the .300 mark five years between 1919 and 1925.

Fred Haney, the former Milwaukee Braves manager, now general manager of the Los Angeles Angels, was a little fellow with very small hands and shy on strength when he came up to the Detroit Tigers from Omaha in 1922. High pitches handcuffed Fred. His strength was low pitches. As his manager, I squatted him down over the plate, got his arms up, and with the pitcher forced to send the ball in low, Fred averaged .352, .282, and .309 his first three seasons.

Now we come to the moment of impact.

A great many young players are convinced that if they stand back as far as possible from the pitcher, they will have an opportunity to see the ball fractionally longer. They retreat in the box until they are almost out of it. But they should realize that a pitcher primarily depends upon his speed and curves, and that a curve will break just as the ball reaches the plate, or just before. If the pitch is a fast ball, it will have just about as much speed on it after it passes the plate as before. The thing to do, lads, is to aggressively meet the ball *out in front of you*; make up your mind to contact the ball before it breaks or as it begins to break. You want to see out in front of you what the ball is doing; you can't do that after the break.

Above all, watch that pitcher's arm and keep your eye on the ball every instant after it leaves his hand. Learn to see in a flash. Handball, incidentally, is one of the great training sports for good hitting.

Don't try to overpower the ball. Just meet it solidly, and follow through evenly without upper-cutting or letting the bat waver from a parallel arc.

The arm position I've described will protect you from swinging the bat at too low a level. Heinie Manush of Detroit used to pop up because he unconsciously held the bat below his waist. Whenever Heinie fell into the habit, I'd whistle at him as a reminder. If the bat is held above the belt, you are in the middle of the strike zone and far more immune to upper-cutting. Heinie wound up leading the league.

The most shocking aspect of modern baseball is that few big leaguers even know how to lay down a good bunt. Some of them actually shove the bat upward at the ball, others can't pivot properly. Many don't even try to learn. Sacrifice plays go wrong again and again and managers do nothing about it. If I was managing today, every member of the team would practice laying down bunts until proficient, or be traded away. For in the late innings with the score tied, or in extra innings, the bunt can be the game-breaker.

If the rival pitcher is going good and you can't touch him, start bunting. This will throw the pitcher off stride as nothing else can do. Bunt to either side of the box. The pitcher must go after the ball, so make him sweat and strain. Remember, it's an entirely different sort of fielding chance for him. He delivers, goes quickly for the ball and his rhythm is changed. It makes not so much difference whether or not you're thrown out or safe on the bunt; you've accomplished your purpose—to make a strictly offensive man (pitcher) turn defensive man and jar him off stride. Many a batting rally has started by a bunted ball that the pitcher couldn't handle.

Remember: with practice, you can bunt a ball easier than you can hit away on it. Also: in advancing a runner, the bunt is much safer than going for a base hit, for the possibility of a fumble is more pronounced. I've seen many a lanky pitcher step on his own hand or trip on his own feet while fielding the ball. What's more, handling a deft bunt is the toughest play any third baseman can face.

As a minor league rookie, as I've said earlier, I worked by the hour to develop the ability to drop a bunt exactly on a sweater spread along the base line. Ordinarily, the ball should be placed far enough to evade the catcher, and frustrate the third baseman. But in a close game, with a teammate on second base, you should bunt a bit harder and force the third-sacker to handle the chance. Certainly, you may be thrown out. But who's covering third? No one. Your teammate advances to third standing up.

The threat in a bunt is a marvelous weapon. Often, I would bunt two or three times in a row, forcing the first and third basemen to move in close. At which I'd fake another bunt, and drive the ball straight at one of them. Neither of these fielders, charging in to field a bunt, can handle a hard-hit ball right at them. They just can't shift that quickly.

Tristram Speaker was no home-run-hunter. He'd drop that bunt one time, then indicate another bunt and whistle a single into left field. George Sisler would use the bunt to lure the infield in, then poke the ball over their heads. Let them drop back and he'd lay down a bunt and beat the throw to first.

Once upon a time, down South, there was a marvel of a speed-ball pitcher named Happy Harry Hale from Happy Hollow, Tennessee. He mowed down everyone. Standing 6 feet 7 and weighing about 150, he was the original buggywhip. When Happy Harry came out of the backwoods to show off his stuff for the big-time scouts, he struck out a dozen men and didn't yield a hit in six straight innings. Then one of the old pros on the team that was getting shellacked decided it was time to call a halt. "Let's buy this boy a bus ticket," he said.

The old pro bunted. Happy Harry had never seen a bunt, and he stared at it as if it was a Tennessee moccasin. He ignored a second bunt. Finally, he picked up a third bunt and threw it over first base into the stands.

The sad pay-off came on a fourth straight bunt. Happy Harry now was desperate. As he unfolded himself to field it, he stepped on his own hand and spiked it to the tune of five stitches. The next bus out of town carried him back to Happy Hollow.

Pitchers are not the natural athletes you find at the other positions in baseball—keep that in mind when weighing the value of a bunt against trying to hit between the agile infielders and race-horse out-fielders.

Young players seem to think the act of bunting difficult. It's most simple. At the pitch, merely move your rear foot up practically even with your front foot, while pivoting to face the pitcher. Keep the weight forward, elbows bent. Break at the legs and extend the arms in front of you. Don't push the bat into the ball, but get the bat in front of the plate to receive the ball. Slide the top hand down the bat, close to the trademark, letting it rest loosely in the palm. Just as the ball reaches you, draw back the bat toward the catcher to make the impact as easy as possible. Guide the direction of your bunt by your arm action. Don't tip off the bunt, but come to the plate looking eager to hit—take a few vigorous swings as if determined to pound the ball to a remote corner of the park. Size up with a glance the position of the third baseman and first baseman. Drop your bunt and run at top speed all the way to first. Don't lag if the bunt is a bad one—there may be a fumble. The fellow who's thrown out by a half-step because he assumes he's beaten on the play never will make a ballplayer.

Let me tell you one of the finest bunt stories in history—one that's been forgotten. It also illustrates the value of carefully analyzing the pitcher, which is quite different from guessing what he'll throw. Never guess with a pitcher.

Paul Waner, then with the Boston Braves, was facing Whit Wyatt, the big smoke-ball thrower for Brooklyn. It was a duel between two extremely clever men. Waner had almost twenty years in the big league behind him, Wyatt fifteen. Holding a two-run lead in the fourth inning, Wyatt knew he'd have to face the dangerous Waner two or three more times that day. No one was on base, so he risked a home run to discover something.

Wyatt began throwing Waner fast balls inside, to find out if he had the power to pull his high, hard one over the fence. If Waner did so, Wyatt still would be a run to the good. And he'd know what not to throw in the clutch.

Thinking right with him, knowing that one run wouldn't tie the score, Waner backed away and deliberately fouled that inside pitch to left field. This gave Wyatt the impression that he was too fast for Waner to pull. And all the time, Paul Waner was setting his own trap for the moment when he could unload on that same pitch.

Came that moment in the eighth inning, with runners on first and second and none out. A home run would win the game, and Waner knew he'd get Wyatt's fast one inside. He did.

Know what Waner did? Even though confident that he could hit it out of the park, he choked up and dropped a sacrifice bunt that advanced both runners. If you can see why, you're on your way to becoming a thinking ballplayer.

Paul couldn't do anything else, for the percentage demanded a bunt. With his team three runs behind, he couldn't take a chance on a pop-up that would nullify those vital runners at first and second. As it worked out, the Braves won.

Always calculate the percentages on every play. Today's power-hitting is all the more foolish because it goes directly against the most obvious percentage situation on the diamond. Ask yourself where the biggest safety zone exists for any hitter. It happens to be right down the middle, over second base or near it. Hitting there, you get the ball past the pitcher before he can act, and you leave the shortstop and second baseman in the most difficult possible position. The shortstop will be caught off balance by the crisp hit down the middle. The second baseman must go far to his right, reverse and make a long throw to first. Often, either will be lucky to get a glove on the ball.

Furthermore, you are hitting back the way the ball is pitched—that is, not pulling against the revolution or spin of a ball that often is curving. Pulling curves constantly results in sliding the ball off the bat, beating it into the ground or popping up. Hit straight back through the second base zone without any fancy touches, if you want to be a high-average batter.

In practice, I've seen many star players swing themselves off stride by staying in the box too long and aiming for the fences. Stay just long enough to rap four or five good sharp drives. Then's the time to quit. Stick around and look for the bleachers and you only get off your timing.

Developing the acumen to size up a pitcher and discover his weakness is something only alertness and practice will give you. Big Ed Walsh is in the Hall of Fame. Walsh's spitball was fast and vicious—he threw it across the knees and the curved spitter broke down, while his fastball spitter broke up. But we had a third base coach with Detroit who finally noticed one small fact about Walsh.

"Watch his cap bill," he told us. "That's the tip-off."

If Walsh put his hand to his mouth, he might be loading up for the spitter, or bluffing. We couldn't guess which until our coach's keen eyes gave us the answer. To apply saliva, Big Ed had to open his mouth. And up would go the bill of his cap. He never knew that we knew, and how it helped. Against a man who'd always been poison to me, I finished with a career average of .307.

Greater even than Walsh—the greatest, in my opinion, who ever wound up—was Walter Johnson. His speed surpassed Rube Waddell's, Dazzy Vance's, Bob Feller's, Lefty Grove's, Van Lingle Mung's or that of any fireballer I ever saw. Billy Evans, the umpire, once said, "Johnson was the only pitcher who ever broke the wires on my face mask with a ball that got past the catcher." On murky days, players would come to me (when I managed Detroit) and moan, "Ty, I've got an awful bellyache today, mind if I lay off?" or, "I'm sore in the legs, think I'll sit this one out." You could bet Johnson was slated to work that day. The boys were scared stiff and they begged off in bunches, and now, at my advanced age, I can't say I blame them. A sidearm Johnson fast one looked about the size of a watermelon seed and it *hissed* at you as it passed.

I never saw another pitcher instill fear as did the Big Train. Just consider, he once threw three straight shut-outs against the Yankees, 3-0, 6-0, and 4-0, in four days.

I'll admit there were times against Johnson when I all but shut my eyes and swung, but then I got to figuring that there must be some way to equalize on him. Bunting worked when he was a green rookie, but you can bet Walter schooled himself to field bunts and plugged that weakness in a hurry.

After several seasons when I had no luck, Johnson accidentally beaned my teammate Oscar Vitt with his curve (not his fastball, thank Goodness) and laid Oscar stiff. Vitt didn't move for some time. Johnson dashed in to the plate and stood there as white as a sheet until Oscar opened his eyes. He was so frightened of his own speed—the fact that he'd almost killed Vitt—that he had to take himself out of the game.

Well, wasn't that provocative? I thought about it, and realized that Johnson was so nice a guy that he never dusted off a batter. He had pinpoint control, along with his speed, and took good care not to split anyone's skull. Very considerate of him. And yet a weakness that could be exploited.

Gradually, I began to crowd the plate on Johnson. From 10 inches or so back of the plate, I moved in until at last I was standing right against it, and even out over the plate with my bent knees and arms. With that plate tucked in under me, I was giving Johnson only a few inches of target. It was cheating, if you will, but also strategy. I was gambling that Johnson would be so afraid of hitting me that he'd work to the outside corner, and that he did.

Now, Johnson wouldn't be wide of the plate by much—he had such great control. But he'd miss the corner a fraction, get behind in the count, two balls and no strikes, and that's when I'd resume my regular stance and whack the cripple that had to come down the middle.

I'd never in a million years expected to dominate Walter Johnson, who pitched a record 113 shut-outs, and yet in a way that's what happened. When I began hitting him, he'd look upset and I'd hear him say, "Gee whillikins!" His confidence dropped slightly. He would bear down on me harder than most batters, yet he never saw through my plate-crowding strategy. Altogether, I faced Walter about 250 times, got 14 doubles and three triples off him, among 80-odd hits, and averaged about .325. Without playing on his unusual weakness, the mark would have been closer to .125.

The moral for young players is self-evident: study and "read" every pitcher you go against, and let the small clues you pick up make *you* the aggressor at the plate. Always have a belligerent, take-charge attitude up there. You can cultivate quite a "mad on" while awaiting your turn at bat, a cold determination to ram the ball down the pitcher's throat. You'd be surprised how effective it is. It will show up in your walk, in your eyes, in the way you hold your head, the stance you take. Now the pitcher is fearing *you*.

They used to say of my cocksure strut, "Look at Cobb—he thinks he owns the park." Well, I'd rather be called a swellhead than a bad hitter.

The winning competitor must get ready in advance. Practice, practice, and more practice is the answer, until you know the fundamentals of the game so well that they become entirely natural and instinctive. Why should a certain well-built youngster with speed and skill fail to get anywhere, while another, without half the qualifications, lands on top? Why should one man be good in a pinch while another, with greater physical assets, be useless? To me, the answer rests in what you might call *lack of conscious thought under pressure*. An example:

Once, Al Mamaux of the Pirates was hit on the head by a foul tip in the third inning. Mamaux could remember nothing until the seventh inning.

And yet in those four innings, he pitched fine ball and struck out six men because instinct and muscle memory were carrying him along.

Mamaux had based himself so well in training and experience that even in a blackout, he didn't have to ask himself how to stand, wind, pivot, deliver, and follow through.

The last boy into the showers after a practice session is the boy most likely to show the early poise that every school coach is looking for. He still uses his brain at all times, but his brain is free and ready for advanced thinking, which is impossible if he is still consciously concerned about the fundamental things he must do.

I see few major leaguers these days who bother to "read" the catcher, who can be even more informative than the pitcher. Catchers, even veterans, fall into patterns or systems. Many receivers, for instance, invariably will sign for a fastball when they have one strike and two balls on the batter. When you first step to the plate, some catchers automatically ask for the fast one. With men on bases, some are sure to call for the curve. Or perhaps you've had good luck with the curve earlier, and the catcher is reluctant to call for one again. Right here, keep a good eye on the pitcher. It may be a change of pace. If you stride too soon on a let-up-pitch, you're out of luck. Watch for any slight accentuation of the wind-up, which will be a feint to cover up a slow ball coming at you. The feint may look most convincing, but the arm follow-through will be less sweeping than with a curve or fastball, and if you recognize it on the spot, you'll be ready.

Ray Schalk was a little man, but one of the two or three greatest catchers who ever lived. He was a system man, but so clever at it that you had to study Schalk, and watch almost every pitch he called to get any kind of a line on him. For example, Ray would get his pitcher ahead of you on the ball-strike count by calling for fastballs. A curve seemed almost sure to come, but again there would be a fastball. And still another. Every fast one was a surprise, because you kept expecting something else. When you were absolutely certain that you'd get a curve or drop next—Ray would feed you another fastball. Then, about the sixth pitch, he'd give you the twister—when you were fastball-happy and convinced he didn't have anything else in his pitcher's repertoire.

A word about slumps. Every young man must expect to fall into a mysterious period when the base hits won't come, no matter what he tries. He sweats and worries and presses and falls even deeper into a rut. He is the most woebegone sight in the world. From all sides, he is fed advice on how to break the slump, much of it conflicting, until after desperate experimenting he often ruins what is a good, sound swing.

Here's how I broke a slump—as simple and foolproof a solution as can be supplied:

In practice, I would resort to my old friend, the bunt. I'd bunt the ball back to the pitcher for half an hour or more, making no attempt to do more than punch the ball toward the mound. Slowly, then, with my timing established, I'd begin hitting a bit harder— but always straightaway. I'd increase the arc of my swing until at last I was hitting hard ground balls and line drives down the middle. After a few such sessions, my timing returned and my slump went away.

Hitters aren't "born." They learn, and one big thing they learn is concentration. Bobby Jones, the best hitter golf ever had, used to walk right past me during a tournament, those milky blue eyes of his absolutely blank. I was an old friend of Bob's but I was invisible to him. He was thinking 100 per cent of the next shot. On the diamond, I'd get a hit and slide into second without even knowing a crowd was present. Then a great wave of sound would reach my ears, and I'd be aware for the first time since I went to bat that I had an audience. This is an act of will power, of concentration that any determined boy can develop and call upon under pressure. When Harry Heilmann was leading the American League with marks of .394, .403, .393, and .398, the earth could have parted under him, and he'd still have completed his swing. Yet there was a time when Harry couldn't reach the .300 class. Concentration, a stance with his feet together, the developed ability to hit to the opposite field all bred confidence, and once he had the ingredients put together, Heilmann made every pitcher he faced quail.

If what I've said here indicates that I think modern kid players should ignore what they see on television and return to the old fundamentals of batwork, I've accomplished my purpose. Science is out the window these days. But we must come back to it if baseball is to remain the No. 1 national game. Today, it's as if two golfers had decided to forget all about the course, with its dog legs, bunkers, roughs, and putting greens, and instead just went out to see who could slug the ball the farthest on a driving range. Modern slam-bang baseball requires very little gray matter. It's time we asked players to use their ingenuity and give the fans a sane balance between brains and brawn. As it stands, the big leaguers of the 1960s era are poor custodians of the sport I love.

Boys, strive to master the lost arts of a great game. Unless you dedicate yourself to that task now, as the old-timers die off one by one, they will have vanished forever.

12

The Ultimate Secret:
Make Them Beat Themselves or
Waging War on the Base Paths

Lou Criger was the batterymate of the one and only Cy Young on the Boston Beaneaters and a rather loud-lipped individual, even in a day when noisy ballplayers were all the rage. Criger never had any trouble commanding an audience of fans and writers.

"This Cobb is one of those ginks with a lot of flash—but he doesn't fool me. Watch him wilt when it gets tough. I'll cut him down to size," stated Catcher Criger.

From then on, it was as certain as the shine on the seat of an umpire's pants that the two of us would clash. Criger kept pouring it on, in every interview.

"Cobb's no star," he told the St. Louis *Post-Dispatch*. "Why, in the last two years, he's stolen only two bags on me. He's a bonehead runner, if you want to know. One time he tried a delayed steal on me, starting when he thought I was about to return the ball to the pitcher, and I had him out by 15 feet, only the shortstop dropped the ball. The other time, I had him out by 20 feet and our second baseman let Cobb slide around him and hook the bag. No, I've got that boy's goat good.

"Last season, when he came to bat, I'd say, 'Look out, Ty, this pitcher of ours is wild as a hawk and he's liable to crack you on the head.' Then I'd signal for one right at his bean. Bing! Down he'd drop, and when he'd get up the fight was all out of him and he couldn't have hit a stationary balloon."

Criger was a slick psychologist. He was aiming to tie me up in so much anger that I'd take foolish chances at bat and against his arm on the bases. And the Beaneater had an arm like a Sharp's rifle.

As a base-runner, I had some pretty radical ideas. Some said I was crazy to take such chances; others were beginning to suspect that maybe I had something. My counter to Criger's challenge had to be something unusual. And when we opened the first Boston series of '08, I watched the Young-Criger battery carefully before coming to the plate. Then I told Criger, "I'm going to steal every base on you today." At bat, I singled and then walked what seemed suicidally far off the base—15 or 20 feet. When Young wheeled to pick me off, I was already on my way back, and safe well ahead of the throw. This happened a couple of more times and Young didn't come close to catching me—despite my brash lead.

"I'm taking second on the next pitch!" I yelled to Criger. At Young's pitch, I was off and with all that lead, beat Criger's fast throw by a good margin.

"Now, you big baboon, on the next pitch I'm going to third!" I hollered at the fuming catcher. With the big jump I had on Cy Young, I beat Criger's bullet peg to third.

"Now on the next one I'm coming home, ice wagon!" I told Criger, who was dripping sweat and venom all over the plate.

As Young wound up, I was halfway down the line and Criger, ball, and I all arrived at the plate together. Out of the dust cloud stepped umpire Jack Sheridan, his palms down. "Safe!"

On four straight Young pitches, beginning with my single, I'd completed a tour of the Boston bases. Our man at bat hadn't taken his club off his shoulder while I was coming around. Criger had been deflated in the worst way that can happen to a catcher—I'd told him exactly what I intended to do, and still gotten away with it.

They wrote about that one for months, and even years, and some commentators even blamed Lou Criger's retirement soon after that to a broken heart. I doubt the truth of that, but I do know that I never had trouble stealing on him again.

But had I really done anything so miraculous?

No, I'd only used my head and employed some pressure of my

own. The secret of the three straight steals was Cy Young. It took me a while to find his weak spot, but then I discovered that Cy not only had a slow wind-up, but tipped off when he was about to try a pick-off at first, and when he was not. Other pitchers might throw a decoy ball over to the first sack, only fairly hard. Then they'd turn, as if to pitch, and sizzle another one to first and catch you napping. Young threw hard all the time—but only when he stood on the mound with his elbows slightly away from his body. When his elbows were pulled in, it meant he was going to pitch.

That one clue was like looking into his brain.

Just to make the percentage better, I warned Criger of my intentions. He couldn't believe it when I went for second just as I'd announced, and the momentary shock caused him to hurry his throw slightly so that it was less than perfect. When I informed him I was taking third on the next pitch—after checking Cy Young's elbows—Criger was sure I was lying. Coming home to score was more of the same, only by now I had him furious and panicky and wondering what the devil enabled me to get all that jump on his pitcher.

At all times on the field, I tried to be as sensitive as a burglar alarm to every pulse of the game. If you weren't, in the days when baseball was a strategist's duel, and not just a lot of cannon shots going off, you'd be beaten by some more nimble thinker. Larry Gardner of Boston, for instance, was one third baseman I never could successfully bunt against. Gardner would be in there pouncing on that ball before I was ten strides down the line. Time and again, he threw me out like I was his bow-legged sister Kate.

Years later, after he'd retired, I was in a fanning bee with Gardner. "How'd you do it, Larry?" I coaxed him. "You can tell me now."

"You clenched your jaw and clamped your lips together, Ty, when you intended to bunt," said Gardner. "Minute I saw that, I came a-running." Only Gardner was observant enough to see that.

Headwork—not the fact that we were supermen—enabled us old-timers to pull off unassisted triple plays and consecutive steals and hit-'em-where-they-ain't base hits that make lyrical reading today and often sound downright impossible. Can you imagine a one-armed pitcher striking out 19 men in nine innings and winning a flock of one-hitters? Hugh (One Arm) Daly, on one of the early Chicago teams, lost his left hand and forearm in a fireworks explosion.

Yet Daly analyzed the hitters so well that he could almost always anticipate a bunt and field it with his pitching hand.

Along with keen observation went a use of psychology that has gone out of style to the point that nowadays I think I'm watching 18 mechanical men out there.

To all youthful candidates for a baseball career, I'd like to emphasize that the greatest weapon of all—*yet the most overlooked force in the game*—is an astute understanding of an opponent's thought processes, and application of that knowledge. Train yourself, boys, to think along psychological lines. Even big leaguers are a bundle of nerves when a game is close, and there are untold ways when running the bases of using that to your advantage. You can set up a conditioned reflex in many players, and make it pay off at a timely moment. Others players are suggestible. In the 1907 World Series, I was camped off first base when another Tiger singled to center. Reaching third base seemed a highly unlikely goal for me, since the ball was hard-tagged and cleanly fielded. As I reached second at full speed, Second Baseman Johnny Evers took the throw-in from center field with his back to the bag, and with Shortstop Joe Tinker out of his line of vision.

Evers heard somebody yelp, "Tag him!"

Wheeling, Evers swept his glove around to get me and touched only thin air. His first thought was Why the —— did Tinker tell me to do that? He was thinking of Tinker, for a moment, not me—and I was still running.

Having stabbed out with the ball, Evers had to recover his throwing position, and I beat his throw to third by a whisker.

It wasn't until then that it dawned on Evers that it had been my voice he'd heard. Sometimes a little suggestion can go a long way.

To steal 96 bases in one season and over 800 in a career, which I managed to do, sounds like quite a physical feat. The truth is that hundreds of players have had the speed and timing to run up such a score, or even more. My stealing was 90 per cent mental. I wasn't extra fast, and I had no mystic powers, or occult gifts. Some of my plays looked downright stupid. I'd let myself be caught flat-footed between bases. Nine out of ten times I'd get out of the jam and advance a base for a most simple reason. All I had to do was make the opposition keep on throwing the ball. Sooner or later, somebody would make a wild throw. "Make 'em throw the ball," should be Rule One in every base-runner's primer—but the steal is unpopular today, and the maxim is forgotten.

My whole plan on base was to upset batteries and infields. How? By dividing their minds, by upsetting and worrying them until their concentration was affected. I was always looking to create a mental hazard—by, as some writer once put it, the establishment of a threat.

The Threat had many sides to it. For example, there is only one base you can steal to win a ball game—home—but there is much you can do on other bases to help win. One of my stunts was to break for the next base when our team was six or eight runs ahead, and the opposition was least expecting it. So what if I was thrown out? I had planted a seed of uncertainty, of confusion in them. The next day, when I'd hit a single in the late innings of a tied-up game, I'd go for two bases and they'd tighten up and fumble. The idea is to get the other fellow nervous, anticipating what he's afraid you'll do.

The Threat includes understanding the mechanical faults and weaknesses of every rival player, and knowing their skills as well, and using both against them. When you're racing a ball to a base, smart infielders do not tip you off on the location of the ball with their bodies. They'll stand limply, or fake the wrong way, then snatch that ball and slap it on you.

But with all their skill, they still have to *look* at that speeding sphere, and when I discovered that simple fact, my base-stealing score mounted rapidly. Riding into a base, I'd ignore everything but the infielder's eyes. They told me what action to take. Against the Athletics in Philadelphia one day, Frank Baker reached for a throw at third that seemed to be coming from behind me and to my left. But Baker's eyes gave his arms the lie. I slid to my right and as the ball struck at the juncture of Baker's glove and the ground, I kicked it clear into the A's dugout. I kept going to score.

The A's screamed in protest, claiming interference, but the umpires ruled that it was an accident—since nobody could deliberately kick a bounding ball while sliding. But Baker and I knew what had happened.

On second base slides, watching the eyes makes it possible to aim your slide as far away from the tag as possible. At third base, you can line your body up with a throw coming from right field and often the ball will carom off your back or hips, and you may make it all the way home.

I always liked to vie with an intelligent player ahead of a dumb one, since the smart player is easier to "read." He will do the correct, predictable thing, invariably. In an earlier chapter, I described the process of scoring from first base against New York on a bunt by the use of unorthodox tactics on Hal Chase, the ace fielder of all time at that position. Some time later, around 1911, I spent a good part of one season setting up a conditioned reflex in Chase. Time and again, when I was the runner on second and a ball was hit to Chase, I'd turn third by 10 or 12 feet. After making the put-out at first, Chase, with his wounderful snap throw, would fire the ball to his third baseman, Pepper Austin. I'd jump back just in time. The thing got to be routine. I'd turn third boldly, Chase would drive me back, and we'd grin at each other. I didn't win anything and neither did Prince Hal.

Until the day I didn't stop. As Chase made his long-accustomed throw across the diamond, and Austin made his automatic dive for me, I pulled out all stops and was across the plate before Austin could get the relay to the catcher.

In baseball's Golden Era, we'd spend months setting such a trap. We'd file away in our minds the slightest details which might mean a chink in the enemy's armor. Players developed amazing memories about one another. George Sisler, at first base for St. Louis one June day, watched me reach third, and made a bluff throw to hold me there. I leaped back to the bag, as if admitting I didn't dare anything else. Sisler thought so, too, what with him holding the ball and each of us the same distance from home plate. He turned his back for a part of a second to return to first. That was enough—I was gone, and Sisler, turning, astonished, threw hurriedly and a bit high and I slid in under the ball for the winning run.

Two years went by and then the same situation occurred in Detroit. But this time Sisler *backed up* into first base, his body tensed, his eyes riveted upon me, his arm cocked to throw. I had to laugh out loud. Sisler was a great artist—not the type to be fooled twice over any span of time.

A great many of major league base-runners of today don't even know how to travel the paths and to slide well; roughly 50 per cent of them make the fundamental, time-killing error of running right over the top of the bag and "going the overland" on the turns —or circling in too wide an arc. The old boys slid from any direction, using one leg as a sliding frame and giving the fielder only an instep or a hand to touch, and cutting corners fine by pushing their left foot against the inside of the bag to execute a true pivot. Today the right foot is used by players, which is a time-waster. Hitting a bag left-footed, you cross over your right leg like a football halfback cutting back and save split seconds. I'm supposed to have invented the fallaway or fadeaway slide—maybe I did. Although Mike (King) Kelly of the 1880-era Chicago White Stockings could let a baseman hold the ball in his hand while standing on the bag and from a distance of 10 feet away win a bet that he'd get back safely. Kelly was that elusive. The secret is to make your move at the last possible second. As a rookie, I watched men leave their feet a couple of body lengths from the base and forfeit most of their mobility. I wanted to see the whites of that fielder's eyes. I'd come straight in, then collapse right or left while throwing in a body feint. Sometimes I'd deliberately slide wide, go right past the bag, then reach back and hook the outside corner with my trailing toe. Or I'd employ a roll slide. I'd go even farther past—as if I'd missed my target—then roll on my rump and sweep a hand backward over a corner of home plate or the sandbag. Five fingers isn't much to give a defensive man who has to catch the ball and put it on you in the same motion.

You don't see the delayed steal used much any more. It was a favorite of mine (but used most selectively) because it depends on a predictable reaction. On an outfield single, I'd turn first, come to a complete stop and at the instant the outfielder was lulled into hauling back his arm to lob the ball to the infield—thinking he had me stopped cold—I was off. I could make book on it that the outfielder would have to check his motion and change both his position and thinking to make a fast throw to second. I gained a full second there. Just enough, most of the time.

You almost always gain that extra base from a psychological standpoint, or from calculating angles. If you have the outfielder worried enough, he'll often take his eyes off the ball for an instant to see what you're doing, and that's fatal. He juggles the apple, and you've got him beat.

Casey Stengel, when he was a young player, came up to me one night and asked, "Ty, on outfield hits how do you manage to take that extra base so often? You don't look that fast to me."

"I'm not," I told Casey. "Rounding first, I look to see which hand the guy has used to field that ball. If he's right-handed, and the ball's in his left hand, it means he has to cross over his body and turn to make the throw. That's my edge, and I take it without hesitating."

In sliding, I used about nine different varieties; hooks, rolls, bent-leg, fadeaway, the slide past the bag, the down-and-up slide, in which you hit the dirt and bound up running, etc. How long since you've seen a feet-first slide into first base on an infield hit? All theory today holds that you maintain more speed by running straight across the initial sack. I take sharp exception to this. With a runner crossing first in an upright position, the umpire has the man and the ball in the same line of vision. If the ball arrives waist-high, or higher, Mr. Ump doesn't have to do much guessing on "safe" or "out." But suppose you're down on the ground. The umpire must change his line of sight from the ball and baseman's glove to look down at the runner—he can't watch both at once. And if the throw is low, the sliding runner will throw up a dust cloud that will confuse the umpire even more. As to speed, if you don't lose momentum sliding into other bases, why should this apply at first?

Mull that one over, boys, and see if Tyrus and the old-timers didn't have something at least worth trying.

Very few fine sliding practitioners are in operation today. The boys go in for football stuff to break up the double play, throwing body blocks on the second baseman or shortstop, and in doing so they come in high and slide right into the ball for a tag-out. If they stayed down on the ground, they'd be safe. It's a lot of bunk, very amateurish stuff that we see in the major leagues, for there are far better ways to move runners around the bases. The neglected run-and-hit and hit-and-run, for example. If a man had tried to use football tactics on one of the old-time keystone men, the next time he charged down the base path he'd have taken a ball right between the eyes as hard as it could be thrown. We slid properly, on the ground, using our feet to kick the ball out of the fielder's hand whenever possible. Or we'd pretzel our legs around the fielder and tie him up beyond any chance of a throw. The idea today seems to be to injure someone by imitating a blocking halfback. That's not baseball as it's meant to be played.

The secret of base-stealing is to watch the pitcher's feet, knees, and hips—for it's against him, not the catcher that you'll fail or succeed. Under the balk rule, if the pitcher moves any part of his body—feet, knees, hips, shoulders, elbows, or arms—toward first, he must throw to first, except in the case of left-handed pitchers, who position their body toward first naturally and extend their arms in that direction as they deliver. If the pitcher moves any portion of his body to the plate, he must throw to the plate.

My cardinal rule was: Watch the pitcher's legs from the hips down. Especially the feet. To throw to first on a pick-off, or to the plate, the moundsman must take a step or he balks. Consequently, I watched the front foot and when I saw that foot move toward first, I leaped back for the bag. When the foot began to move to the plate, I lit out for second.

Occasionally, a sharp pitcher will use a move that calls for lifting the back foot off the rubber, spinning and throwing and stepping with the front foot simultaneously. But my eyes were fixed on *both* feet, and I could always get back in time with that warning. No matter how tricky his motion, no pitcher should outsmart a base-runner—if the latter is focusing every instant on the feet.

Urban Shocker and Big Ed Walsh, two of the greatest, had very quick, clever moves, yet their feet always constituted a clue. Shocker had a peculiar head motion that used to dazzle base-runners. He'd stand out there and shake his head toward first base—as a boxer feints. This entranced many a runner, who kept watching Shocker's head. His purpose was to hold his man near the base—but not to pick him off. When the steal attempt came, Shocker's catcher had a much better chance to nail the runner at second.

Because I was always prepared to slide back into first base, I could take leads that were termed fantastic. "You haven't got a good lead off first," I used to argue, "if you don't have to slide back to the bag." A 10-foot or even a 12-foot lead is no good. You must get out there 15 to 20 feet and still be protected. I stayed low, kept on the balls of my feet, like a dancer. I kept my arms loose, waving them back and forth to create some momentum when I was ready to run. And every pitcher in the American League was a bird I couldn't learn enough about. I studied them constantly. There was a right-hander with Washington, I recall, who had a habit of stiffening his right leg when he was going to move toward the plate. He did this to get more push off the rubber. A perfect tip-off—as soon as he stiffened his back leg, I was off to second. Stole the poor devil blind for years, and he never did get wise to my discovery.

We don't often see the long lead and the dramatic duel between pitcher and runner these days, because the lively ball and home run mania makes it unnecessary to place a premium on manipulating just one extra base into the offensive pattern. Thus the fans are robbed of their birthright once again.

Base-stealing has fallen into limbo and the thrills that go with it are no more. But it'll return, as surely as I'm writing these words. The trend that way already begins to show—the Pittsburgh Pirates of the last two years being an example. Boys love to tear around the bags, and, if these sandlot kids are listening, I say to them— go to it, and go to it with your brain ticking all the time.

Do the unexpected. Break when it doesn't seem logical, and fail to break when they expect you to run. Around 1909, they were still calling me "crazy in the head," but I remember one day when Hughie Jennings, managing Detroit, gave me the "hold-up" sign as I raced for third on a short outfield hit. The ball was almost to the infield relay man from the outfield, but I kept going like a seagull late for lunch. Jennings was so appalled that he moved in from the coaching box and I knocked him flat on his back as I swerved for home.

"Well, I made it, and Hughie told me later, "Sorry I got in your way. But I could see the ball and *you* couldn't, and I figured—"

"Hughie, I could see the ball," I assured him.

The secret was that I'd been practicing for hours running full speed while training myself to look over my right shoulder, and keeping tab on the whereabouts of the ball. I see big leaguers do this only rarely any more. They run blindly and depend on coaching signals, often misunderstood, instead of depending on the fact that the human neck is built to swivel, and it only takes a lot of hard practice to make it your most dependable base of observation.

Be consistent in your unorthodoxy. I did the unexpected every day, not as an exception, until the defense could count on being suddenly shocked at some point in the contest. There was a rookie Cleveland outfielder who was briefed on an "unwritten law"—never to throw behind Cobb. One day I lined a simple single to the boy and as I turned first, he didn't hesitate. Without an instant's delay, he wound up and whipped the ball with everything he had to the catcher. I wasn't going to outmaneuver him!

Psychology and headwork develop from application to detail. When the Tigers arrived in a road-trip town, I learned beforehand whether some of the old-time, retired stars of the game lived there. Or perhaps it'd be a veteran manager or ex-coach. While the crap-shooting and beer-drinking went on back at the hotel, I'd be with these old boys, picking their brains. They were tremendous store-houses of knowledge. Sitting at their feet, I got all sorts of tips and inspiration.

The base, itself, for instance, often wasn't strapped down tight. The writers used to mention my "superstitious" habit of kicking the bag after I'd arrived at a base. Others thought it a nervous habit. What they didn't know that with each kick, I moved that bag a few inches closer to me, after I'd taken my lead-off. If I had to dive back, that inch or two could be the difference. Never overlook the smallest percentage.

Another trick, good for one or two times a season, was to fake an injured knee or ankle on the base paths. I'd writhe around on the ground, in agony. Then I'd call time and hobble to my feet and limp around painfully. It was logical that I was hurt, for I played hell-bent-for-election at all times.

When the game resumed, I'd go on the first ball pitched and steal second.

The hardest catcher for me to steal on was Billy Sullivan of the Chicago White Sox. I'd swiped only two or three bases on him in half a dozen seasons when I decided to try dividing his mind.

"Billy," I said, one day at bat, "when I get on, and I will, I'm going down on the second ball pitched. Remember, I warned you."

Sullivan snorted, and when I went as promised, his throw was a shade wide and I was standing there at second as safe as a J. P. Morgan stockholder.

Next day, I smiled genially at Sullivan and gave him another solemn promise. "Today, I'm going on that second pitch again."

Did Sullivan believe me? He must have, because he didn't even cut loose when I went down—on the *first* ball pitched.

Little white lies can make big black numbers on the scoreboard for your team, if you've first set the stage for them.

Flattery is an art, in itself. George Moriarty, the New York third baseman, liked to tempt me to do something outrageous after I reached his base by tossing the ball into the air and catching it. He'd toss it up two feet or so, giving me a challenging look while the ball was in the air.

"Oh, no you don't, George," I said, grinning. "I wouldn't go for home on *your* arm." And he had an arm, too.

One day I dared him back, "Toss it a little higher, George." Knowing he had me in his power, Moriarty increased his tosses and finally lobbed the ball a good four feet. I hotfooted it for home on the instant and Moriarty couldn't wait for that ball to come down— he began grabbing for it as it descended, bobbled it, and by the time he had it by the handle, I was into my slide and scoring as enjoyable a run as I can remember.

At the bottom of it all is the aim of making them fight themselves, beat themselves, and an overlooked baseball truth is deeply involved here. *A defensive play is at least five times as hard to make as an offensive play.* An error by a fielder can come from a bad throw, a bad hop of the ball, the muff of an easy chance, the ball hitting the runner or a mix-up in responsibility between shortstop and second baseman, or two outfielders, on a given play. But on offense, a man can run a play 100 times without variation or error. About the only mistake you can make is to stumble. Weighing those odds, I became highly aggressive on the paths. Runners, until then, had been the hunted, the prey of the defense—but my idea was to go on the attack and never relax it. Not for me to fight for my existence on the bases. An offensive attitude is the key to making any play, and if it meant gambling and getting tough, I was willing. If they roughed me up, I knocked them kicking with my spikes. I used my legs like an octopus when I was thrown out. Donie Bush of Detroit was a fast man. With Bush the runner on first and me at bat, I'd signal for the hit-and-run, then drag the ball through the infield for a single. Second base would be impossible to reach, but I'd make the dash, anyway, which drew the play away from Bush, now approaching third base. As Bush kept going for the plate, I'd slide and scissor my legs around the second baseman who'd tagged me out, wrapping him up so tightly he couldn't make any sort of throw. It looked accidental, was anything but. I'm out, but Bush had scored.

Base-runners today forget they are an adjunct of their teammate at bat, one of his most valuable assets if they'd stop thinking of home runs and start using their noodle. On base, I always sought to give our hitter an edge on the pitcher. I'd show every sign of larceny, which often would force the moundsman to pitch out in hope of catching me going down. But I wouldn't go. Ball one. Next, I'd make a false dash, check up, dive back to first, and draw a throw or two. Unsettled, the pitcher would serve ball two. Now, our hitter had a tremendous advantage—he knew the next serve had to be in there, and he could plant himself for a straight fast one. This may seem simple, ordinary baseball, but it wasn't done until around 1908, when the Tigers made it a regular part of our attack.

When you're on second or third and a hit drives you around to the plate, don't just slide—get a wrestler's leg lock on the catcher, mess him up, and pull the hitter from first base around to second.

Scheme, scheme, and keep scheming. In the outfield, I'd pretend I'd misjudged a drive, to get the runners started around the sacks, and then with a fast change of pace I'd make the catch and nab some sucker between bases.

Mickey Cochrane—few catchers to match him ever breathed air—used to accuse me of even calculating the number of bounces a ball could take to shortstop which would still enable me to beat the throw to first. I don't recall getting quite that mathematical. But one day in the 1920s I had a little chat with Emil Haisman, the Detroit groundskeeper.

"Emil, we can't match the Yankees' power, with Ruth and Gehrig and Meusel and the rest," I said, "so let's see if we can work out an equalizer."

"I could get a gun and shoot the Babe," said Emil. "What else can we do?"

What we did, prior to the Yankees' arrival, was to take advantage of the fact that Detroit had speed merchants, if not power hitters, and the Yanks had only one man, Earle Combs, who was outstandingly fast. We let the grass grow for five or six days down the third base line until it was nice and shaggy. Then Haisman mowed it down real close for about 10 feet from third base toward home plate. When the Yanks took the field, if their third baseman, Joe Dugan, stayed back, we'd bunt into the high grass and leg it. If Dugan charged in, we'd slap one onto the close-clipped turf and it'd skip past him into left field.

We also built up the third base foul line and beveled it just enough so that line bunts would roll fair. We soaked the infield with water so pitchers would find it sticky going when they had to field those chances.

And we consistently gave those tremendous Yankee teams of the 1920s more trouble than any other club, even though they had us far outclassed for brute strength and in pitching. We gimmicked the field and bunted, we pulled the hit-and-run from second base as well as from first, we sacrificed to put a man in scoring position and we invented new strategies. Take the double steal.

Eddie Collins and Jack Barry, the keystone combination of Connie Mack's champion Athletics, were masters at breaking up a two-man steal. With runners at first and third, the former would break for second. The catcher would fire toward second, either Barry or Collins would neatly cut off the throw back of the pitcher and shoot it home to catch the man coming in from third by an easy margin. Nothing so unusual about that. It was the old maxim: Protect home plate at all times.

"How can we counter this?" I asked myself. For every action, there's a reaction, as the scientists say, and baseball is a precise science.

I found two counters, and both worked when properly executed. When I was the runner on third, I'd take a short lead off the bag. When the Tiger at first started running and the throw was on its way, I'd break as if on my way to the Promised Land. Collins or Barry would cut off the peg and slam it right back to the catcher. But, while that went on, I'd have wheeled in a flash and raced back to third.

Result: men on second and third. Our man coming down from first wouldn't even have to slide.

But we hadn't pulled a double steal. How could we do that?

Here's how—and it drove the Athletics crazy trying to figure out how we worked it:

There is an optical confusion involved in an absolutely immobile body in relation to another object. From second base, given only a quick glance, an infielder cannot closely judge a runner's position in relation to third base—if that runner stands completely still. I would take a rather long lead-off, and then freeze myself. As the catcher threw to second, Collins or Barry would have time for no more than a flash-look at me. Time didn't permit them to figure my distance from third base. They saw me stock-still, not even leaning toward home—presumably fairly close to the bag and thus not representing a scoring danger. Barry would pass up the cut-off play and let the ball go through to Collins, for the play on our runner.

And the moment I saw Barry's head duck to let the ball pass, I'd be off and sprinting. In actuality, I'd taken a lead of 10 feet or so, and that meant only 80 more to go to beat the hurried throw that would come from Eddie Collins when he realized my deception. Five times out of six, I'd beat that throw.

A sublimely beautiful play, with both men safe, based on (1) my deceptively long lead; (2) not a movement from me at the critical moment; (3) the eye's inability to define distance in a split second.

I haven't seen that one pulled in years, and the way things are going in the National Pastime, perhaps I never shall again.

Here's another one, a fine point, lost to base-runners these days. How is it possible to score from third on a short fly ball to the outfield which is handled by an infielder? The shortstop or third baseman hustles back under the ball to make the catch over his shoulder. I see no runners who'll take advantage of that situation. They stick at third, glued down by lack of analysis of the play.

The point is—the infielder is running away from the plate to make his catch. Which means he'll need a couple or three steps after the catch to brake his momentum. After tagging up, I'd tear for the plate on such a play. My percentage edge was that the fielder needed a couple of seconds to recover, turn, aim and throw. And you should have seen some of the throws that resulted when Mr. Shortstop saw me better than halfway down the base line. Again: *make 'em throw it.*

To youngsters, I can't overstress the need to study opponents until you can tell how many times they blink their eyes per minute. One year, I noticed that certain Washington Nats weren't hustling down to first with the usual vim. They weren't loafing, but there was a perceptible difference in their willingness to hustle. In one game, given the lucky break of sharply hit drives straight at me, I threw out three Nats at first base from right field, to set a record.

The Great American Game should be an unrelenting war of nerves.

175

I guess that's what I miss most in it nowadays. In the battle of wits I was lucky enough to join in, you sat up nights plotting ways to win—and it was on such a night that I won a league batting championship that it seemed I was about to lose.

With the 1911 season about finished, Shoeless Joe Jackson of Cleveland topped me nine points in the averages; all nature had to do was take its course, for Jackson was the pluperfect hitter of all time, and my string of four straight batting titles would be broken.

Jackson was a Southerner, like myself, and a friendly, simple, and gullible sort of fellow. On the field, he never failed to greet me with a "Hiyuh, brother Ty!"

One time, a pitcher, with malice aforethought, threw two straight balls squarely at Joe's head. Jackson turned to the catcher and drawled, "Golly, that man's wild today." With the courage of the innocent, he slammed the next pitch against the fence.

So now we were in Cleveland for a season-closing six-game series, and before the first game I waited in the clubhouse until Jackson had taken his batting practice. I had one of the clubhouse boys tip me off when he was finished, so I couldn't miss him.

Ambling over, Joe gave me a grin and said, "How's it goin', brother Ty? How you been?"

I stared coldly at a point six inches over his head. Joe waited for an answer. The grin slowly faded from his face to be replaced by puzzlement.

"Gosh, Ty, what's the matter with you?"

I turned and walked away. Jackson followed, still trying to learn why I'd ignored him.

"Get away from me!" I snarled.

Every inning afterward I arranged to pass close by him, each time giving him the deep freeze. For a while, Joe kept asking, "What's wrong, Ty?" I never answered him. Finally, he quit speaking and just looked at me with hurt in his eyes.

My mind was centered on just one thing: getting all the base hits I could muster. Joe Jackson's mind was on many other things. He went hitless in the first three games of the series, while I fattened up. By the sixth game, I'd passed him in the averages. We Tigers were leaving town, but I had to keep my psychological play going to keep Jackson upset the rest of the way.

So, after the last man was out, I walked up, gave him a broad smile and yodeled, "Why, hello, Joe—how's your good health?" I slapped his back and complimented him on his fine season's work.

Joe's mouth was open when I left.

Final standings: Cobb, .420 batting mark, Jackson, .408.

It helps if you help them beat themselves.

13

*Away from the Park—
A Wonderful World*

The old Ponchartrain Hotel bar was my first "club." In my younger days, Detroit lacked an athletic club and the Ponchartrain was the blue-stocking hangout of the town.

I used to wash up after a game and head for that watering hole, where I was all eyes and ears for ways to augment my baseball income.

As I had no trouble seeing, ballplayers who were dependent entirely on their meager salary to feed the wife and kids never would be able to bargain strongly with their ownership. Those team owners had held a contractual whip hand since the game was in its incubation stage. Almost no one remembers the name now, but a Boston magnate named Arthur H. Soden invented the reserve clause, which even today binds a player to a team just as long as said team requires his services. Soden devised that legal clamp in 1879. He was widely admired by his fellow owners, but hated by the players. He blacklisted one player, Sadie Houck, because he wouldn't tip his cap to Soden. If Soden disliked a player, he refused to pay him. If the player hollered, he got the bum's rush out of the league.

Right from the break-in season of 1905, I was determined to put myself in a powerful bargaining position. How? Simply by earning some important money on the outside.

I had no idea where to start. What with my magnificent salary of $2400 a season, I lacked the cash to invest in anything that looked good. Just about the only commodity traded on the Detroit exchange that I knew much about was cotton.

At the Ponchartrain oak bar, all the rising tycoons of the newborn auto industry did their drinking and dealing. Having no big baseball reputation at the time, I wasn't invited to join their select circle. Anyway, I couldn't have afforded to set up a round of whisky for the boys. But a ballplayer still could stand at the end of the bar and use his "rabbit" ears to advantage.

I had a buddy in these expeditions.

"Walter," I'd say to my young friend, "how are your funds at the moment?"

"If I had aces wired, I couldn't make a bet," Walter would moan.

"Well, I've got a dollar or two," I'd say. "Let's go mingle with the big boys. But don't order anything more than a sherry flip."

Walter had been a clerk at the Malcomson coal yards, now was checking coal for the Michigan Central Railroad. We'd sip our ten-cent flips and watch such men as Alex Malcomson, John S. Gray, John Dodge, Ransom E. Olds, the Stanley (Steamer) twins, J. W. Packard, Alexander Winton, and Billy Durant, who were about to put the country on wheels. The Dodge brothers, for instance, had arrived in Detroit as itinerant iron puddlers. They'd land a contract to build motor shells and before many years were worth $155,000,000. The senior Fisher was an immigrant buggy-builder. In 1908 he established the Fisher Body Company and all his sons became multi-millionaires. John Kelsey made imitation staghorn hairbrushes in a tumbledown warehouse and went broke at it. Kelsey began experimenting with wheels for autos. There came a day when he was worth $18,000,000 or $19,000,000 and when he sold out his company, Kelsey hadn't changed much.

When the people who were acquiring his firm came to his hotel to hand over a check for several million, they found John washing his socks in the bathroom bowl.

My friend Walter, the coal-checker, was Walter Briggs. He was on short change at the Ponchartrain bar, but after Walter got into the auto body-building business, he could have bought the hotel. He and Kelsey acquired a half-interest in the Tigers in 1920. Briggs Field, Detroit, is named for my once-poor chum.

Fortunes were made overnight in early Detroit. You could toss your money in almost any direction and not miss.

But I had little or none to toss.

There was a hotel man, for instance, who ran for the city council and was grateful that I voted for him. Since he'd been giving me a $10.50 per-week rate, I felt it was the least I could do—even if I wasn't yet twenty-one years old and not registered.

"Want to take a ride with me?" my newly elected councilman friend said one day. "I'm about to make your fortune."

He drove me out over the Belle Island Bridge into the Fairview section, where there was only open acreage. Not a building in sight.

"Ty, on that corner," he said, pointing, "the Fairway Savings Bank is going to erect a branch building. Other big concerns plan to build here. You can take options on corners around here for not much money, hold them for six months or a year and sell at a handsome profit."

It was an open-and-shut tip from a man who knew the score, but I didn't have the cash to acquire even one lot. Those who did invest cleaned up.

At the Ponchartrain bar, I was tipped by Louis Chevrolet, himself, to buy stock in the projected Durant-Chevrolet company. Durant's plan was to come out with the Chevrolet in competition with Henry Ford's Model T. I knew about it long before the combine was formed—again I missed out for lack of investment money.

It was agonizing to lose such chances. Charley Hastings, sales manager of the Hupmobile Company, gave me a chance to get in on the ground floor. Hupmobile began in a rude shed where it manufactured milling machines.

"I can arrange for you to take over the Hupmobile agency in Augusta," Charley said. "You'll have to put up $50 for each car delivered to you, which will be $2500 initially. Then, you'll need to put up another $2500 for stock in the company."

As a family man, I couldn't take the gamble. So went another wonderful chance out the window.

Same thing happened in the case of the Hudson Motor Car Company—and other similar opportunities.

Since I'd worked for a cotton factory in Georgia, I began speculating in a small way with that commodity, and made a profit of a few thousand dollars. Later, after World War I left cotton supplies desperately short, I cleared $155,000 in one year off cotton. In the early days, though, I was strictly a small-time investor with big ambitions.

Away from baseball, I had a lot of fun, and much of it came in pitting myself against the odds found in the financial world, which are somewhat longer against success than getting a base hit. United Motors was small potatoes in 1907, when I bought 50 shares. A year or two later, United was taken over by General Motors and my shares became worth $180 apiece. Down South, I invested in real estate deals which prospered. All in all, I was on the road to independence from baseball by 1918 when an unexpected offer came my way.

Down in my home state, a country-town soda dispenser and druggist, Dr. J. S. Pemberton, had concocted a soft drink that caused all the kids to clamor for more. Pemberton sold the formula for less than $2000 in 1887 to Asa Candler. Ernest Woodruff, who was in ice, coal, and cotton, acquired the drink from Candler in 1919, for $25,000,000. As you can see, the drink had prospered greatly in thirty-two years. Still, I took a dim view of putting any money in it.

I knew the stock market big board pretty well by now. The drink wasn't listed there. Candler hadn't developed the product as a sales item outside the South, and, as I saw it, there were better speculations available by the dozens.

One rainy day in 1918 at the Ansonia Hotel in New York, I was pinned down by Bob Woodruff, son of Ernest, and my great and good friend for many years.

"Ty, you've just got to buy some of this," Bob argued. "We've formed a syndicate to buy out Candler, after which we'll capitalize the company strongly and sell stock. If you buy now, the price is only $36 a share. You'll see it boom like nothing else in the market."

I demurred. "I can't afford it right now, Bob," I said.

Bob wouldn't take no for an answer. He argued with me and I gave him every excuse I could think of, short of the blunt reply that I didn't like his soft drink as a stock investment.

"What will I use for money?" I asked Bob. "That's $10,800 you're asking me to put up for 300 shares."

"We'll get the Trust Company of Georgia to loan you the money," came back Bob Woodruff. "You'll be able to pay it back out of dividends."

So it went, back and forth, all that rainy day, until I finally capitulated, mostly from sheer weariness.

That soft drink, Coca-Cola, has been awfully good to me. It has enabled me to build a hospital for the ailing and the indigent and put many boys and girls through college, in the form of the Cobb Memorial Hospital of Royston, Georgia, and the Cobb Educational Foundation of Atlanta. It has secured the future of many friends of mine, whom later I was able to bring into the Coca-Cola picture. After I bought a small block of the stock, I realized that Woodruff was absolutely correct. We had a drink that the whole world wanted. I bought more shares and still more, until in time I became one of the major shareholders in Coca-Cola. My one regret is that so many close friends refused to listen back in the early 1920s when I urged them to get in on the "Pause that Refreshes."

A lot of them, by merely investing to the tune of a few hundred shares, would have cleared $250,000 to $300,000 in less than ten years.

Coca-Cola, to settle a misunderstanding about me, wasn't the start of my good fortune in the business world. This has been widely printed. But it certainly capped the climax. I shudder to think of that day at the Ansonia when I made every excuse I could think of to avoid buying into a bonanza.

Away from the ball diamond (and I slipped away to indulge this hobby more than once), slamming a big racing car around a track at high speeds appealed to me as a sport.

"You'll get yourself killed," my friends argued.

The point was: they'd never strapped themselves behind the wheel of a powerful Mercedes, Pope-Toledo, White Streak, Thomas Flyer, Lozier, or Fiat and experienced the hair-raising thrill of mastering the roaring beasts. Those who feared for my life were the pedestrian type. You have to do it to appreciate it.

I've always felt that my friend, Barney Oldfield, was one of the most courageous men who ever lived, driving the equipment he did at the speeds he hit—as high as 131 mph in 1909. Also William K. Vanderbilt, Ray Harroun, Howdy Wilcox, Tommy Milton, Ralph De-Palma, and other pioneers of speed. I never entered the Indianapolis 500-miler, but I used to hit it up there on the bricks at 100 mph and more whenever I could sneak away from the ball game. At the Atlanta and Savannah speedways, I indulged myself. As I recall, my best time for a "flying kilometer" was in a National 40 at Indianapolis: a mile in 45 seconds flat.

Brick Owens, the umpire, served as my mechanician that day. The landscape was just a blur and when we rolled to a stop, Brick had a green complexion.

"Never again," whispered Brick.

"That's just the warm-up," I said. "Now we make another run and really open her up."

But Brick was hanging over the rail, losing his breakfast.

I squared accounts with all umpires that day.

At the Georgia-Carolina State Fair in 1914, I was head starter of the racing events. The job paid $50 a day, but didn't include a chance to drive. After spending a dusty day getting the boys off, we came to one of the last races on the card, and I couldn't contain myself. As the field departed in a cloud of smoke, I grabbed an old pal, John Wheeler, of the Bell Syndicate, and jumped into my own car. "C'mon, John, let's catch them!" I yelled.

We had to take some corners on a pair of wheels, almost pitching Wheeler into the dirt, but we caught them—and won.

At Savannah's famous 16-mile speedway, which wended over hill and dale, I was roaring along one day in a big National with Bill McNey, the noted race driver, as my mechanician. McNey reached over and turned off the ignition switch. "You're too damned reckless for me," said McNey.

We'd hit about 105 on the stretches that day, and I hadn't seriously thought of the danger.

But a few days later, the newspaper carried a story: RACING STAR McNEY KILLED.

Over that same course, and not so far from where he'd shut off my switch, McNey had been going close to 100 when a farmer drove across his path. To miss him, McNey had to swerve off course and up a hill. He hit a tree and telescoped car and himself.

I thought: Just three days ago we were riding along together and now he's dead. And me a man with a family.

That was my last race against time.

Great men of science seem to be fascinated by baseball. One 1927 day while the Philadelphia A's were in spring training at Fort Myers, Florida, we were invited to tour the laboratories of Thomas A. Edison. The old gentleman was celebrating his eightieth year on earth.

After showing us some fascinating experiments with rubber and vegetables that he was conducting, he said to me: "Mr. Cobb, you are involved in a very exact science. I wish I knew more about it."

I couldn't very well invite Mr. Edison to grab a shillelagh and step into the batting cage for a workout, but one of the Athletics' press agents hatched a bright idea. For a publicity shot, Mr. Edison would stand at bat while I served him up a pitch. Edison agreed with alacrity.

At the park, Edison watched closely while we ran through batting practice. Then, while the cameramen got set, Edison selected a bat and slowly walked to the plate. Mr. Connie Mack was the catcher.

Now, I'm as certain as a man can be that Edison hadn't held a bat in his hand in fifty years, if ever. And he was a very old man. So my first pitch was right over the plate and without anything in it. Yet the pitch was moving with enough speed to require good timing, and it also described a bit of a parabolic arch.

Something went past my ear with a *whssst!* I didn't have time to blink.

Tom Edison really hit that one! He had cowtailed the pitch— but how? It was because, while watching, he had analyzed the components of the batter's swing, quickly deciphered the necessary footwork, appreciated the need for follow-through, and put them all together to hit one right on the nose.

As I'd always argued, hitting is mostly mental. Edison proved it beyond any argument.

I played a good deal of poker with Warren G. Harding and William Howard Taft when they were President.

Near Augusta, on a private lake, was a club where for more than one hundred years the gentlemen of the South and their celebrated guests had convened to enjoy themselves in stag activities. No woman ever set foot in the place over the century, to my knowledge. It was an honor to be invited there. No money ever showed on the table. All gambling was done by chits, with a check promptly in the mail next morning. The hand of a winner never was questioned, when he'd bluffed his opponents into throwing in. You didn't even look at it unless it was displayed. Nor did you treat the President as anyone holy. He was just one of the boys down there.

But some of those characters around Harding were a caution. The hangers-on who checked into the hotel with him near our club jumped their bills and local people had to take up a collection to pay them.

Although his administration has caught hell from the historians, I believe Harding was an honest man. I saw him up close often. If there were crooks involved, they were those who hung to his coat-tails.

Taft was three hundred pounds of relaxed jollity. After a huge dinner, of goose or pheasant, he would attend Masonic rites with the rest of us. Amid the proceedings, a steady snore could be heard.

Mr. President was catching up on his sleep.

One of the quaintest characters in California, where I made my home for many years, has been Parkey Sharkey. He is, among other things, a professional picket. Also a cab driver who claims to have collided with the only streetcar in Palo Alto.

Parkey, whom I'd never met until one unusual night, threatened to sue me for 15 cents.

He wrote a letter to the papers about it, which went:

"Other nite when I leave my parkey lot Ty Cobb the ex-football playler, park his car on my lot. So I sit and wate for him to comeback. Whin he come back I say, hey you, you owe me 15¢ for parking. He called me a hole-up man. I felt ambrassed very much. He say to me how I know you run this parkey lot, never see you around. It burn me up whin he say that after I have been in bussness 2 years and no bussness yet. I get mad. So he take me for ride to police station to find out if I really run lot. So I tell him I go sue him.

"P.S.—Ty Cobb give me his autograft."

The case was settled out of court when I paid the $1.50 cost incurred by Parkey in filing suit. Case dismissed.

At that, Parkey was a bargain, compared to a situation in New York's Central Park long ago. I was driving through the park at a moderate pace when a policeman dashed up and yelled, "You're under arrest."

"Why?" I inquired.

"Never mind why! Get down from that seat!"

When I refused, the copper climbed up, grabbed my coat and began dragging me from the car.

Well, at that point I made a little pugilistic history. When the smoke cleared, the man in blue was sans his helmet and coat and bleeding variously. Picking himself up, he vanished over the horizon.

I'll get 99 years for this, even if he had it coming to him, I thought.

Imagine my relief when I spotted a photographer, hiding in the bushes. The thing was a "plant." At the time, I was appearing in the George Ade comedy, *The College Widow*, at the Lyceum Theatre. The play's publicist had seen a chance to grab off some Page One space. The backfire had come when I'd knocked his phony cop loose from his teeth and uniform.

The photo was supposed to show me being collared and dragged off to jail. Fat chance!

As an actor—very briefly—I didn't threaten Edwin Booth or John Drew or Eddie Foy, and I wonder now how I ever got talked into treading the boards. Vaughan Glaser, the producer, kept after me to try the Thespian art until, in 1912, I agreed. I played Billy Bolton, an All-American halfback, opposite Sue MacManamy, who played the college widow. The stage lights were murder on my eyes. The work was grinding. Seven nights a week, I was Bolton, from Boston to Augusta. It proved to me that actors of my day, more than ballplayers, had to be iron men.

We had one wowser of a laugh in the show, though.

My father in the show, a railroad president, arranges for me to attend a Baptist school named Atwater College. Upon returning from a trip abroad, he discovers that I'm enrolled at a rival Methodist college. Not only that, I'm a football hero and up to my ears in courting the president of the Methodist college's daughter.

Once he's fully grasped the full total of my defection, my father steps back one pace and exclaims:

"Well, you're a hell of a Baptist!"

It seems that the Sunbeam Motion Picture Company, around 1916, also caught me in a lightheaded moment and thrust me in front of the Hollywood cameras. The result was an opus titled *Somewhere in Georgia*. No review is necessary here. Just let it go that I was attacked by thugs, bound hand-and-foot in a remote cabin, made my escape, commandeered a mule team and raced up to home plate just in time to save the ball game for my team.

It was fun, though, getting to know Doug Fairbanks and Fatty Arbuckle.

186

No man ever possessed more pure inspirational punch and self-confidence than Knute Rockne. And self-control under stress.

I was with him at the Auditorium Hotel in Chicago one 1928 evening, after he'd scouted a future opponent at Soldiers Field. Feeling sure his Notre Dame powerhouse would easily whip light-weight Carnegie Tech, he'd given up command for the day and sent the Irish to Pittsburgh under an assistant coach, Hunk Anderson.

A man walked into his room and told Rockne that Notre Dame had been beaten in one of the biggest upsets of all time.

Anyone else would have shown *some* emotion. Rockne just blinked and went on playing host.

"That hurt," I said.

"Sure it hurts!" snapped Knute. "And *next* week, we'll hurt some-one else!"

And Notre Dame did, again and again, because they had a leader who never once wavered.

Rock was hired as a consultant for the Studebaker Company, which wasn't doing well. All the top sales executives were gathered in a room when he arrived for his first lecture. Ignoring them, he walked to a window and stood there for a good ten minutes, staring out at the parking lot. Then he turned and let them have it, machine-gun style.

"I see a lot of cars out there! New cars! Shiny cars! Executives own them, the men who draw their pay from Studebaker! You men! And what do I see? Not one Studebaker in ten parked out there!

"If you men don't have confidence in the product you're selling, why don't you quit?"

And Rockne walked out.

On April 2, 1931, I was scheduled to make my first airplane trip— out to California from the Midwest. I had my ticket and reservation when I heard the news broadcast—*Rockne killed in Kansas plane crash*.

I canceled the flight and didn't get into a plane for several years.

Many a night I sat by a glowing deep-woods campfire with Jack Miner, one of the rarest men I've ever known.

Miner was a great hunting guide, a master of woodcraft, a game slaughterer who turned champion conservationist, a man so dedicated to saving wildfowl that his work earned him a royal title from King George V of England.

A Canadian, Miner killed anything he could shoot to keep his larder stocked until one day in 1910 a crippled goose landed on his pond. Miner cared for it until it was tamed. The goose called in other geese, all seeking refuge. It got so that the wild honkers would eat from Miner's hand. Curious to know where the birds migrated, Miner began the first banding operation. He was years ahead of any federal wildfowl service banding operation. In time, he traced 55,000 birds and famous men came to see his methods.

When a boy strayed away and was lost in the wildest of country, Miner went in after him. He found the lad, who was the son of a Canadian Pacific Railway executive. From then on, nothing the CP could do was too good for Miner.

"I want no reward," he said. "Just ask all your people to be on the lookout for the birds."

From division heads to section hands, the CP employees scanned the skys across Canada for any sign of bird movements, and the moment they spotted a flight, Miner received a wire describing what was happening. With such an observation system working for him, he was able to plot the movements of wildfowl throughout all Canada.

Miner's prestige was so great that one year, after covering the World Series for Christy Walsh's syndicate, I left for the deep Canadian woods aboard the *Winnipeg Flier*. When we were five hundred miles from nowhere, the train ground to a halt. I alighted with all my hunting gear, to be greeted by Jack Miner and his two sons. Stopping a crack train to deposit one ballplayer in the wilderness was nothing in the way of a feat for Miner.

One day when Jack was playing host to a group of British notables in Jasper Park, he threw back his head and out came the sound of a howling wolf.

From the rim of a butte nearby came an answering cry.

Jack Miner was closer to nature's wonder than any man I ever knew. A king knighted him for that. Just to know him was one of the finest things that happened to me in the wonderful world I found away from baseball.

14

A Whiff of Gas: a Job I Didn't Want

I saw Christy Mathewson doomed to die. None of us who were with him at the time realized that the rider on the pale horse had passed his way. Nor did Matty, the greatest National League pitcher of them all.

We were at Hanlon Field near Chaumont, France, when it happened.

Along with other sport figures, I enlisted in the Chemical Warfare Service in 1918, was given accelerated training in defense against and the use of poisonous gas and was shipped overseas, pronto. George Sisler, Branch Rickey, Matty, myself, and athletes from the gridiron, polo fields, and race track were assigned to the "Gas and Flame" Division as instructors. I wore a captain's bars. We wound up drilling the darnedest bunch of culls the World War I Army ever grouped in one outfit.

The doughboys who came our way largely were hard cases and rejects from other services. The theory was that they would listen to well-known sport personalities—and to some extent it was effective. Those that gave us trouble and didn't heed orders didn't last long, for we weren't fooling around with simulated death when we entered those gas chambers. The stuff we turned loose was the McCoy and meant to train a man to be on *qui vive*—or else.

Back in April of 1915, the Germans had first employed gases that poisoned and asphyxiated in the form of chlorine cylinders lobbed into the Ypres salient. Allied casualties were heavy. Then came mustard and sneeze gases, frightfully successful. Protective masks that were rushed into use were a joke at first. They were cumbersome affairs consisting of a mask which fitted around the face, attached by a tube to a canister suspended around the soldier's neck and hanging in front of his body. He breathed air through a tube held in his mouth, from which the poison gases were filtered through charcoal and soda lime contained in the canister. A nose clip was supposed to prevent breathing through the nostrils. But men forgot the procedure or panicked. What's more, all that gear impeded a doughboy's movements, especially his ability to burrow into the ground when under machine-gun fire.

By 1918, we had improved masks and a growing knowledge of the stuff coming out of the Kaiser's laboratories. One of our training techniques involved marching men into an airtight chamber in which gas was released almost without warning. At a hand signal, everyone was supposed to snap his mask into position. Alertness and speed was the goal.

I'll never be able to forget the day when some of the men—myself included—missed the signal.

Men screamed to be let out when they got a sudden whiff of the sweet death in the air. They went crazy with fear and in the fight to get out jammed up in a hopeless tangle.

As soon as I realized what had happened, but only after inhaling some gas, I fixed my mask, groped my way to the wall and worked through the thrashing bodies to the door. Trying to lead the men out was hopeless. It was each one of us in there for himself.

When I staggered out and gulped in fresh air, I didn't know how badly my lungs had been damaged. For weeks a colorless discharge drained from my chest and I had a hacking cough. When the draining stopped, I felt that Divine Providence had touched me.

For sixteen men were stretched on the ground after the training exercise and eight of them died.

I can recall Mathewson saying, "Ty, when we were in there, I got a good dose of that stuff. I feel terrible." He was wheezing and blowing out congested matter.

Christy Mathewson had been a hero of mine from the day I broke into the American League. He was truly magnificent in every way—no other phrase fits. I rarely had a chance to hit against him, since he was with the New York Giants in the other league, and I've often regretted I didn't see more of his fastball and fadeaway. That fadeaway was imitated by half the boys in America. "Big Six," his nickname, came from a famous New York fire engine carrying that number. Matty stood 6 feet 1, weighed 195, was one of the most commanding and romantic figures the game ever knew. He came from Factoryville, Pennsylvania, the son of a gentleman farmer, one of the first college-breds to reach the big league. Matty was handsome, classy, and as rugged a competitor as ever stepped on the hill.

"Nice guys finish last," Leo Durocher once had the effrontery to announce. Well, Matty was as nice as they come and he is tied with Old Pete Alexander for most National League games won in a lifetime (373). He won 30 or more games for three years running and for 12 years in a row, and 13 in all, he won more than 20. Matty had the kind of control that's gone from the game. He pitched the record number of consecutive innings without allowing a base on balls, 68. Once, in 1913, he pitched for a solid month without walking a single batter. And listen to this one.

In the 1905 World Series, my rookie season, he set a mark as impossible to equal as Bob Jones's grand slam in golf. Just a little matter of beating the Athletics three straight games—*each one a shut-out*. Matty worked 27 consecutive frames against a team of the highest skill without permitting a run to cross the plate.

Where do you stop with Mathewson? He won 83 games by pitching a shut-out. He struck out 2505 batters. He won 16 games in one stretch without a defeat, struck out 18 men in one World Series game. Once, he beat the Phils with only 67 pitches used in the game. He even edged Walter Johnson for most seasons of winning 20 or more games. Only Cy Young topped Matty in the latter department.

That day in Chaumont, he inhaled just enough chemical gas to weaken his lungs. It left him wide open. When he returned to the game, at age thirty-eight, he became John McGraw's right-hand man with the Giants. It wasn't long until doctors discovered he'd developed tuberculosis in both lungs. Matty went up to Saranac Lake, New York, for the "cure," which didn't take. In a short time, he could move only his fingers and forearms.

He had a will, did Mathewson. "When a fellow can't read or write or talk and barely move," he'd say, "it takes a little doing to keep his mind off his troubles. So I've started working out a baseball game, on paper. I figure the odds on any given play, just the way it happens on the field. I spend every day at it and I've learned a lot about the game I didn't suspect."

There you had an old-time ballplayer talking. With his body gone, his head never stopped working.

With all that heart, Matty rallied and came back to the league as president and part-owner of the Boston Braves. By now, one of his lungs had collapsed. It was only a matter of time. He made his fadeaway from life on October 7, 1925.

So I want to salute Matty here—a salute from another of the old school who somehow miraculously has survived. I don't remember him as a list of statistics. I think of Matty as one of the great men and competitors sport has had.

As for me, the war presented no further hazards, other than a shell fragment which came close to removing one of my eyes. I was on the first ship home from Brest, France. Back with the Tigers, I found them bidding for another championship. In August of 1919, we moved to within four games of first place. Then we faded and wound up fourth. Now nearing my thirty-third birthday, I won my twelfth batting title at a .384 mark, and felt unusually pleased about it. None of the youngsters who'd come along to crowd me finished within 29 points of my average. It was obvious, at the same time, that the Tigers weren't right. After fourteen years as manager, Hughie Jennings had lost his grip. In 1920, we collapsed to seventh place. The fans began barking and everyone knew—including Hughie—that he was finished.

It was an inglorious thing to witness. Jennings belongs with the most successful morale-builders in baseball history. The Scranton Irishman was redheaded, generously freckled and, as Tim Hurst the umpire put it, had a perpetual grin that echoed. Having experienced men when he took over, he didn't turn our squad meetings into rundowns on how to pitch against or attack an opponent. He kept us eager to conquer at all times, maintaining our spirit and fight and imparting a tremendous urgency into what can easily become a dull task. On the coaching line, Hughie's wild cry of "Eeeyah!" and his shrill whistles let us know he was with us and on top of every play. He'd dance in glee at a good play and tear up grass. Just as an historical footnote, next to "Eeeyah!" Hughie's

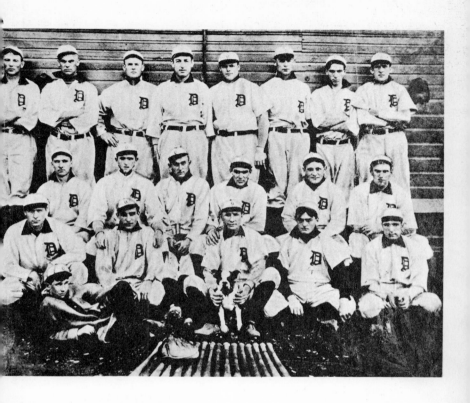

TEAM that set Detroit "baseball crazy"—the American League champs of 1907. third from left, middle row. Some of the men who'd hazed me as a rookie ar or two earlier are shown here: Ed Killian, far right, top row; Ed Siever, eft, bottom row, and Charlie Schmidt, fourth from left, bottom row. Schmidt, broke my nose with a sneak punch, later became my good friend. That's the "Wild Bill" Donovan, an iron-man pitcher, fourth from left, top row. Edgar lett, who was my roommate briefly (until the hazers drove him away) is sixth left, top row.

AT THE WHEEL of the Chalmers.

ᴇʀ NAP LAJOIE virtually tied me for the batting championship in 1910, I
ived this de luxe Chalmers car. Lajoie was such a close second that the Chalmers
npany also awarded him a Prize Automobile. That's the Frenchman sitting
t to me.

ᴏᴠᴇᴅ a fast car—here I am at the wheel of a 1910 Owen—and did some high-speed
ng at Indianapolis Speedway and elsewhere.

Bob Jones of Georgia, a fine friend of
was fresh from scoring his "Grand Sla
golf when we posed for this shot at High
S.C. in late 1930.

Frank Navin, in 1934.

WIDE WORLD PHOTO

ONE OF THE last times I ever pulled on a uniform came in 1950 when with Tris Speaker, left, and Duffy Lewis, right, helped open the Dallas Eagles' Texas League season. We three old birds took the field for one-third of an inning.

A GREAT MOMENT in my life—the opening of my hospital in my hometown of Royston, Georgia, built in loving memory of my mother and father. My friend is the late Dr. Stewart Brown, noted Royston surgeon.

I WAS ELECTED to the Baseball Hall
Fame at Cooperstown (N.Y.) in 1936.

ONE OF MY favorite photos: with Walt
(Big Train) Johnson. Taken around 19
when Walter won 23 games and I hit .38
We were friends at all times—on the d
mond or across a poker table.

N OUTFIELD THROW—not made with as much power as I had when young. I all but ined a fine throwing arm by fooling around with trick pitches. This was circa 1923.

A PAIR of my all-time all-stars: Lefty
Grove, who won 300 games and lost only
141, and Pie Traynor, the deadliest fielding third baseman of them all and a .320
lifetime hitter.

favorite cry was "That's the boy!" This shout of approval became condensed into that enduring bit of American lingo—"Attaboy!" He'd charge the umpires, his eyes blazing and with every sign he was ready to rend them limb from limb. In actuality, Hughie couldn't have whipped a cripple. But his fiery state of mind was catching, and it whipped us into playing better than we knew how. This is the critical requisite of any great manager. Not very many men have had it. In singling out the leaders of note, baseball writers rarely mention Jennings. To me, he belongs near the top. He led the Tigers to first-division finishes in ten of his fourteen years, won three pennants, was second twice.

To be faithful to the facts, I must relate some incidents never before revealed.

I did not want to manage Detroit. I had every reason in the world to take that stand. Running a team is one of the cruelest, debilitating, all-consuming assignments you can accept. My conception of a ballplayer always was that of a man free of outside worries. Playing and managing rarely have mixed. In this century, Fielder Jones, Tris Speaker, Bill Carrigan, and Fred Clarke are just about the only successful examples. I was determined to wait until I was on the downhill grade as a performer, knowing that off my record I'd always have a managing position waiting somewhere in the big league. For that reason, I flatly turned down repeated urgings that I succeed Jennings.

Hughie, personally, worked on me in August of 1920.

"Ty, I don't want to go on. I can't take it any longer," he confessed. "I've got to get out and everything points to you. There just isn't anyone else who knows the situation well enough."

"Hughie, I won't consider it," I said. All I needed to help cement my decision was to look at this good friend of mine. The effect of fourteen years' pressure stood out all over him. Jennings was a well-rounded man, one who'd taken time to improve his mind by attending St. Bonaventure College and matriculating at Cornell's law school. As he stood now, he was in bad shape. Sad to say, he'd found relief in the bottle. And you could tell it from a distance of a few feet. He was only fifty years old, but pathetically tired, ineffective, and with the old grin faded. Eight years later, he was dead of the same disease that took Matty—tuberculosis.

Navin came at me next. With the season over, I was managing

in a California winter league along with Rogers Hornsby, George Sisler, and Harry Heilmann when Navin phoned me. "The job is yours," he said, as if he was handing me $50,000,000. "All you have to do is say yes."

"No, thanks," I answered.

After his arguments failed to change my mind, Navin, to keep the iron hot, asked me to recommend four or five minor leaguers who might be acquired by Detroit. I named Ray Kremer, Lefty Cole, Suds Sutherland and Carl Holling, pitchers, and Johnny Bassler, catcher. "Kremer is the catch of the lot," I told Navin. "He'll be one hell of a pitcher in a couple of years."

Navin went out and got all of them except Kremer, whose purchase price was too rich for his blood. It was typical Navin economy. Kremer went to Pittsburgh, became a first-line star who won 18, 17, 20, 19, 15, 18, and 20 games in straight seasons. Had Detroit signed Kremer, we'd have won a pennant in 1924, instead of finishing five games behind Washington.

Aside from a lack of confidence in Navin, I had other reasons to sidestep his offer. By the end of World War I, I'd accumulated a tidy fortune outside baseball. The newspapers had a stock line they used, "Ty Cobb, the only millionaire player in history," etc. By 1920, I was interested in stocks and bonds, cotton shares, the automobile industry and real estate, along with Coca-Cola; was independent of my baseball salary; and wasn't at all tempted by the substantial pay raise accompanying the manager's job. It was almost a unique position for a ballplayer. And it seemed only common sense to me to take advantage of my independence and devote all my energies to getting base hits.

What about my children? I had four of them growing up in Georgia by now, who saw so little of me that it was a shame. My style of play sent me home exhausted each winter. Add the weight of bossing the Tigers and I'd be surrendering even more that was precious.

The plight of Jennings and the team preyed on my mind, nevertheless. We were in Boston one day, trailing by three runs in the ninth inning with none out, runners on first and second and dependable Bobby Veach at bat. Jennings flashed a sacrifice-bunt sign to the startled Veach. Donie Bush and others came running to me in the dugout, pleading, "You're not going to let him do that, are you, Ty?"

I ran out to the coaching line. Reaching Jennings, I dropped to one knee, fiddled with my shoestrings and talked fast. "Don't bunt, Hughie," I whispered. "We're three runs down in the ninth and that's Veach up there. Let him hit away."

Jennings seemed unable to grasp the simple percentage involved. "There's none out, Hughie!" I hissed at him.

He heard me at last, removed the bunt sign and Veach took a full cut, driving the ball into the stands for the game-tying home run. We went on to win in the 10th inning.

We all had such high regard for Jennings that we kept such incidents secret; the newspaper boys never suspected that he'd lost all confidence and decisiveness.

At night, I'd sit in Hughie's room while he slugged down drinks to drown his sorrows. I'd advise him on how to handle his pitchers, try to buck him up, hoping that he'd snap back. But there was no chance. The 1920 Tigers came within an ace of becoming the first Detroit team ever to finish in the cellar.

That winter, I was duck-hunting at a private club near New Orleans when, at the Roosevelt Hotel, I ran across E. A. Batchelor, a close friend and Detroit sportswriter. "Batch" was in town with the University of Detroit football club, which was slated to play Loyola.

"No two ways about it," said Batch, "you've got to take the job. The team needs you in the worst way."

"I don't want it," I repeated for the fiftieth time. "I've recommended Kid Gleason. If Navin can get Gleason, we'll be in good shape. He's as smart and popular as they come."

Gleason then was non-playing manager of the White Sox, after earlier serving as Pants Rowland's assistant with that team. The Kid, we all knew, was the real brains of the White Sox. He'd spent twenty-one years as a player, graduating from the Baltimore Oriole and John McGraw school—a brilliant baseball thinker and a grand man.

"It won't be Gleason," said Batch. "It'll be Rowland, if you don't accept. Do you know that he's in Detroit right now talking to Navin?"

That was a jolt. I couldn't play under Rowland, nor could anyone who knew the facts. Pants Rowland never had appeared in a game of big-league ball, in fact had been running a short-order grill in a small Illinois town until 1915. He was a typical fan, up until the day Charley Comiskey and Ban Johnson arrived in his town on a hunting trip. Rowland fell into the most fantastic lucky break in the history of managing. Comiskey took a fancy to him and shocked baseball by naming Rowland his new manager. To cap the cockeyed story, the White Sox won a pennant and World Series in Rowland's third year. Posies were tossed at Rowland for that, but everyone around the league knew that Kid Gleason had been the actual tactical genius behind the victory. Big-leaguers called Pants Rowland "the bush-league manager." When the White Sox fell to sixth place in 1918, he was released in favor of Gleason.

When Batchelor saw the expression on my face, he said, "Before you'd play under Rowland, would you take the management?"

"I'd have to think that over," I answered. Batch needed no more. He hippety-hopped to the phone, called Navin in Detroit. In a few minutes' conversation, I reluctantly agreed to meet him in New York and discuss the job.

That was an error I'll always regret. Rowland or no Rowland, I wish now I'd never stuck my neck into the noose that the Tiger management represented.

As it happened, when I sat down with Navin and signed away my independence as a ballplayer, the date was December 18, 1920, my thirty-fourth birthday. Although the newspaper boys recognized my reluctance, and were puzzled by it, I couldn't mention Jennings' decline, nor my feeling about working under Rowland. "This is quite a birthday present you're getting," Damon Runyon remarked, noting that my pay went from $20,000 to $35,000. "Tris Speaker and Babe Ruth aren't getting within $10,000 of that."

"Anything *but* a present," I told Damon cryptically. "This thing has been forced upon me."

Runyon, nor any other baseball expert, ever deduced what I meant; the revelations I am making here are expressed for the first time.

The seventh-place team I inherited had dropped as many as 13 games in a row the previous season, had batted .265 as a group (next to worst in the league). We had aging veterans at second and short-stop and the pitching corps was down to just two dependables, George Dauss and Howard Ehmke. I knew I was saddled with a likely candidate for the league basement unless we could pull in some standout rookies fast. So when spring training opened in San Antonio, Texas, I had combed the minor leagues for anything that looked capable of raising even a loud pop fly.

Navin's support I couldn't be sure about.

"How much help are you prepared to give me?" I asked him.

"Whatever you need to win," he came back.

Taking him at his word, I went after talent and shook up training camp with some ideas called "shocking." Instead of putting pressure on the boys, I abolished morning workouts. "Sleep until noon if you like," I announced. The Tigers, who were used to 9 A.M. drills, were flabbergasted. For years, big-leaguers had been routed out of bed at 6 A.M., served a heavy breakfast, then sent through a stiff morning drill. My theory was that the body wasn't tuned up for exercise that early. Circulation hadn't reached its normal gait, muscles hadn't been brought out of nighttime retirement and stomachs heavily loaded with food were unreceptive to violent physical effort. Moreover, as any doctor could vouch, baseball managers doubled the mistake. After the fatiguing morning workout, players would "rest up" for the afternoon practice period. During that time the body would begin replacing nerve and muscle tissue expended in the A.M. But before the process of reconstruction could near completion, they were shooed back on the diamond. They were forced to call upon muscular energy not yet returned to normal and in no condition to be taxed.

I abolished skull practice. To me, it was time wasted. I wanted a fast-thinking, clever team. But I saw no profit in hashing over strategy for thirty minutes or an hour in the clubhouse, after which the players would forget what had been said when the situation arose on the field. A far better system is to plan the attack on the spot, put it into execution immediately, and run less risk of mental errors. Also, an on-the-spot plan is far more likely to fit the situation at hand than something conceived an hour before the game.

When we opened the season, I struck a blow for the poor, beleaguered pitcher. I removed my bull pen to the back of the grandstand, where my pitcher couldn't see a relief man warming up.

This isn't done in baseball today, although in some cases bull pens are distant from the diamond. How would you like to be at work at your job, under extreme pressure, and have a replacement hovering just behind you, waiting for you to fail? Consider what happens when the pitcher is working hard, the opposition bunches some hits, and out to the bull pen hurry the relievers. That pitcher needs every bit of concentration he can apply. Instead, you unnerve your own man. You tell him that he may get the hook any moment. My own relievers worked out of sight of my man on the mound. Far better that my pitcher see the opponents warming up a new arm, which could only be good for his confidence.

At San Antonio, and later in Detroit, I also saw to it that we kept intact a tradition as old as old-fashioned baseball, a tradition that since has tragically withered and died. Namely, you don't go in for a lot of hearts-and-flowers fellowship with other teams. Nowadays, I see rival big-leaguers practically strolling arm-in-arm. Off the field, these rivals are buddies instead of bitter opponents. They play cards and have drinks together. When baseball lost its toughness, the attitude of go-to-hell-with-you-guys, it lost a lot.

Even the New York Giants of the other league were included in our combative frame of mind. John McGraw had the Giants in training camp at San Antonio, too. McGraw sent word that a scheduled series of exhibition games between the Tigers and Giants might not be played unless I personally paid him a visit and asked for such games. McGraw hadn't liked me from the time I whipped his catcher, Buck Herzog, in a Dallas hotel-room fight four years earlier. The Little Napoleon, as they called him, was looking to make me eat humble pie.

"McGraw can go take a jump for himself," I came back. "From now on, the Giants don't exist."

Between our hotel and the Giants' hotel was Alamo Plaza. Believe me, no Tiger crossed that square to talk with any Giant, and vice versa. If one had, his head would have fallen. Every civic organization in San Antonio tried to make peace, for the series was a natural, but we left town without even recognizing that New York was there.

That feuding spirit made baseball the idolized game it once was. That spirit is all washed up now. The lust of battle has passed from the hearts of men, the passion is gone, the spirit of Mars has vanished. Love and kisses have replaced crossed swords.

And, believe me, it doesn't fool the fans. They know synthetic drama when they see it. Thus each year American baseball slowly loses more ground to pro football, the game that threatens to replace baseball as our No. 1 sport. For shame.

We didn't have any unsophisticated fans in the Detroit stands on Opening Day—my first game as manager. They were not there to judge Cobb the player as much as Cobb the field general. My fifteen years of service wouldn't save me from their hatred if we played poor ball.

I count this game as one in my managing career when everything went right. Facing the White Sox before 25,000 fans, we were in a seesaw battle all the way. Twice I called on pinch-hitters, Larry Woodall and Ira Flagstead. Each responded with singles that scored runs. A kid pitcher just up from the Coast League, Suds Sutherland, set the White Sox down with dispatch. An in-and-out hitter named Harry Heilmann, who was soon to become a tremendous man at bat, remembered what I'd told him about his swing and the position of his feet. Harry's smashing ninth-inning triple won us the opening game by a score of 6–5 and left Detroit delighted.

As for me, I was so busy at my new role that I almost forgot to swing that bat. But a sacrifice and a double in the late innings atoned somewhat for earlier failures to hit. When we roared into the clubhouse to celebrate the victory, a question crossed my mind.

Were my high-average days as a batter ended now that I had the responsibility of governing the actions of almost thirty men?

Thinking it over, it didn't seem too important. Not when I could take a boy like young Heilmann and by rearranging his feet and arms create a hitter in a million. As Plato believed, he who carries a torch passes it on, or fails himself.

15

Sabotaged

How would you like to be within reach-out-and-take distance of a pennant and World Series and then be thrown down cold by your owner?

Detroit hadn't run such a championship fever in fifteen years as it did in '24. We were beating the hated Yankees game after game, fighting like fools, and the town loved us for our hustle and ability to overcome glaring holes in our line-up. My pitchers were mainly overage, shopworn vets or untried rookies, my second basemen were two highly inadequate glove men, Del Pratt and Les Burke, and with six weeks to go in the race, my crack first baseman, Lu Blue, twisted his knee. Lu was lost for the final 40-odd games.

Ignoring our handicaps, we held first place in July, fell back a notch in August, then took the lead again, and entered September bunched tightly with Washington and the Yanks. The injury to Blue was one crisis I couldn't handle by filling in with one of our utility men. We hadn't a man in our dugout who could begin to do a job at first base.

Picking up the phone in Washington, I called Frank Navin. He seemed depressed, rather than excited over our place in the standings. "What are you going to do?" he wanted to know.

"Only one thing we can do, and it'll save us," I told him. "We own Johnny Neun at St. Paul. Get him for me fast."

Neun, twenty-three years old, was abusing American Association pitching something fierce. We owned First Baseman Neun, outright. So there was no problem.

"Oh, I hate to do that," answered Navin. "St. Paul is right up there in the Association race and Neun is one of their mainstays."

"For God's sake, what league do you think Detroit is right up there in?" I yelped. "We're in the American League, and we can win the money with a little help! Neun's our property! Don't worry about St. Paul—worry about us!"

Navin replied, weakly, "Well . . . I'll see what I can do."

After a few days and no Neun, I phoned Navin back, learned he was procrastinating, and tried to shame him into calling up Neun. I said: "If it'll keep St. Paul happy, take $5000 out of my salary and give it to them. I want that player!"

His weak spine showing all the way, Navin did nothing of the sort. Our first base hole continued, we slipped to third place and finished there, six games behind the victorious Washington Senators. The Yankees also edged us, although everyone recognized which was the better club. On the season series, we beat them, thirteen games to nine.

Navin was content to finish "in the money." It cost the Tigers cruelly. That 1924 World Series, in which we should have played, was worth nearly $6000 to each man on the winning side, $3800 to each loser.

Neun? Oh, we acquired him the following year, when it was too late, and he hit for fine averages thereafter.

Where he should have backed his team with the same fine desire shown by Jake Ruppert at New York, Sunny Jim Dunn at Cleveland, and other owners, Navin consistently defeated my purpose. In six years as manager, I had the worst ownership any manager ever suffered. Navin weighed 275 pounds at this time. He was well-fed, highly prosperous in Detroit and grew more so during my tenure as Tiger manager. In 1920 he took in as partners the wealthy automobile wheel-maker, John Kelsey, and the equally affluent Walter O. Briggs, auto body manufacturer; for $500,000, they bought 50 per cent of the Tiger stock. Attendance went crazy as we contended for the pennant in '22, '23, and '24. The enlarged Navin Field couldn't handle the throngs. In 1921, Detroit's population was 993,678 and within two seasons we drew 990,000 at the gate. In the season in which Navin failed to supply me with Johnny Neun, we passed the million mark in home attendance for the first time—1,015,136 paid. Keep in mind, that was in 1924. In 1960, in a much-larger park, the Tigers drew only a few more fans: 1,168,000. Navin erected extra circus seats at the season's opening of '24 and never took them down until October.

Meanwhile, at the Windsor Jockey Club, across the river in Canada, Navin's plump figure could be seen day after day at the $50 and $100 win windows. A one-time sheet-writer of horse races himself, he would stuff as many $1000 bills in his pocket as there were races on the day's card, and bet the works. He was a plunger of the big-time variety, despite Baseball Commissioner Kenesaw Mountain Landis's thunderous denunciation of gambling by anyone connected with baseball. Navin got away with it, even developed an intimate relationship with Landis.

Harry Salsinger, the late, great Detroit sportswriter, used to tell of accompanying Navin to a Chicago track, where the bookies swarmed around him. In one race, Navin bet $10,000 with one book, $5000 with another, and $10,000 with a third.

His horse ran second by a head. "What looks good in the next heat?" asked Navin, without turning a hair.

This same jovial spender cost Detroit one of the seven greatest hitters of all time by refusing to reach in a modest way for his bankroll.

In the winter of 1925, Dr. Charles Strub and Charley Graham, owners of the San Francisco Seals, met me in New York. We discussed a Seals outfielder who'd tagged the ball for a .401 average that past season, knocking in 130 runs in 174 Pacific Coast League games. As old friends of mine, Strub and Graham gave me first refusal on the player for the sum of $45,000.

"The deal is as good as made," I assured them. Every manager in the big leagues was Irish green with envy over my landing the young sensation.

Furthermore, when we landed this boy, I planned to conclude a deal all set up with the Chicago White Sox by which we would surrender Fatty Fothergill, an overweight outfielder, and Red Wingo, another outfielder, for Si Blankenship, the sort of relief pitcher we desperately needed.

Navin objected to the $45,000 price set by San Francisco for their .401 hitter.

"It's a terrific bargain," I told Navin. "The White Sox paid San

Francisco $75,000 last year for Willie Kamm, and he's not the ball-player this boy is by a long shot."

"Well, I can't pay it," said Navin, the long-shot $25,000-a-race devotee.

And so we lost Paul Glee (Big Poison) Waner, who single-handed could have brought us two and maybe three pennants. Waner went to Pittsburgh that winter and successively batted .336, (rookie), .380, .370, .336, .368, .322, .341, .309, .362, .321, .373, and .354. Read those figures and weep. I'm still weeping. Waner is seventh on the all-time list of base-hit makers, with 3152. One of the greatest who ever drew a bead on a ball.

So help me, Navin even dealt away a player of real class whom we already owned, George Grantham, *to the National League.* Selling Grantham, a rising second base star at Omaha in the Western League, was inexcusable enough. Selling him to the Chicago Cubs for a paltry $30,000 was downright treason. I have no other word for it, unless it be sabotage. Passing talent to the other league, which all American Leaguers viewed with contempt, just wasn't done in baseball's Golden Era.

Grantham put together eight straight .300-and-better hitting seasons with the Cubs and Pirates. At the time I lost him, the hole at second base was costing me game after game.

Kremer . . . Neun . . . Blackenship . . . Waner . . . Grantham . . . any one or two of them could have lifted Detroit to the glory of the pennant. Those omissions are not all of it, however. I could go on, repetitiously, for several pages of mismanaged deals, opportunities squandered, pennies pinched. In the spring of '21, I could have landed Jim Bagby from Cleveland for cash and Bernie Boland. Boland hadn't won a game for Detroit the previous season. Bagby won 14 that season, after we lost him. To Navin, an outlay of $13,000 for Earl Whitehill, a pitcher, and a good one, was a major transaction. He stuck me with kids, many of them not even with a Class A or AA minor-league background, and aging merchandise others had cleared from their shelf. We had plenty of hitting on my Detroit clubs, but no pitching. When I demanded pitchers, Navin got me men waived out of the National and American Leagues, such as Roy Moore and Rip Collins. Moore won no games for the Tigers before leaving the majors, Collins was a "nightwalker" (couldn't hear a curfew) and an in-and-out performer.

Came one season when the Tigers were chewing on the tail of the front-running Yankees, with a fine opportunity to overhaul them in the final weeks of play. We were a tired team. And yet we kept winning. On an Eastern road swing, we scrapped our way to one of the best records ever made—13 wins in foreign parks in 16 games—and returned jubilantly to Detroit.

Navin's corpulent paunch appeared and then the rest of Navin behind it, and he inquired, "Who'll pitch the first game when we open with New York tomorrow?"

"The staff is shot," I said. "We have no rotation left. Every man is fagged out. I'll have to use Lefty Cole with all those left-handers, Ruth and Combs and so on, in their line-up."

Navin chewed on his lip and looked glum. But not about our pitching shambles. "You know, it'd be a real problem if we won the pennant. We haven't large enough press box facilities," he said complainingly.

On my honor, that's what the man said.

I stared at him with disgust. "Don't worry about us winning it," I snarled, before walking away. "We're too worn out to cause you the trouble of enlarging your press coop."

With his negative, defeatist attitude, Navin could have caused worse damage, by infecting the entire club, so you can imagine how often he got in my clubhouse. He ruined our chances again and again. But he did it at a distance. If he'd come selling his gutless philosophy in the clubhouse, I'd have ordered him out.

It got so that I couldn't stand to look at Navin. In my years of managing, never was I allowed one cent of expense money. All big league managers are provided with an expense account, to cover special occasions, but Navin wouldn't budge. If a player temporarily needed a loan, or a newspaperman's grouch could be cured by a bottle of booze, I paid for it out of my own pocket.

When I took over the Tigers, they were spiritless. The clubhouse looked like a morgue and gloom was spread around like a London fog. My first job was to sell myself to the players, make them believe in me, and this I set out to do. There are managers who, when they become boss, feel it's up to the hirelings to make the advances. They're aloof and set apart in their own mind. And they err, badly. One reason Casey Stengel had such a magnificent managing record was his habit of seeking out his men, learning or sensing their problems, and lending help. Your players must be sold on you, or they won't put out for you. I went the limit to gain the confidence and respect of my men, and so build morale.

Each big leaguer is a study in human nature under high pressure. Each is different in his reaction. There's the lad who thinks he's having bad luck, that a black jinx has him down for good. You've got to get at him from every angle—cheer him up, make him believe he's good, appeal to his loyalty to you and the team. Then there's the non-hustler. Oftentimes this fellow has more ability than anyone on the team. Find the key to his laziness. Maybe it's really a psychological withdrawal, because he's concealing an injury, is sore at his manager or is getting bad news from home.

A frame-up can help such a condition. I'd arrange to have another player or coach jump all over the man who wasn't hustling. With the whole clubhouse watching, I'd walk up and stoutly defend the player. I'd get under his skin, show him I was his friend, and usually he'd begin talking out his troubles with me.

Playing on an athlete's emotions, in the manner of all great managers, is tricky business. How well did I succeed?

Despite all the handicaps, in my first season Detroit gained 68 points in the win-loss percentage column, from .396 to .464. The next year we gained another 49 points. The next year, 26. And the fourth year, 19. Meanwhile, St. Louis, Boston, Chicago, and Cleveland lost ground. New York and Philadelphia stayed about even. Only Washington, under Donie Bush and Bucky Harris, gained commensurate ground with Detroit.

My only hope of keeping the Tigers up there—and they stayed up there most of the time I was in charge—was to develop fresh talent from the youngsters our scouts dug up. I always spoke to these youngsters from a player's angle, rather than as their boss, since I was holding down a full-time outfielding berth while running the show. "Listen," I'd tell them. "Many of you boys, like me, come from small towns where the chances are pretty slim. Don't ever waste the wonderful opportunity you have here. Take care of yourself physically, improve every way you can and save your money." When I caught any of the lads sporting about town at night, I took the position that the front office should dispense the punishment.

But Navin had trouble getting the idea through his head.

"The higher the authority that tans their hide, the more effective it'll be," I explained. "Also, if the club president punishes them, it won't be of my doing. I can go on being their manager with good feelings, instead of having them hate me."

I gave Navin three culprits to deal with. They were Rip Collins, Herm Merritt, and Roy Moore. Strolling along the bench, all I had to do was look them in the eye to detect their guilt. Their eyes were red-rimmed and puffed like a piece of French pastry beneath the lower lids from closing too many saloons. "You deal with them," I told Navin.

"How?" he said.

"Hire a detective. Get the proof and then fine them plenty."

The "Big Jap," as some of the players called poker-faced Navin, hired a slewfoot, who trailed the boys from bar to bar, typed up a long report, and submitted it to Navin. He lost his aplomb when he read the verbatim conversation the detective had overheard. It went:

"I wonder what Old Icewater Navin, the —— would think if he knew we were sitting here, having drinks. I'll bet the old —— would bust wide open. Well, the hell with him. He's nothing but a —— and a ——." (Laughter followed.)

The report included the information that one Tiger had been detected emerging from a damsel's room at 4 A.M., said damsel not being accredited by the Amateur Athletic Union and the sort that could jam up a player seriously.

I'll give Navin credit for blowing up. One of his few effective acts as owner during my regime was to crack down hard on the nightwalkers; when his own pride was stung, he could be a strong man.

No one understands what a sincere manager suffers when he lacks just a few of the tools necessary to make a strong contender a champion. Beyond that supreme disappointment, I've had to live for years with the allegation that I wasn't a capable manager. This old saw has been widely printed and has a number of teeth in it. Some of them are:

1. I lacked patience with my men, believing that all of them should do the things on a ball field of which I was capable.

2. I thought every player should have my "insatiable" desire to win; if they didn't, I had no use for them.

3. I was playing the stock market more than I was managing.

4. I failed to see the great promise in Carl Hubbell, and got rid

of him; likewise, failed to see the potential greatness in Charlie Gehringer as a rookie.

In no way do I consider myself a failure as a manager; I resent the claim and want to clear up the controversy once and for all.

First, to the record. A bunch of statistics can be juggled to prove anything. But these are very simple, unequivocal figures I'd like to present.

When I was forced to take the Tiger reins in 1921, the team was in seventh place with the second-lowest group batting average in the circuit, .265. After my first season in charge, the Tigers showed a .316 batting mark. Not only was that figure the *highest* in the major leagues in 1921, it tied the all-time record *and remains the American League record today*. (It is still the second-best of both leagues.) With the single exception of Topper Rigney at shortstop, every regular on the club hit .300 or better and showed a marked improvement—in some cases, phenomenal. This was accomplished in the course of just one season.

I took the boys, one by one, kids and vets, and worked to improve their plate styles. Bobby Jones, a .249 hitter under Hughie Jennings, jumped to .303 in '21. Lu Blue, whom the Tigers twice before had farmed out, hit .308, .311, and .307 under me. Johnny Bassler, a bust at Cleveland, and who'd dropped out of the majors for seven years, returned to us and blasted the ball for .307, .323, and .346 marks, while catching 120 or more games for five years. My other catcher, Larry Woodall, climbed from .245 to .363 in one season, and averaged .344 the next year. Harry Heilmann, not so long ago, testified as to what he learned under me:

"Ty was the one who taught me to hit with my feet together. He stopped my overstriding and got me to swing the bat above my beltline. He jumped my average from the low .300s to almost .400. He did the same with the whole ball club. It's one instance where you can absolutely prove that a manager definitely was able to pass on his own skill to his players."

There's more to the Heilmann story than that. The big San Franciscan joined Detroit back in 1914, and was unimpressive with the bat. No one could decide where he should play defensively, first base or the outfield. This indecision helped set back Heilmann several years. His technical faults with his big black bat were many— but he was always willing to take advice. During games, I'd whistle piercingly at him from the bench when he let his bat droop below his waist. I settled his indecision by putting him in right field to stay, since he was a bit cumbersome at 205 pounds to handle an infield job. He was an overswinger when I got him. Harry would try to pull the ball against fastballers such as Lefty Grove, with many a pop-up or bounding ball on the ground the result. "Cut down your swing, and learn to hit to the opposite field," I told Harry. And I showed him how in many a long practice session.

How well he learned is in the books. With all his raw power, Harry Heilmann didn't go after home runs, but listened to my advice: "You're not paid to hit homers. If you change your stance to take a toe hold and go into competition with the home run specialists, you'll never be a top hitter."

Result: Heilmann is in the Hall of Fame, with a .342 lifetime average (Babe Ruth's was .341). Few men ever put together such marks as Harry's .394, .403, .393 and .398, which gave him four American League batting championships.

Joe DiMaggio led the American League twice: Ruth, once; Lou Gehrig, once; Jimmy Foxx, once; Al Simmons, twice. Heilmann led it four times.

Big Harry wasn't the only kingpin batter I developed at Detroit. Heinie Manush, who started out to be a plumber in Alabama, was an apt pupil. As a rookie, Manush adapted to my choke-and-slash style at bat, averaged .344, and in 1926 was the American League's premier hitter with a .378 mark.

In all modesty, I could teach hitting. And teaching batwork requires the highest order of patience, a quality my enemies have claimed I was without. Over the years 1917–27, an eleven-year span, Detroit dominated the league batting crown. In that time, through the efforts of Heilmann, Manush, and myself, we won it eight times. During my six managing seasons, we won it four times. Charley Gehringer, who broke in under me, was still another who became skilled enough to lead his league—but that came somewhat later.

Let me review, briefly, the case of Gehringer—whom I am charged with discouraging and failing to recognize as a rare prospect.

Fowlerville, Michigan, had a population of about 400 souls. Bobby Veach, one of our regulars, played some after-season games in that area and came to me the next spring to say, "I've seen a

208

busher that's hard to believe. He looks like Lajoie in the field and he hits everything."

Veach found Gehringer. Not me, Navin, or anyone else. What I did was to check into the tip, have the 20-year-old Gehringer signed by Detroit and then put him through close analysis. He was a find, all right, but far from ready for moving into a key major league position like second base or shortstop. I farmed him to London, Ontario, in '24, brought him up late in the fall for a few Tiger games, then returned him to Toronto for another year of seasoning. When we pulled him in to stay, we had a great second baseman. Had I rushed him into the line-up, Gehringer, a raw country boy with a rather shy personality, could have been ruined.

He was spoon-fed, all the way. I turned him over to Dan Howley, my chief assistant, with strict orders to handle him slowly and carefully.

The green youngster didn't explode all over the league at the outset, as some "experts" claim, but averaged .277 his first year under me. From then on, though, it was Katy-bar-the-door. Charley played second base for Detroit for so long that I had been retired for fourteen years when he finally hung up his spikes. I am the only Detroit player ever to appear in more games than Gehringer (2323 he chalked up). He drove in more runs than any Tiger who ever wore the uniform, with one exception. He is second on the all-time Detroit list in total hits, at-bats, doubles, runs scored, and total bases. He is third in triples and lifetime batting mark—the latter figure being a splendid .321. He is in the Hall of Fame.

Yet I am supposed to have stifled his development and failed to recognize his merit, when I farmed him out for two seasons.

Charley barely could cope with life in the majors even after I permanently assigned him to second base, for he was so young and reluctant to protect himself. One day I saw him leaving Navin's office with a long face.

"What's the matter?" I asked.

"I wanted to get a copy of my contract," said Charley, "but Mr. Navin won't let me have it."

Gehringer was so hurt about it that he was on the verge of leaving the team and returning to Fowlerville.

I marched him back upstairs and confronted Navin. Any time a ballplayer asked to see his papers, Navin interpreted it as the prologue to a demand for a salary hike, and would pull any delaying tactic he could. Charley was due for a raise at the time.

"Give the boy his contract," I said wearily. "He isn't trying to work you for anything. He's only proud of being a big leaguer and wants a copy to show to his folks and friends back home."

Charley got both the contract copy *and* a raise—I saw to that.

I'm wondering right now, however, what might have happened if I hadn't come along that day when he emerged browbeaten from Navin's office. I wonder if Gehringer would have become the second-ranking player at his position in history. The only man I'd pick ahead of him is Eddie Collins.

Altogether, in six seasons, I believe that I developed some 27 players who were valuable to Detroit, many long after I was gone. They came from baseball's lower stratifications, in numerous instances, and endured to be solid, good-earning major leaguers. I can't give enough credit to Dan Howley, my aide. Since I had to perform in the outfield each half-inning, I was wide open to sniping on the bench by malcontents on the club—and every club has them. Dan was my bench protection. He kept the troublemakers under control, while working incessantly with young talent. There never was a finer, more loyal assistant, nor much smarter baseball man than Dan. He showed it again in 1928, when he took the St. Louis Browns managing job and lifted a seventh-place-bogged team into third place.

Still another favorite attack point of my fault-finders is the accusation that I demanded of all my players the same urge to win that I possessed, and, finding it lacking, marked them down as inadequate. I give you only one case (of many) in rebuttal. When George Cutshaw joined us in 1922, he was a ten-year veteran no longer able to do acrobatics about second base. His arm wasn't much any more. He was nearing the end of the trail. But Cutshaw was a master of the position in many other ways. And so he played 177 games for me at second, having for a while almost a rebirth of his fine talent. At age thirty-five, Cutshaw showed me he was giving everything he had left, and that was all I could ask.

We were almost exactly the same age in 1922. That year I averaged .401 at bat. Cutshaw's average was .267. Far from jumping down his neck for his light average, I was happy to have him around. Without my asking him, he worked unceasingly with the other infielders, showing them stance on fielding a ball, where to throw on bases-jammed situations and the technique of whipping that arm around the face on a double-play throw to first base. George was simply great, in ways that didn't show to the fans and sportswriters, and he knew that I knew it.

You'll also read in most of the baseball histories that I'm the manager who released Carl Hubbell, the fellow who later won 253 games for the New York Giants, was nicknamed "The Meal Ticket" and who set a mark in 1933 of 46-1/3 scoreless innings pitched. "Cobb never could see anything in Hubbell's side-arm pitching," the story goes.

This is a very strange charge. Every bit of evidence you could ask to see shows that Hubbell still was the property of the Detroit organization in 1926, when I departed as manager. He did not become a Giant until the winter of 1927.

And the man who let him go was George Moriarty, my successor as manager. Moriarty, who had been umpiring in the American League, took the Tigers to spring training at San Antonio in '27, wasn't impressed and farmed Hubbell to Decatur, Illinois, that season. Hubbell wound up at Beaumont, Texas, a club in which Detroit was interested, later was sold to the Giants for $40,000.

But though I was gone from Detroit, I still take the rap for that colossal blunder.

The plain fact is that one of my last acts as manager was to urge Navin, "Never let Hubbell go. He may be wild and not ready now, but he's going to be one of the best. Any man with his speed who can turn the ball loose below the belt side-arm only needs control to succeed."

And so, for a summation . . .

I was a "bad" manager. I was that "bad" manager whose seventh-place inheritance of 1921 became the best-drawing attraction in the league, next to the Yankees, and packed them in at the rate of a million fans in a season. I was that "bad" leader whose teams finished in the first division four of my six years in office, who ran second in 1923 and third in 1922 and 1924 and fourth in 1925. I was that "bad" teacher who taught a few tricks to Heilmann, Manush, and Gehringer, who among them had 38 seasons of batting .300 or more. I was that "bad" manager who pleaded with Navin to buy Paul Waner, who saw George Grantham sold from under him.

Naturally, a man of my outlook on baseball yearned to win a pennant. I count the fact that I didn't win one when managing as the supreme disappointment of my professional life. Nothing could better have rounded out my twenty-two years spent in the game up to that point. But we did *contend* four of my six years, and did it with intelligence and desire. No Tiger team I ran was a down-at-the-mouth, slipshod, discouraged outfit—despite our woeful pitching and patchwork defense. After I left Detroit, the Tigers stopped contending for seven years. In that span, they finished seventh twice, sixth twice, fifth three times, and once fourth.

Therefore, no man alive can ever tell me that I did a bad job of managing. My view being inevitably suspect to prejudice, any doubter can ask one of my ex-players, such as Fred Haney, the latter-day successful manager of the Milwaukee Braves, for an opinion. Haney is a friend of mine—true. But he's also a man of candid expression. He and others of Detroit background *as players* take strong exception to the critics, and that, I believe, is the best authority one can quote.

It is a terrible thing for any manager to approach his job aggressively and determinedly, while frustrated by an ownership which turns up its toes when a crisis appears. The name of Flint Rhem is one more on a long list of my bitter memories. In 1922, I received a letter from Rhem, then pitching for Clemson College down South. His spelling didn't indicate he was about to graduate *magna cum laude*, but young Flint cited a flock of one- and two-hitters he'd pitched and asked for a tryout with Detroit.

"Let's get this boy, if his story stands up," I urged Frank Navin. "I know what kind of college ball they play in the South, and it's first-rate. Rhem isn't winning these games against a bunch of humpty-dumpties."

The boy's story did stand up. He was a regular Frank Merriwell at the college level.

Navin didn't do a thing about him. Rhem went to the St. Louis Cardinals two years later, won 20 games one season and became a star relief man.

Just about that time, I led the Tigers into St. Louis to meet the Browns, in one of our typical games. I have the box-score before me now. It says this:

Harry Heilmann collected a triple, a double, and two singles for our side. Bobby Veach contributed a triple. Ainsmith hit a double for our side. I had a pretty good afternoon for a battered old gaffer in his mid-thirtys—a home run, triple, and two doubles good for five runs. Together, the Tigers slammed the ball for 13 hits.

And the final score?

Believe it or not, the Browns slaughtered us, 16–8. They collected 17 hits off three of the second-rate pitchers I was forced to use and nullified all our efforts in a manner most depressing.

And that's how it went after I stuck my head into the managerial noose.

Oh, what we could have done with a couple of pitchers in those days. If I'd had them, the Yankees would have had to wait a few years to become the terrors of baseball. In every other way but pitching, we spit in their eye and showed them the scientific way to use a bat, a glove, and a ball.

16

The Babe and I

I can see Babe now, a glass of Scotch in his hand and a challenging look on that big flat pan of his as we sat one day in his Riverside Drive apartment in New York. It was 1943 and golf was the subject of controversy between us now. I was fifty-five years old, Ruth forty-seven. We'd never quite settled our rivalry as ballplayers, and so, on this evening when Ruth invited me to dinner, he tossed me a teaser.

"How about a match—you and me?" he suggested. "We'll do it for war charity. Ought to draw quite a house."

"I'm here for the World's Fair, with my children," I came back, "but if there's time to work it in, it suits me fine."

Babe pulled on his cigar and I could sense what he was gunning for: my scalp. I'd heard that Ruth shot golf at a 6 or 7 handicap, in the 70s, whereas my own game was more on the ham side, in the 80s, normally. On the diamond, I had been rough on Babe. I'd never taken my spurs out of his hide and one day he'd come looking for me in the Detroit clubhouse with fistic mayhem in mind. We'd won and lost duels to each other way back since 1915, when Babe had been a rookie pitcher with Bill Carrigan's Boston Red Sox. To add heat to the situation, some press association or other was always holding a poll to pick between Ruth and Cobb as the all-time star player.

Over the years—and Babe was well aware of it—I'd discovered his one vulnerable point. And how I'd worked on it. You could play Ruth like a zither, if you'd studied him closely enough.

He figured to even it up by giving me the beating of my life out on the links.

Let me bow my head in George Ruth's memory. I never saw a man who could beat you so utterly—and do it every day, virtually—with his mere presence on the field. The fact that he was apt to break up any game with one home run swing was only half the story. Think of the psychological effect of having Babe going against your team. Your pitcher always feared to walk the man who batted ahead of him for fear Ruth would drive him home. That meant that the pitcher had to work hard and worry excessively about that man. Then by the time he was through that ordeal, up came Ruth, and the pitcher went through another exausting few minutes. By then he was apt to relax when the next hitter stepped up. When Ruth batted, he helped the man in front and the man behind.

Not much is remembered of Ruth, the pitcher, but I can testify that he was left-handed dynamite and could have ranked among the greats had he not turned to outfielding and slugging. In 45 or 50 times at bat against him, I never touched him for more than a single. He had a pretty fair curve, a big fastball and excellent control. Look at his earned-run average. In 1220 innings pitched, Ruth had a 2.26 ERA. In 31 World Series innings, it was a remarkable 0.87, and Babe won all three games he pitched. As usual against a powerful thrower, I choked up the bat and somehow managed to average around .325 against him over a five-year-period. But I never hit him for extra bases.

The season after Babe became a Yankee (1920), I took over management of the Tigers, and it became incumbent upon me to try to do something to stop his batting rampages. The best solution seemed to be to distract him—to get his goat. Along those lines I proceeded.

Whenever I'd pass near him on the field, I'd make some little remark or gesture, such as, "Do any of you fellows smell something? Seems to me there's polecat around here." My fingers would be applied to my nose. Ruth's neck would swell and he'd roar back an insult at me.

Another sensitive point was his large belly and thin legs—if you mentioned that he looked like an egg on stilts or a beer keg balanced on two straws, he'd turn purple. Babe could be distracted, all right. At least, when I heckled him, he always answered the call.

We used to tell him, when he was running bases against us, "Heard that little Johnny Rawlings ran you out of the Giants clubhouse? That true, big boy?"

"You — — can go to —!" Babe would bellow. "It ain't a — bit true!"

The reference was to an incident of 1922, the year the Giants whipped Babe and the Yanks in the World Series—not only beat them, but humiliated the Yanks by winning four games and playing one to a tie. Rawlings, a lightweight infielder, bench-jockeyed Ruth the whole Series. And Babe hit only .118 for the five games. After the third game, he barged into the Giants clubhouse and threatened to wring Rawlings' neck. Several of the big, tough Giants moved in, and in the end, Ruth left without swinging any punches.

But the way the Tigers poured it on Babe, little Rawlings personally had chased him out of there.

It came to a point where Ruth didn't like Cobb very much, and, now and then, it helped us win a ball game.

One afternoon, Babe hit a two-bagger against us, and Emory (Topper) Rigney, our second baseman, protested violently when the umpire called Babe safe on a slide into the base. I ran in from center field, aiming to cool off Rigney so that he wouldn't be asked to leave. However, upon arriving, I saw another possibility. Ruth was giving Topper what-for, with one foot only touching the base. And Rigney still held the ball.

"Say, Topper, what smells so awful around here?" I asked. "Do you get a whiff of something striped?"

Rigney sniffed. "By gosh, there *is* something in the air."

Babe blew up and started for me. If he'd continued that lunge, I'd have departed from the vicinity in a hurry because I never wanted to fight Babe. Secretly, I admired him greatly. While I was razzing him, I was always half-laughing to myself.

But in the midst of his lunge, just as Rigney was ready to catch him off base and tag him out, a cunning look spread over his face and he stopped at the last moment, his toe still touching the bag.

I tried again: "Man, what a stench around here!"

Ruth only glowered at me. He'd finally seen through my polecat gag, and in this case, in the nick of time.

"Cobb, do you know what you are?" said Babe.

I didn't wait around to find out. Ruth had a vocabulary that stuck out, even in baseball.

Everyone in the American League cherished the hope that the Big Guy would eat and drink himself into a stupor and be unable to get the bat around his stomach, but it was the falsest of dreams. He absorbed enough punishment off plates of food and out of bottles to have killed an ordinary man. I've never seen such an appetite. He'd start shoveling down victuals in the morning and never stop. I've seen him at midnight, propped up in bed, order six huge club sandwiches and put them away, along with a platter of pig's knuckles, and a pitcher of beer. And all the time, he'd be smoking big, black cigars.

Next day, he'd hit two or three homers and trot around the bases, complaining all the way of gas pains and a bellyache.

Once, around 1924, Babe and I came somewhat close to settling a situation with our fists. My pitcher that day was a slender youngster named Earl Whitehill, who had the Yankees beaten, 2–1, in the ninth inning. Lou Gehrig was at bat and Whitehill's pitch speared him in the midriff. There was no chance that the pitch was deliberate, for hitting a man in the final inning when you're holding a short lead is the last thing you want to do. Yet Gehrig took umbrage and went for Whitehill and a general fight broke out.

When the game ended with no heads broken, more trouble erupted, and I dashed in from the outfield to save my little fellow, Whitehill, from any injury. In the dark player's tunnel leading from the field, I came across two bodies all tangled up on the ground, and the top one was Gehrig's. I assumed Whitehill was on the bottom. Seeing a white shirt and a leg sticking out, I reached down and gave a heave and yanked with all I had.

Out popped nobody but Ruth. "For Criminy sakes, what are you doing there?" I asked him. Babe was spluttering indignantly. "Trying to stop it, dammit!" he roared at me. "Lou doesn't know what he's doing." Babe had clamped a headlock on Gehrig and was trying to restrain him from further assault.

"Sorry," I apologized, "I thought you were my pitcher."

In the Yankee clubhouse, word of the incident got around, and his teammates began baiting Babe. They claimed I'd shoved him around and kicked him during the earlier melee, and because there'd been so many people involved in the Brannigan, Babe couldn't be sure they weren't right.

"You gonna let Cobb get away with that?" the Yanks demanded.

Babe came charging into our clubhouse while I was showering, and next thing I knew there he stood, bristling for a fight. "Listen, Cobb," he yelled, "I've had enough from you. You laid *hands* on me out there!"

Before he could say another word, I jumped right back at him. "Why, you big baboon, I was only trying to stop a fight, same as you. We were in agreement for once in our lives. So what are you doing in here? Now get the hell out—before I throw you out!"

I guess Babe saw I was sincere. He hesitated a moment, unballed his fists and walked out.

And now (to return to my opening remarks) it was close to twenty years later, and I was sitting in Babe's apartment, as his guest, and we were enjoying a drink and some small talk. He was up to around 240 pounds and filled a big easy chair. Babe liked to sit with his feet parked on an ornamental beer keg from Jake Ruppert's brewery. We drank from oversized tumblers, and I will say that Babe's wife, Claire, kept them steadily refilled. After an hour or so, Babe got around to challenging me to a war charity golf match, or matches.

Nothing happened just then, but not long later, out in California, I was playing in the amateur division of the Oakland Open when I ran across Fred Corcoran, who directed operations for the Professional Golfers Association. We were in a smoke-filled locker room and I was chatting with friends when Corcoran said, "Say, do you think you can beat Babe Ruth at golf? He claims he can trim you with no trouble."

"Tell you what I want you to do," I replied. "You challenge Ruth for me to a match. I'll play him any time, anywhere, for any amount of money."

Naturally, my reply appeared in the newspapers with the twist that I'd said, "I can beat Ruth at anything." The big publicity build-up was started. Each of us was quoted on fire-breathing statements that made what was just a joust between two aging ballplayers who played golf for a hobby sound like the battle of the century. From New York, Babe was quoted as saying, "For years Cobb has been broadcasting that he could beat me at any game, anywhere. I've never seen him play, and I'm not boasting about my ability. But tell him to stop talking and come on East and settle this."

Next, a telegram arrived at my Atherton, California, home reading: IF YOU WANT TO COME HERE AND GET YOUR BRAINS KNOCKED OUT, COME RIGHT AHEAD. RUTH.

The ballyhoo boys didn't fool me, but I was beginning to get interested in meeting Babe with a different type of weapon in our hands. We were both southpaws, and although he figured to outdrive me, I hoped that my short iron and putting game would even things out. The newspapers jumped on that angle—Babe's home-run power versus my so-called "deadly" ability to hit singles and bunts, as translated into tee shots, approaches, chip shots, and putts. Corcoran arranged two 18-hole matches—the first at Boston's Commonwealth Country Club, with proceeds going to Golden Rule Farm, the New England version of Boys Town. Our second meeting was scheduled for Fresh Meadow Country Club on Long Island, with the USO the beneficiary. If a "rubber" match was needed, we'd play that in Detroit.

Reaching New York, I found that Ruth fans had the long needle out for me. In my hotel room, the sportswriters informed me that Babe's last four rounds over metropolitan courses had been 77, 74, 73, and 72. Babe was blazing hot, they said, and asked what my best score had been. "A 71 over the Ocean course at Lakeside in San Francisco," I told them honestly. "But a week later, I took an 84 over the same layout. Boys, I'm only a fair golfer. Looks like I'm licked."

It was Ruth's 6-handicap against my 9, and it sure looked as if I'd bitten off too much.

"Where is Babe?" I asked.

"Oh, he flew up to Boston to get in some practice rounds at Commonwealth," was the reply.

This was getting serious. I began to apply a little pressure of my own. The story got out that I'd been taking lessons from my old pal, Walter Hagen, and that Jimmy Demaret, the great pro, would "second" me during the Ruth matches. I was asked, "Do you plan to heckle the Babe the way you did in baseball?"

"Well," I answered, "you can say that I'll do everything possible to win."

219

Headline resulting:

COBB PLANNING CRAFTY TACTICS: TY SO PERTURBED
HE TAKES GOLF LESSONS FROM HAGEN
BY TELEPHONE

Referee of the match was to be Arthur Donovan, the famed fight arbiter, with Bette Davis, the screen star, to present a suitable award to the victor. By now, a gallery of thousands was assured. Wow!

Although it might seem silly, I went into those Ruth matches as determined to win as I ever was on the ball field.

When I got up to Boston, to shoot some warm-up rounds, I would usually be teeing off just as Babe was finishing up. "How'd you do today?" I'd ask him.

"Not so good—had a 76," Babe would snort.

"Oh, my gosh! There's no use my playing you if you're shooting like that," I'd say indignantly. "These people are expecting to see a real match, but we'll just be plain gypping them."

Babe would smile happily and head for the clubhouse and bend the elbow for an hour or two. When I came in, my score would be in the 80s, you can bet I saw to that. By the time we teed off in the opening 18-holer, he was beaming and full of confidence.

Babe started the match convinced he'd wrap it up in a hurry. He went 2-up on me on the fourth hole, when he hit a spectacular 60-foot chip shot that dropped into the cup for a birdie 4. But on the next hole, a hunch of mine about Babe paid off. If an opponent pulled off a difficult putt, Ruth felt the pressure. In this case, I dropped a nine-footer downhill. Babe's ball was only 12 inches from the cup, but he jabbed at it and missed the hole and wound up with a double bogie 5.

I also discovered that I could come close to matching Babe's 260-yarders off the tee, but I didn't bother trying it. I let him outdrive me. Which meant I got first crack at the second shot. When I lofted it up onto the green—and iron play was one slight golf strength I had—the heat was on Ruth to match my shot. And that he didn't like. He'd swear and wiggle around and cuss himself when the shot went astray.

Not once did I open my mouth to heckle him, as he'd been expecting. Just: "Good shot, Babe."

At the 9-hole turn, Babe's margin had been erased and we were all even. I tried a little distraction technique. Pulling an iron from my bag on a long second shot, I prompted him to object. "What the hell, Ty, that's a wood shot," he said.

"Well, maybe so," I said, "but I'm superstitious."

For a top-flight golfer, a wood was the club to be used, but I wanted the control an iron brings—due to a fringe of skunk cabbage along the fairway. But I didn't tell Babe that. I blamed my dumb club selection on superstition. And he got so interested in watching the result of this oddball affliction of mine, that he dumped his next shot in the cabbage.

And in the end I beat him, 3 and 2.

Babe rushed by plane to Fresh Meadow on Long Island to prepare for match No. 2, but I waited for the midnight train and leisurely made my way to the scene. We had another tight match, and this time Babe took no chances. He stayed away from the bottle, had his hair fastened down with a big bobby pin and concentrated like mad on his putts. We battled 18 holes to a deadlock. On the extra nineteenth, the Babe defeated me with some beautiful shots.

For the big rubber match, action moved to Detroit's Grosse Ile Golf and Country Club, where we were to play man-to-man, but in company with Waltar Hagen and Mysterious John Montague. First, however, we played a tune-up match at Canterbury in Cleveland, with Tris Speaker as my partner and Billy Burke teamed with Ruth. Again, I went to the old psychology. Time and again I messed up shots that weren't difficult. Around the green, I'd undercut with my niblick. "Don't know what's wrong with me, I'm sure off," I'd moan. My putts wouldn't drop, I was in the rough more than a highway hobo.

That night, going over on the boat to Detroit, Babe again was all smiling confidence and he killed a good part of a quart of Scotch.

And the next day at Grosse Ile was streaming hot—in the nineties. Babe began to sweat ferociously before we even started and he looked slightly ill.

Hagen, the greatest nerve-twister in the history of golf, had tipped me to another trick in the earlier matches. "Give him some putts," advised Walter. "Concede some tough ones until he gets to expect it." So, at Boston and Flushing Meadow, I'd knocked Babe's ball away from the pin several times when he was facing tricky two- and three-footers. He ate it up.

At Grosse Ile, I conceded nothing, and it made Babe boil—sort of like taking a kid's lollipop away from him when it's half-eaten. Also, my bad shots of Canterbury suddenly became good ones. Each accurate chip or dropped putt was like a nail driven into the Babe's heart. I was holding his nose to the grindstone, and he hated that. Babe was a roaring lion when he was ahead and could play relaxed, but you could break him by forcing him to play from behind. In a team game like baseball, that was anything but true. The Yanks could trail, 3–0 in the ninth, load the bases and then Babe would clean them with one swing. In highly personal and individualistic golf, he was another man.

My putter got hot and after dropping the opening hole to Babe, I turned him at the halfway mark leading by five strokes. On the fifteenth hole, he was desperate. I had an uphill 10-foot putt and tapped it with the bend of the green and dropped it.

"He's a puttin' fool!" bellowed Babe, throwing both hands up. Actually, I was playing rather poor golf, but Babe was so far off that he made me look good.

When the play-off match started, Babe had offered to bet me $5 a hole, but I'd declined, indicating that I didn't think I had a chance. When I took a substantial lead, I said, "Okay, Babe, I'll bet you now. How much?"

"——!" said Babe. He refused the wager.

That's when I knew I had him.

It was all over on the sixteenth hole—the match and Has Beens' Golf Championship of Nowhere in Particular was mine, 3 and 2.

Babe didn't have much time left on earth after that final meeting between us. Less than four years later he was afflicted with cancer and within six months he was dead. I can't honestly say that I appreciate the way in which he changed baseball—from a game of science to an extension of his powerful slugging—but he was the most natural and unaffected man I ever knew. No one ever loved life more. No one ever inspired more youngsters. I have reverence for his marvelous ability.

I look forward to meeting him again some day.

17

You Field with Your Head Too

At Comiskey Park, Chicago, early in the season of 1920, a ball hit midway between Ira Flagstead and myself in the Tiger outfield set up the sort of situation of which all young fly-chasers should beware. But for a fluke second accident, it might have ended my career.

Both of us charged full-tilt for the ball and we collided with a crash that could be heard in the bleachers.

Outfielders almost invariably warn each other away with the cry, "I'll take it." The first man who sees he can get to the ball calls for it, the flanking man replies, "Take it," and veers off before they come together. But outfield chances can be of the in-between variety, splitting the two men's positions and setting up a collision course more fraught with danger than any slide into a base or bean-ball. This was such a case.

As we crashed together, I was flung into the air, did a somersault and landed on the back of my neck and shoulders. All the ligaments of my right knee were torn from place. They carried me off, and after a cast had been applied and I'd been hospitalized a few days, it was another four or five weeks before I was ready to move on crutches.

"We can't promise you a thing," the doctors reported. "Possibly you'll never again be able to run on that knee with speed."

"Anything I can do to help it?" I asked, feeling that strange sensation a ballplayer gets when he sees the foreshadow of his end as a major leaguer.

One of the doctors advised me to go home, get some beer hops and vinegar, brew it on the stove and apply hot packs. Pushed from the depot to the train in a wheel chair, I headed for Georgia. I had my cook down home keep dishpans steaming with the hops-vinegar compound and poulticed my knee more religiously than Mother Fox treated the earaches of the little foxes in the bedtime fable. When I could get around and walk a bit on the leg, I saw a bone specialist. He suggested that I put some real pressure on the knee, and said that if it collapsed, he would operate and cut loose the adhesions and start the healing process all over again. "It's a gamble, admittedly," he said, "but sometimes you can force Nature's cure."

The Detroit management was highly doubtful when I suited up again. We were on an Eastern road trip when I urged manager Hughie Jennings to let me back in there. "I can't do any base-running," I argued, "but I can run well enough to get down to first with a hit now and then. Then you can send in a pinch-runner."

"Let's wait," said Hughie.

I kept after him, and in Boston, he let me pinch-hit, and the leg didn't buckle. Soon later, I was on base with a single when one of the boys lashed a hit, and I forgot myself completely, and made a four-alarm rush for second. The play required a hard slide. When I hit the dirt, a million stars exploded. The pain was agonizing and I didn't have a doubt that I'd ruined myself for good and all.

Examined, I was found to have torn loose all the adhesions—which, medically, are the union of fractured or severed parts. The trainer put enough bandages on me to immobilize me and my death knell sounded in all the newspapers.

Two weeks later I was running like an antelope.

That's an amazing fact: within ten games, the injury disappeared, I was back in action. The knee remained perfectly serviceable until my retirement 994 games and eight years later.

A flukish and very lucky break, and one I wouldn't attempt to explain.

But it does have a bearing on one of the most important pieces of advice I can give any young player hoping to develop into an outfielder. Most collisions out in the pasture are needless. Keep your ears open while you're concentrating on running toward the ball and stick to the tested formula, boys. When you shout "I'll take it!" or "I've got it!" shout it loudly and clearly. Give that signal the instant you feel the play belongs to you, and not your teammate. After that, the responsibility for the catch is yours. If you call for it, you have the confidence to play the ball, knowing you are on your own and safe from injury. The collision hazard is eliminated almost entirely.

Don't invade the other fielder's territory, unless he is caught unaware by a fly ball, line drive or grounder, or loses the ball in the sun, or falls down. Otherwise, stick to your assigned area. Don't be a fly-hog. When a chance appears that neither of you can rightfully call for, remember that your career can end in the next few seconds. Hustle for the ball, but try to keep track of the other man by being extra-alert. If you hear him call, immediately forget the ball and locate him. Once in a while, it'll be necessary to throw yourself to the ground to avoid a crash.

If I had it to do over again, knowing as much about baseball as I have learned through the years, I would again want to become an outfielder. The advantages and remunerations are many. One is longevity. Outfielders last longer. They do not have to take the body-contact beating of an infielder and their chances of injury, limited mostly to collision with a fence or another outfielder, are less than any position on a club.

To be an outfielder you must be a player who delivers at the plate. You must be a good hitter, consistently in the .300 class; but you should not try to enter the door of modern, streamlined baseball through offense alone. You should be capable of doing something besides hit and catch a fly ball.

The term "fly-chaser," often applied to outfielders, is one of baseball's most glaring misnomers. Outfielding should be as much a specialty as playing shortstop or second base. An outfielder is called upon to field as many ground balls as he is flies, and the improper fielding of them causes more errors and allows more runs than missed fly balls.

You must be gifted with a good arm because you are called upon to make long throws. Also, speed of foot is essential, particularly if you are going to be a center fielder. If you have speed you can learn to run.

The fellow with a nervous disposition should be an infielder or catcher. A player who has to be "doing something every minute" will wear himself to a frazzle trying to play the outfield. The ideal outfielder must be endowed with a stoical nature or acquire the knack of being a "good waiter" in a relaxed, though poised sort of way. Be nonchalant yet set. Be alert yet not tense. Ideal outfielding temperament demands this.

Fact is that some of the most happy-go-lucky, relaxed, personable stars of history have been gardeners. Going 'way back, there was Wild Bill Lange, Jesse Burkett, Joe Kelley, Jimmy Sheckard, Mike Donlin, Gavvy Cravath, Oscar (Happy) Felsch, and Fatty Fothergill, and later on Casey Stengel, Harry Heilmann, Babe Herman, Pepper Martin, Lefty O'Doul, and Hack Wilson. Nobody ever accused any of those boys of being victims of nerves or tension.

When Bill Lange was bothered by the snores of his teammates during Pullman trips, he bought a sack of lemons. Soon as the snorers were in full chorus, Bill sliced the lemons in half and started down the aisle. At each berth, he opened the curtains and squeezed lemon juice into the wide open mouth of the snorer.

"All you could hear from then on was funny little splutters," Bill said, in telling about it. "None of them woke up. But they sure stopped honking and I got a swell night's sleep."

Mike Donlin didn't like the pay offered him one year. So he quit the Giants and announced he was making his debut as an actor. Everybody laughed heartily at Mike's plan to become a Barrymore. But he married Mabel Hite, the stage queen, joined her touring company and scored a big hit tromping the boards all over the country. Mike stayed with acting two years, nonchalantly returned and hit .333 his first season back with the Giants.

Outfielders come in all shapes and sizes. Even roly-poly, like Fatty Fothergill, whom I managed at Detroit. Fatty's food tabs looked like we were keeping an elephant in right field. But one day, after hitting a homer off George Earnshaw of the Athletics, Fothergill waddled his 220 pounds around the bases, yelling insults at the A's with every step and then turned a complete somersault in the air at home plate. Didn't use his hands at all, but landed on his feet with the grace of a Pavlova.

The boys who played the fences in my day were in the game every moment—using their heads to annoy hitters, and often leaving the fans limp with their stunts. One day Gavvy Cravath watched Babe Ruth come to bat in an all-star game. Cravath shrugged, and sat down with his back against the center-field wall. Sam Crawford, in right field, found a shady spot and stretched out on the grass for a nap. Irish Meusel, in left field, turned his back and fell to conversing with the bleacher fans.

Ruth was so burned up that he took a swing against slow-balling Paul Fittery that was terrible to watch. He popped up to the infield.

A perfect job of inserting the needle, I call it.

If you have the build, the stoicism to fight off nerves, a strong arm, speed, and can hit, then the outfield is where you belong. First, you should form the right outfield habits and learn the fundamentals early. Once acquired, those habits stick with you the longest.

One of the habits is your practice routine. Infielders, necessarily, waste a lot of energy in infield practice. I made it a practice that when I was going well, and in my stride not to use up too much energy in pre-game work. In my case it paid off.

But don't go to the other extreme. There is plenty of work to be done before a game. Do plenty of throwing in practice but don't be a Fancy Dan. Many outfielders like to consider themselves great pitchers who missed their calling. Take advice from me, who, in this respect, was a dumbbell. I spoiled a very good arm by throwing knuckle balls and spitters. I succeeded in injuring a good outfielder's arm by this unnecessary skylarking.

It happened in 1915 when I was experimenting with knucklers, shine balls, spitters, and the like, under the impression that a great pitcher had been lost when I turned outfielder. After the season ended, I took the mound in a game against the Bushwicks in Brooklyn. One of them bunted. I fielded it, but threw off balance, and something went, "Snap!"

My arm went entirely dead at that moment. I left the game, keeping the extent of the injury a secret, but, privately, frightened to death. All that winter I self-treated the arm. I'll never know what ailed me—possibly a chipped elbow bone.

As late as November, I couldn't throw a rock across the street. By January, I was lobbing a ball against the brick wall of my Augusta home. Came spring and the arm improved and finally was usable again. Yet the day when I could throw out three Senators at first base from right field in one game was finished.

After 1915, however, I piled up more assists than when I was sound of arm. Can you figure why?

227

The reason is simple. Once the boys learned I was weakened in the arm, they began to take chances on the bases that they hadn't earlier. By charging balls hard and getting my momentum behind the throw, by getting a fast jump on long flies and by throwing to the bases intelligently, I was able to take advantage of what the opposition thought was a fatal weakness.

Save that arm. Use it as an outfielder's arm, not a pitcher's. Pitchers can come to the same grief trying to emulate an outfielder. Remember the distance and trajectory of the two throws are vastly different.

Before a game make a few throws to the plate from varied distances. In making throws to the plate I found, as a general rule, it was better to aim just beyond the pitcher's box from center field. A bounding ball, one that skips in, is generally easier for the catcher to handle with a base-runner attempting to come home. I have always thought a bounding ball increased speed after it hit the ground once. This has been argued pro and con. Most catchers think it does and prefer a ball that skips in.

Don't end your throwing exercise with a toss or two at the plate. Try yourself for accuracy at second and third and make the ball come in on a straight air line.

With the lively ball of today, outfielders have to play farther back and the defense is more concerned with keeping a base-runner from taking that extra bag. You can rarely throw a runner out at the plate any more, but you want to keep him from going from first to third on a single. Remember, the relay is the thing today. In my time, we rarely relayed. Get your infielders to team with you in practice. Make throws, short and long, from various parts of your field.

In dead-ball days, outfielding was more of a challenge to speed, ingenuity, and instinct than it is today. Outfielders had to develop amazing skills. Good men played remarkably shallow, almost in the infielder's shadow, in some instances, and caught thousands of line drives and bloopers that are base hits in the 1960s. What's more, to protect against deep drives over our heads, we had to perfect a knack of taking a look at the ball, turning our backs, then running at breakneck speed to haul it down. Two of the best at this were Fred Clarke, the Pittsburgh manager, and Tris Speaker. In a game in April 1911, Clarke made ten put-outs in left field against St. Louis. He was the first National League outfielder to score four assists in one game. And what a rifle for an arm had Clarke. One August day in 1910, he threw a strike from the deep outfield to nip a man sliding at second, picked off another runner at third and two at second. He did this without the help of relay men, who are infielders who run out and pass on the outfielder's throw. Today, playing deep, against the jack-rabbit ball, the garden men make many a "sensational" catch. To me, though, those catches are like picking cherries. Positioned deep to begin with, outfielders make those exciting fence catches while running parallel to the wall and need only jump and pull down the ball with one hand, to which is attached a piece of leather so wide and heavy that it becomes an artificial trap. Those huge gloves worn today account for many an astounding put-out.

After the catch, the fielder has only to throw to his relay man, who guns it to the baseman or catcher. In my time, an outfielder had to make the throw all the way from right field to third base or home plate, or left field to second or home without help—in a day when distances to the fence were much longer than in the home-run epoch.

That makes it all the more remarkable that Tris Speaker could play in tight behind the infield, where in one month in 1918 he made two unassisted double plays. That meant he had to make the line-drive catch and beat the runner, who'd been on second base, back to the bag. The mechanics of the maneuver are impressive enough. But even more a tribute to Tris is the fact that the runner never would have left the bag had he thought there was even a possibility of the ball being caught.

And even while stationed in so close, Tris could turn his back and get back there for long fly balls. I see no one around today with that capability.

The most overlooked and neglected detail in practice is the attention given ground balls. Spend a reasonable portion of your daily practice charging in on them. A little infield practice will help an outfielder and I advocate it.

I have seen outfielders go year after year displaying weaknesses on ground balls, weaknesses which in most cases could be corrected by application and practice. It is appalling the number of games that are lost in a season in this manner. Some otherwise good outfielders are so poor at it they practically have to get down on their knees to make sure a ground ball does not go through them. They have never troubled themselves to learn the simple technique of fielding a ground ball.

Practice on ground balls is just as essential to an outfielder as an infielder, though you do not play them the same as an infielder. I stress this point—rush in on the ball always, and shorten up the distance. In so doing make sure you are in a position to block it in case you don't field it. Play the ball in such a way that you knock it down, preferably in front of you, so you can still pick it up in time to make a throw.

By charging in on a ball the danger of a bad hop is far less than if you wait for it, and when you charge in you will discourage the runner from taking that extra base.

Outfielders have variable styles for catching a fly ball. I had ideal success by adhering to the principle that any ball that could be caught above the belt should be caught with both hands receding toward the body. Your safest catches are those made with hands somewhat above your shoulders. Your eyes are better focused on the ball that way. Pull a ball into you, never try to punch it. This applies to both flies and ground balls.

Any put-out you make with men on base, ready to advance after the catch, should find your feet in such a position that when you receive the ball you can make the throw. Always shift your feet to where you are in a position to make a throw. If you've thought out where the play is going in advance, as you always must, you can accustom yourself to have your feet positioned for the throw automatically.

I mentioned catching a ball with your hands above your shoulders as the "safest" kind of put-out. But you can't always catch a ball that way. The toughest outfield play is a low, line drive where you have to come in on the ball. Again, the important thing is that you pull the ball into you and not punch it out.

On a "last-ditch" play in the final inning where the game is wrapped up in a catch in which you must leave your feet and make a dive for it, fall with your whole body free and not tense. Throw everything into it and don't try to protect yourself. This is one of those plays where you do or you don't, but practice will polish it up.

A very important thing with an outfielder who is conditioning himself by running around the park is to practice the same kind of moves you are going to make in a ball game. Practice everything—making a quick turn, going back for a ball, cutting across, pivoting, charging in on a ground ball. Sort of a shadow-boxing routine, while legging it around the park. It will strengthen your ankles and improve your agility in making any kind of a turn.

You've seen halfbacks weaving their way around a series of rubber tires on a football field to perfect their pivoting. Learn to pivot. Just imagine the tires are there. It will help you get a quick start on a ball hit to the outfield.

Perhaps the most important factor in outfield play is figuring in advance of a pitched ball what you are going to do if it is hit into your territory. Before you do this it is vital that you know what kind of ball is going to be pitched. Insist that the second baseman or shortstop signal you behind his back what the pitch is going to be and break for the ball the very split second the bat is applied to it.

For example, you have a left-handed pitcher throwing to a left-handed hitter and the sign comes up that it is going to be a curve ball. You know very well that if it is hit at all well it has got to be hit toward left field from your position in center. The percentage, at any rate, is against the hitter pulling it. Therefore you can take a step, or lean, or start in the direction the ball is likely to come.

Curve balls are more likely to be pulled than fast balls. An outfielder should get the sign from the shortstop, watch how the infielders are playing a hitter and "shade" to the right or left, accordingly. You should shade right-hand hitters toward their power area, the left-field side, and left-handed hitters to the opposite side. Tris Speaker, Earle Combs, Mel Ott, and other all-time defensive outfielders studied the dampness of the turf, the angles of the fences (to handle caroms), and location and intensity of the sun. They missed no smallest detail.

Go in for some bluffing. Use trap and decoy plays. It was my style to make the easy chances look hard, giving the base-runner a case of the screaming jitters as he tried to decide whether to stay put or take off. I'd make a production of catching a fly I could have stuck in my pocket. Or I'd do the opposite. The bluff catch on Texas Leaguers—flies hit between the infield and outfield—is not difficult. You merely charge the ball with arms outstretched, giving the impression that you've got the catch made. Naturally, the runner or runners will hold up, and often you can take the ball on the short bounce and nab one of them for a force-out. At the least, it prevents the runners from taking a big lead and so getting an extra base on the Texas Leaguer.

I can't stress too much that you should study all hitters. Find out what each does against a certain kind of delivery. It will pay dividends. Another thing. Watch those flags atop the grandstand. They will indicate the direction and velocity of the wind. Don't place all the burden on your natural ability, your legs and your eyes. The wind can be more of a help than a hindrance if you study it and make it your ally.

Furthermore, you have to play a park as well as a ball. There are air currents which cause swirls and they vary in different parks. And parks aren't uniform in size. You may have a short right-field fence which will call for you to play the position entirely different than in a more spacious enclosure.

If you give up on a ball, or a base-runner, you might as well give up outfielding. I've raced back for many a ball on an educated guess where it'd come down, reached a wire or rope barrier with screaming fans standing beyond, got a flash of something white, taken a dive with hand outstretched and felt the thrilling impact of ball in pocket of glove as I went tumbling head over heels. Miracles don't happen on "blind" or semiblind catches. You make them happen by trying to the last ditch.

Mule Haas, about the year I retired, was in center field for the Athletics with his team leading 7–6 in the ninth inning. One out. The Yankees got two men on base, and up came Babe Ruth. He busted one off Rube Walberg that was stamped home run and game-winner from the moment it left his bat.

Getting a fine break on the ball, Haas sped for the fence. He had to run up an embankment, leap, with both hands outthrust like a football end catching a pass and with his back to the plate. He caught it, crashed the barrier, and fell to the ground, still holding the ball.

The Yankee runner on second tagged up and was off with the catch. Not a chance in this world for the stunned Haas to regain his feet and cut off the tying run at the plate. The Yank runner was confidently waved in by his third-base coach.

Imagine his consternation when he found catcher Mickey Cochrane putting the ball on him as he slid home—for the final out of the game. Haas, who didn't quit, had rolled over and up and thrown on a line to Max Bishop, who relayed to Cochrane for as improbable a put-out as you'd ever hope to see.

Make your catches two-handed whenever possible. My rule is never to use one hand when you can use two, but I don't shun one-handed catches. There are times when that's the only way you can make a catch. You can reach higher for a ball with one hand, and your balance is better jumping to make a one-handed catch. Gloves nowadays are so improved over the old type that there is more safety in making a one-handed catch on certain plays. But no matter how you catch it watch the shifting of your feet. In fielding the ball you must get your feet in position to throw the ball toward the proper objective. The ability to do it in advance of the catch is very important.

Use your eyes to follow the ball from the moment it is hit. Once you have a ball judged and see you can catch it, never take your eyes off it. There are times, of course, when you've got to make tracks in going back after a long fly, but the sooner you can turn and get your eyes focused on it the better.

No outfielder should balk at wearing sunglasses. In some fields they are absolutely necessary. A little practice will accustom you to the use of them. Don't get the idea it's "sissy" to wear sunglasses. I wore them without compunction. A sun field can be played without glasses by using your free hand for a shade, but glasses make a catch easier.

The ideal outfielder is impossible to define. In modern times, Ted Williams can't be rated perfect, nor Stan Musial, Joe DiMaggio, Willie Mays, or Hank Aaron. All have had or do have some weakness, such as inability to hit to all fields, lack of defensive speed or failure to develop themselves to their full potential. As close to the ideal as you can get would be a player of the 1888–1906 era who was the picture of perfect assurance in the field and at bat. He was small, but was a terrier on anything hit his way. He broke into the majors with a .311 average in his second season and hit .438, .352, and .378 in other seasons. Naturally, he's in Baseball's Hall of Fame. He was Hugh Duffy, a name almost forgotten nowadays.

All outfielders can learn a lesson from Duffy.

Once, when his Boston team was playing Cleveland, Chief Zimmer hit a long drive over Duffy's head. Catching up with it near the fence, Duffy found that the ball had rolled into a tomato can. He gave it one shake, but the ball was wedged tight in the can. Did Duffy give up? Zimmer was tearing around the bases, headed for a home run.

Without hesitation, Duffy wound up and spiraled the can-with-ball to Bobby Lowe, the Boston second baseman. Lowe was pretty astonished when he saw what had arrived. But he took Duffy's cue and threw the whole mess to Charlie Bennett, the catcher, who made the put-out. But the umpire wouldn't allow it. He claimed that there's nothing in the rules that says you can get a base-runner out by jabbing him in the ribs with a tomato can. "The man is safe," he ruled.

Safe or not, Duffy was the ideal outfielder. He always went and got the ball and made the play and more often than not beat his man to the base. If a man who hit and fielded like Duffy was around right now, he'd be a freak.

Fly-catchers never will replace specialists.

18

A Year of Agony:
The Frame-Up That Failed

I'd ruptured all the ligaments in my right knee in 1920.
I'd spoiled a good throwing arm by pitching knucklers in 1915 and
feared I was going blind in 1910. I had more scars distributed over
my legs than a Hindu fire walker. Now it was the winter of 1925
and time for more trouble. Every five years, it seemed, my otherwise excellent luck in regard to preserving my health deserted me.

Snow fell in my beloved Georgia hills that December, and when
1926 arrived, the dust of a thousand ball fields was in my eyes. I
headed for Johns Hopkins Clinic at Baltimore to undergo surgery
for an optical ailment that had troubled me for more than a year.

Before I went under the knife, a poem appeared in the papers
that expressed what some people were expecting to happen any
moment:

> *The curtain's going to drop, old chap*
> *For Time has taken toll,*
> *And you could never play a part*
> *Except the leading role.*
>
> *You might go on and play and play,*
> *But why go on for folks to say*
> *"There's old Ty Cobb, still on the job,*
> *But not the Cobb of yesterday."*

I'd been around a long, long time. I was forty, an age that had sneaked up on me like Big Ed Walsh's spitball; an age when they say a man's inward fires are banked and he's no longer physically capable of satisfying the fans' demands or his own binding sense of pride. Looking around, I saw only Eddie Collins and a few others left of the old gang who'd broken in twenty years before. By the hundreds, the boys had played out their string. Frank Chance was dead, and so were Willie Keeler, Eddie Plank, Rube Waddell, and Christy Mathewson. Three of my rookie-day Detroit teammates had passed on—Wild Bill Donovan, Davey Jones, and Germany Schaefer. From the dead ball to the cork-center ball to the jackrabbit ball, I'd played through three eras of the national game. Each time I took the field, the record-keepers revised the book.

One by one, I'd toppled the all-time longevity records, some of them dating to the previous century.

Back in 1923, the Hans Wagner record of batting .300 or better for 17 straight seasons had become mine. I ran my string to 18 that year and by 1925, I could show 20 straight years of .300 hitting. In '23, I also caught up with Wagner's 3430 lifetime hits and went past it, heading for 4000. In 1924, I passed Willie Keeler's all-time high of 200 or more hits accumulated in each of eight seasons. By 1926, I'd topped Wagner's endurance feat of playing in 2785 games. Two thousand, eight hundred times, I'd hauled myself into uniform. Tris Speaker and Eddie Collins weren't far behind in the department of total times at bat, but neither had reached 10,000 . . . a figure I was looking back on by the mid-1920s. I had the most singles, triples, total bases on hits, extra-base hits, stolen bases, and runs scored of anyone in the books.

All of this seemed to prove I was ready for the shawl, the slippers, and the pipe. I was cartooned with a scythe and whiskers, the palsy, with spavined legs and tottering to the plate on a cane. There was a great deal of sentimental outpouring for Cobb, the fading warrior. It was good to know that the American public hated to see me fade, yet it was galling.

Because—dammit, if you'll pardon the word—at thirty-seven, thirty-eight, and thirty-nine, I didn't feel I'd slipped. I felt I was demonstrating this fact from time to time. And I had a few witnesses who hadn't buried me quite yet. Westbrook Pegler, reporting for United News Syndicate, was one. Peg wrote:

236

"The poor old guy! On Cobb's right eye there is a filmy cataract, his knees are stiff with the stiffness of age, his old fingers are knotty, and after a generation of toil in American League parks, it's only reasonable to suppose that his throwing arm can't reach the infield any more. When he was young, he was quite a ball player. But when you sit on the Tiger bench and observe him closely, you feel sorry for the poor old guy.

"The poor old guy can't hit 'em any more on account of that cataract obscuring his vision. The other day in Boston, old fans felt a clutching sensation where they used to get laryngitis cheering for him. You could see he was slipping and it was kind of tragic, because all he got was five hits in five trips to bat, including a homer, triple and double, which brought his lifetime bat average to .372. The poor old guy!

"Down in Washington a few days later, there was another occasion to jerk loose some tears for poor old Tyrus Cobb. He went to bat 11 times in a doubleheader, and to save his life, he couldn't make more than seven hits and drive in five runs, the poor old guy with the cataract in his eye.

"And what he did in St. Louis only makes it all the more evident that the Tiger's ancient manager is ready for the boneyard. Need I mention it?"

Peg was having his fun, and I still thank him for it, since at the time a premature funeral didn't appeal to me much. The St. Louis episode came on May 5-6, 1926, seven months before my 40th birthday. George Sisler, managing the Browns, used Joe Bush, Russ Vangilder, and Milt Gaston on the mound in the first game. I'd been hearing so much about Babe Ruth's fence-busters that I switched to a long grip on the bat. And I called my shots in advance. To the newspaper boys I said, "I'm going to give you a little demonstration, just to settle a point I think you've been missing."

Off Bush, Vangilder, and Gaston, I hit three home runs, a double and two singles in six times at bat for a total of 16 bases, which broke Eddie Gharrity's league record of 13.

The following day produced a pair of home runs and a single. The two-day total of five homers, 25 bases toured and a dozen runs scored or batted in gave the experts quite a turn.

"Hell, he didn't do that well when he was young!" exclaimed Bozeman Bulger.

It was true enough, even though a filmy growth medically labeled pterygium had settled over both my eyes, and I had trouble following the ball. But slipping? I couldn't believe it, despite growing signs of physical and mental fatigue.

There was a game with the Yankees, whom I loved most to beat. My Tigers jumped on them for 13 runs in one inning, a slaughter to remember. My end of it that day was two home runs, a pair of singles. At Boston, we smothered the Red Sox with 21 hits, 10–4. The poor old guy got two doubles and three singles, if the official box score is correct.

No, I wasn't ready to fold up just yet—not on the ground that I'd gone back, at least. In 1922, I was thirty-six years old and averaged .401. That was my best mark in ten years. In '24, I tied for most-games-played in the league, appearing in 155 of the 156 on the schedule. That year I also led the league in fielding average with a .986 mark. In '25, a .378 average at bat seemed to indicate a little mileage left in me. The challenge of managing—a job I hadn't wanted, but felt deserved my best effort—helped hold me up. So did the faults of many of my young hitters I was seeking to develop.

If the old-time hitters of my youth had any one distinguishing characteristic, it was their fearless attitude. They stood right up to the pitch. Their position was absolutely commanding. They invaded the pitcher's mind, making *him* fear *them*. None of this plate-shy bobbing in and out of the box, pulling away from curve balls, standing with the tailbone anxiously extended rearward and whining to the umpire that you see these days. At the same time, the great ones like Lajoie, Jackson, Collins, and Wagner weren't fools. They knew the peril of beanballs, for they dodged them every day. But they had the perfect balance, because of their feet-together stance, footwork, and weight distribution, to move clear of a ball aimed at their head, and this, in turn, gave them an advantage in boldly standing in there and striding forward with the precise right timing. Personally, I never was hit in the head in 11,429 times at bat. My cap bill was turned around on occasions, and two ribs were broken, but never was I skulled.

Still the day had to come when I couldn't be sure of my ability to duck in time. In 1925, my Tigers were putting my hitting theories to good use. They were looking the pitchers right in the eye and swinging boldly and they registered a league-leading .302 team average. In my case, I had several narrow escapes from fastballs that shaved my head. I knew I should have moved away from them with more alacrity. By the following February, I had to admit that my eyes weren't right.

Up at John Hopkins, the celebrated Dr. William Wilmer found that an accumulation of dust particles and other foreign matter I'd absorbed through the years had developed a pterygium condition, commonly called proud flesh. The surgical treatment included slitting the growth, burying one end of it with a very fine suture and allowing it to grow away from the pupil. The operation was simple enough. The aftermath wasn't.

When Dr. Wilmer finished, he swathed me in a head mask which left me in darkness. "After a few days, we'll take off the bandages," he said. "You don't have a thing to worry about."

Oh, no? I worried, and fretted, and wanted that mask off to assure myself that Dr. Wilmer's knife had done its job. When the mask came off, I held my breath. Everything looked blurry at first, then slowly began to clear.

A pert little nurse came in to medicate me.

"Not on your life," I told her. "I'm getting out of here."

"Why, you can't leave!" she gasped. "Your eyes need to be treated for several days."

"Lady, I have a ball team in spring training at Augusta, and I'm late now," I told her. "So just don't bother, and get me my clothes."

While she sped off to tell the doctor, I prepared to depart. Then I felt a slight twinge at the back of my eyes. Then a worse twinge. All at once, the hammers of hell began to pound behind my eyeballs. The pain was head-splitting, intolerable. I leaped up and ran into the hall and groped my way to the nurse's desk. My eyes were on fire.

"Get me that medicine fast!" I pleaded.

They rushed me first aid and I collapsed back into bed, the most co-operative patient from then on that Johns Hopkins could hope to have.

The recovery period was torture. Joining the Tigers in Augusta 14 days late for the 1926 training period, I wore smoked glasses. Any bright light or the smoke from a cigar or cigarette gave me fits.

To avoid such irritations, I'd go to bed at midday and pull up the covers. I dreaded the first fastball I had to face on a sunny day.

It came soon, since my job was to teach hitting, as well as perform it, and that first training pitch I hit over the right field fence for a home run.

However, the pitch had been grooved for me. Ahead was another long, weary season when I'd be exposed to the fire power of Lefty Grove, the young sensation of the Athletics, Herb Pennock and Urban Shocker of the Yanks, the still-dangerous Walter Johnson, and others almost as fast. I didn't like what I was thinking: that I could no longer afford to take chances. When a ballplayer can't take chances, he ought to quit.

There were other considerations. That past winter, seated at home before a blazing fireplace, I would find myself reviewing unusual plays I'd made. I'd forget that I was in my big armchair. My muscles would become rigid, I'd make the play all over again, and then fall back in my chair a trifle exhausted. The mental effort sapped some of my strength. I tried to keep from thinking of baseball, yet my mind seemed on it constantly. If I did manage to forget for a short time, some visitor or friend was bound to remind me. I was saturated with baseball talk. My Augusta home was a Mecca for sportswriters, pals, and old ballplayers. I was always on edge, irritable. People pestered me day and night. I knew that in Detroit I wouldn't be able to sit down and chat with a friend for ten minutes without being interrupted. And I couldn't get proper rest at home.

Temperamentally, I was always on edge, unable to take things easy, once the bell rang on Opening Day. I always figured every play to be close, and shot the works, which was both successful and a terrible physical drain. Playing the game to the hilt had—odd as it might seem—saved me from any permanently crippling injury. A burning, vying spirit makes you the attacker, and he who takes the attack is least vulnerable to injury. Meanwhile, though, the tension can't be escaped. I was like a steel spring. The slightest flaw will cause an overworked spring to fly apart, and then it is done for.

I could see a growing and dangerous flaw in me. I was thoroughly tired, no longer baseball-wedded, and I had to have a rest.

Nothing of the sort was possible. I'd contracted for $50,000 of Frank Navin's money to manage the Tigers again in '26. Had I known what the year was to bring, I'd have found some way to have hung up my spikes. I'd seen the seamy side of baseball before. The year 1926 topped all. It remains my most agonizing memory.

My old antagonist, Navin, with his usual craftiness, had set the stage a bit earlier. To commemorate my twentieth anniversary in a Bengal uniform, the fans of Detroit held a banquet at the Statler Hotel. Two combined banquet rooms overflowed with well-wishers. From the city of Detroit, paid for from the civic treasury by special appropriation, came the gift of a beautiful $1000 hall clock, and from many other sources I was given wonderful presents, each one something to treasure forever.

Naturally, the Detroit Baseball & Amusement Company was expected by the fans to make some sort of gesture on this occasion.

My contract with Navin called for $50,000, but with an unusual and secret arrangement involved. American League President Ban Johnson drew $50,000 pay per annum. As Navin had put it to me earlier, "It won't look right to Johnson if you're drawing as much as he does. All contracts must clear his office, so he'll be sure to spot it. So let's put you down for $40,000, and at the end of the season I'll pay you an additional and separate $10,000 in the form of a bonus."

While recognizing that this wasn't strictly orthodox procedure, and had some element of subterfuge, I saw no harm in it. Neither could I very well refuse. For three years, Navin and I had this private arrangement. Ruth, Speaker, Sisler, and other stars were paid less than $50,000 at the time. As long as I collected the full stipend, I saw no reason to make an issue of it.

Came the night of the testimonial banquet. Navin sidled up to me and said, "I have a check here for $10,000—the bonus that's due you at the end of the season. Would you mind if I presented it to you tonight as a gift from the team ownership?"

I gave Navin a long look. Of all the brazen, penurious acts this man had performed, this one took the cake. In a few weeks, when the season ended, Navin *owed* me that $10,000. He didn't even have the grace to blush.

"Do as you like, I'm the guest here," I replied, and walked away from him.

A few hours later, Navin stood up before more than 2000 people, delivered a ringing eulogy of me, announced that the Detroit ball club wished to honor me for twenty years of continuous service and with a grand flourish handed me the $10,000 check. That was my total "gift" from my ownership.

There was a roar of approval from the audience. Navin beamed down at the fans, the picture of an appreciative and generous boss.

The phony act soured my stomach, detracted from one of the finest evenings of my life and increased my urge to retire.

With the season's end, I had lined up a bear- and moose-hunting expedition into the Grand Teton country of Wyoming with Tris Speaker, Garland Buckeye, and a few other friends. Just about then, rumors reached my ears. A plot so evil in design that I could scarcely believe it was being hatched against me. The chief characters involved were Hubert (Dutch) Leonard, a former Detroit pitcher, Frank Navin, Ban Johnson, and Baseball Commissioner Kenesaw Mountain Landis. The shape of the plot began to take form when Navin announced in late October that I would "not be retained" as Detroit manager for 1927. He stated that the team was riddled with dissension—a totally untrue statement—and that I'd made some bad deals as manager.

Shades of the sale of Charley Grantham, the Paul Waner fiasco, the failure to sign Flint Rhem, to acquire Johnny Neun!

One month later, Tris Speaker, the idolized Gray Eagle, was let go as manager of the Cleveland Indians with another unacceptable explanation, and the fans buzzed with shock and curiosity. At this point, the wraps came off the real story.

It stunned the country at first. Then the man in the street, political leaders, judges, lawyers, business leaders, and sportswriters angrily rose up to denounce Leonard, Johnson, Navin, and Landis.

These four were accusing Tris Speaker, pitcher Joe Wood, and me of having fixed a Detroit-Cleveland game played seven years earlier, in 1919, and of having bet money on it.

In a letter to Ban Johnson, Leonard claimed to have witnessed a scene under the stands wherein it was arranged between Speaker and myself that the Indians would allow Detroit to win a late-season game; and that bets of a few hundred dollars had been made. Landis asked Leonard to come to Chicago, face Tris and me and make his accusation directly. Leonard refused. He hid out like a cur dog in his California home throughout the whole sickening affair.

Just the same, Landis, Johnson, and others made a two-month

witch hunt of the Leonard lie. While they dealt in hypocritical sensationalism, my honor hung in the balance.

I was in a rage. "I hope God will vent His curse upon me if I ever did one dishonest thing in baseball," I told the newsmen. "How can any sane man believe Leonard for even a second? Look at the facts."

First of all—who was Dutch Leonard? He was a left-handed pitcher with the Tigers whom I'd dropped from the roster in 1925 for good and sufficient reason. I had traded him to the minor league Vernon, California, club after Speaker, as Cleveland manager, had refused waivers on him. For this, Leonard openly had vowed revenge on both of us. Billy Evans, the well-known umpire-commentator, accurately pegged Leonard in his newspaper column in December 1926 as follows:

"Only a miserable thirst for vengeance actuated Leonard's attack on Cobb and Speaker. Balked in his efforts to stick in the big show, he decided to drag down with him those whom he believed had cast him aside. As a pitcher, he was gutless. He refused to face the tough teams and picked the soft spots. We umpires had no respect for Leonard, for he whined on every pitch called against him. It is a crime that men of the stature of Ty and Tris should be blackened by a man of this caliber with charges that every baseballer knows to be utterly false."

Next—the game we were supposed to have fixed, itself. The nation took a look at the record and saw this:

Played on September 25, 1919, the game was won by Detroit, 9–5. Leonard alleged that Speaker's Indians had agreed to let Detroit win. If so, would not Tris have gone easy with his bat and wouldn't I have been fed some easy pitches?

In actuality, Speaker had a field day. He drove outfielder Bobby Veach of our side to the fence for a first-inning fly-ball out, singled to center in the third inning, tripled to center in the fifth inning to score a run, and tripled to center in the seventh inning, later scoring.

My own performance was poor. I flied out once, grounded out three times and collected a single in five times at bat.

Smokey Joe Wood, the Cleveland pitcher also named as a conspirator by Leonard, and head coach at Yale University in 1926, certainly would have been involved, had a fix been on. Wood didn't even appear in the game.

243

Everything threw the lie back into Leonard's teeth. I was a man of independent means, able at this point to buy a major league club interest, had it been my desire. The paltry profit in betting on a game was the last thing I needed. Likewise Speaker, who was a man of substantial means. Moreover, Leonard claimed that only the three of us were involved. For any trio of men to attempt to rig a ball game is ridiculous on the face of it.

The cowardly Leonard continued to decline to come out of his California hiding. Commissioner Landis announced he would make a ruling on the case shortly. But weeks went by without relief. Without going into details, let me say here that many men high in baseball acted toward me in an eminently vicious and dishonorable way. After twenty-two years in baseball, I did not deserve to be treated as even a *possible* culprit. In my anguish, I issued a statement to all fans:

"Is there any decency left on earth? I am beginning to doubt it. I know there is no gratitude. Here I am, after a lifetime in the game of hard, desperate and honest work forced to stand accused without ever having a chance to face my accuser. It is enough to try one's faith.

"I am branded a gambler on a ball game in which my club took part. I have never in the 22 years I have been in baseball made a single bet on an American League game."

Engaging legal counsel, I fought back to force the stalling Landis to make his decision. I was particularly incensed at Navin's open insinuation that I had been "released" as manager because he put credence in the gambling accusation.

The New York *World* had something to say about this:

"Most damnable of all the charges against Cobb, Speaker and Joe Wood is that statement of Ban Johnson and Navin that they 'dropped' the two idols of baseball because they were 'thinking of Cobb's wonderful family, of Woods' two sons at Yale and of Speaker's aged mother.' Thus do the league officials, quite notorious as 'flannel mouths,' pronounce the men guilty of a crime that no one else accepts in the least or dignifies. That a man who fought so hard to win as Cobb could do anything crooked is unthinkable, except to those who are his sworn enemies."

The Cleveland *Press*, among many papers which editorialized in my behalf, said:

"Whoever is acquainted with Ty Cobb and is any judge of human character knows that he would do nothing to dishonor the sport in which he stands pre-eminent. All his career he has worn with unstained chivalry the greenest laurels of the baseball world. Always out to win, a flaming zealot in this regard, he has been upright in all dealings, has proved himself a good citizen as well as a great athlete, a man foursquare."

At my Augusta home, for weeks mailmen and Western Union boys arrived in a stream, delivering hundreds of letters and telegrams of support from big and small supporters everywhere. Will Rogers wrote in his national column: "I want the world to know that I stand with Ty and Tris. I've known them 15 years. If they are crooked, it shouldn't have taken them 20 years of hard work to get enough to retire on. If they had been selling out all these years, I would like to have seen them play when they weren't selling!"

Jurists from far and near urged me to file suit against Organized Baseball for defamation of character, among them being Charles Evans Hughes, later to become Chief Justice of the United States. All my rights had been mangled by Landis and Johnson. The investigation had been strictly *ex parte*, emanating from Leonard's side only, in violation of everything in the Bill of Rights and the Constitution.

Ban Johnson branded himself as such an aging, two-faced incompetent during the various hearings held on the matter that American League club owners repudiated their president, and voted him an enforced vacation. It was the end of Johnson's reign in the league. On January 8, 1927, he turned in his resignation. In one breath, he had announced stentoriously:

"When I found that two of our managers were not serving us properly, I had to let them go. Now isn't that proper? As long as I am president of the league, neither one of them will manage or play on our teams."

In the next, Johnson had performed a back-flip and said:

"I love Ty Cobb. I know he hasn't a crooked bone in his body, but the situation is such that he has to go."

Eventually, it became clear to all fans that behind the persecution was Ban Johnson's long hatred for both Speaker and myself, plus Navin's acute desire to slide out from under my $50,000-a-year contract, plus Kenesaw Landis's phobia for projecting himself into the limelight and making headlines. And one thing more. The Philadelphia *Daily News* made this quite clear in a page-one editorial:

"Landis and Ban Johnson wanted to make a grandstand play in which the two veteran stars were to be ruthlessly sacrificed to prove that baseball is honest. It was expected that this pure and holy stand would elicit tumultuous applause from the fans, whose interests—for publication, at least—were being guarded. But the dear old public, instead of cheering baseball's nobility of character, found its sense of common justice so outraged that it clamored for the blood of the accusers instead—both of the direct accusers and those whose failure to defend the players implied a belief in their guilt and a concurrence in their apparent banishment from Organized Ball."

If crookedness was the subject, I told the press, I could say a few things about fake turnstile counts and juggled ticket-counting as practiced by major league owners. I had certain proof that World Series tickets had been scalped through agents of club owners. A long, thoughtful silence fell over Organized Ball when that offer hit the headlines. Landis, on January 27, at last broke silence with:

"This is the Cobb-Speaker case. These players have not been, nor are they now, found guilty of fixing a ball game. By no decent system of justice could such finding be made. . . ."

Very decent of the judge. For weeks, I had been agonized by the scandal, sick of heart and convinced that my baseball bow-out would always be tainted with a question. I'll reveal something here never before told. That famous Landis "verdict" was dictated to him by attorneys representing Speaker and myself.

Well, we won. The verdict of guiltlessness and my full reinstatement left me in a position to file suit for any sum I cared to name, and to collect. And baseball was frightened out of its shoes that I would take that step. From all sides, owners and managers of National and American League teams came at me with offers calculated to get me back in uniform—and to circumvent a legal disaster.

"Come and play for us, Ty," they said to me, a forty-one-year-old ballplayer. "Name your own price."

I went into the pine woods of Georgia with my dogs and gun and thought how much finer is Nature than the human beast.

19

Vindication with Mr. Mack

If the men who dominated American League policy, and their watchdog, Kenesaw Mountain Landis, ever blundered into a hot box and got scorched, it was in the case I've just related. Exoneration of Speaker and myself wasn't enough to calm the anger of the public. Nor was the polite invitation to me—followed by pleas—to reconsider my announced retirement nearly enough to move the case off page one.

A Kansas City clergyman arose in the pulpit and delivered ten commandments for Landis which were loudly applauded. Among them were:

"Thou shalt not credit evidence in baseball which thou wouldst not consider on the judicial bench in a court of law.

"Thou shalt not make a mountain out of a molehill of allegation and back-yard gossip.

"Thou shalt not hold lightly the hard-earned reputations of men who have been the idols of the baseball world for twenty years.

"Thou shalt not allow thyself to be used as a cat's paw to pull hot chestnuts out of the baseball ashes for discharged and disgruntled players and ungrateful club owners."

A "baseball bloc" sprang up in the United States Congress. The members smote baseball owners hip and thigh. Senator Pat Harrison of Mississippi, Senator George Wharton Pepper of Pennsylvania, Senator James E. Watson of Indiana, Senator James Couzens of Michigan, and Senator William J. Harris of Georgia were almost as furious as yours truly, and said so in an official way:

247

"We find the action of Judge Landis and Ban Johnson outrageous, the act of publicity-seekers who were not only unjust, but dishonest. This country is not going to be satisfied with baseball's plea that it made a mistake about Ty Cobb and Tris Speaker, and kindly pardon its travesty on justice. They are entitled to legal redress for the great wrong done them, and we urge them to take this step."

On all sides, I was informed by experts that any defamation-of-character suit I might file against the game was preordained to succeed. The sum didn't matter. Any jury would find for me, even if the amount was $5,000,000.

What you've given your life to, you don't tear down. I could not sue baseball, maliciously wronged as I had been. But I gave no clue to the American League of my intentions. The owners could only mitigate their mistake, and show regret, by luring me back into uniform. And so they came at me from all sides with apologies and checkbooks in hand.

Clark Griffith, an old friend and Washington Senators owner, was the first in line. Griffith offered me $50,000 for 1927, just to show up at his park and appear on the field when I felt like it. Phil Ball, owner of the St. Louis Browns, rushed my old assistant, Dan Howley, to Georgia with a higher offer than that. Stock in the club? A percentage of the gate receipts? All I had to do was name it. The offers rolled in.

I yearned for retirement. I wanted to sit by a fire with my family and rest my very tired bones. As far back as 1925, I'd seriously contemplated calling it quits. Under Navin, there was no chance to bring in a pennant winner. Short of buying the Tigers—and they weren't for sale—I was hamstrung by his defeatist policies. In '25, we'd had a chance to bid for Tony (Poosh 'Em Up) Lazzeri, a San Francisco kid with fine promise. Navin had nixed it, Lazzeri went to the Yanks and made second-base history. It was the Lazzeri case, on top of many others, which convinced me that Detroit's future was hopeless. My dream of managing a champion, of seeing another World Series, had long since gone up in smoke.

Setting more individual records had lost its appeal for me. Only one motive remained which could make me change my mind about entering my twenty-third season in 1927.

Vindication.

I could not and would not leave the game with the slightest

248

cloud over my name. Even if I appeared in only one more major league game—on my own terms—I would have proved for the all-time record and generations of youngsters to come that baseball wanted Ty Cobb right to the last.

Weighed against this compelling thought was my inability any longer to take chances. My reflexes at age forty-one were not good enough to guarantee I wouldn't be beaned by a fastball. I thought of Ray Chapman, who'd been killed at the plate, and of others hit and badly hurt. My own cap had been turned around several times lately. Dwelling on this wasn't pleasant. I was torn in making the decision.

Right here, in February of '27, baseball played its ace. The owners knew how much I revered Mr. Connie Mack. And when he arrived in Augusta, and asked me to sign with his Philadelphia Athletics, I was hung on the well-known dilemma's horns.

"I don't want to play more ball, Mr. Mack," I said. "I've had enough. I gave all I had and you've seen the way I was treated. If some wise guy fan should mention 'fix' to me from the stands, I'd probably go right up there after him."

"There isn't a fan who isn't for you, Ty," said Mr. Mack. "We have a pennant contender in Philadelphia, and with you in the line-up, I just know we can win it."

Lean years had come to Mr. Mack. He'd won many a title in the old days, but now, at sixty-five, he hadn't managed a winner in a dozen seasons. Grand veteran that he was, the symbol of everything decent in the game, he deserved to be on top again if any man ever did. And he thought I could help him get there.

We rode together from Augusta to Philadelphia, where I was to be honored by the Philadelphia Sport Writers' Association at a banquet. I didn't tell Mr. Mack that even while I talked to him, the Brooklyn Dodgers had made me a most flattering offer.

"Ty, can I have your answer?" said Mr. Mack when the train was between Philadelphia and Washington. "As to money, just tell me what you want and it's a deal."

"I can't tell you," I replied. "I still haven't decided what to do."

He pulled a blank contract from his pocket and handed it to me. "Anything you put down goes," he said.

When I made no move, Mr. Mack named a figure, higher than any ever offered a player. The sum was $70,000 in salary and bonus, plus ten per cent of the receipts of all Athletics' exhibition games. I still said nothing.

Mr. Mack opened his mouth to raise the ante, and suddenly my mind was made up. "That's enough," I said. "I can't take any more of *your* money."

The next night, in the Crystal Room of the Hotel Adelphia in Philadelphia, I announced to an overflow crowd that I'd decided to cast my lot with the Athletics. It was a strange twist, indeed. I'd battled and feuded with the A's and their fans most of my career, needed police protection at Shibe Park and received a good dozen anonymous death-threats there. When I made my announcement, I wasn't sure how the local hotbloods would take it.

Well, they were very nice. A lot of them stood on chairs and cheered. In fact, the room was in bedlam for a good ten minutes.

"This is my year of vindication," I told them. "I regret that I am not ten years younger, but I promise you that I will give Mr. Mack the best I am physically able to do."

Speculation ran pretty high that "two master strategists" such as Mr. Mack and myself couldn't inhabit the same club and would be bound to clash. Mr. Mack's famous habit of shifting his outfielders about with a wave of his score card from the dugout was supposed to be something I wouldn't be able to take. "Cobb has always been a law unto himself. Poor, gentle Connie has caught himself a tiger, and an angry, old tiger at that, by the tail," one soothsayer wrote in a Philadelphia paper.

Once I'd been measured for the first uniform of my big league life that didn't read *Detroit*, and had reported to the A's at their Fort Myers, Florida, spring training camp, I had a long talk with Mr. Mack.

"I'm playing for you now," I said. "The years I managed don't mean a thing. I want to assure you that I will never refuse any order from you. Any time you want to move me in that outfield, just give me the sign. Even if my judgment on how to play a batter doesn't agree with yours, there never will be any contest between us. You're the boss."

The score card was used on me, many a time. I can testify—as to Mr. Mack's managerial ability—that not once did he err in moving me left or right, deeper or tighter. There were instances when I seriously questioned his thinking. But the man was uncanny. I've caught line drives again and again that I'd never come near if I hadn't obeyed Mr. Mack's order to shift position. I've picked them off the fence or hauled them in down the foul line when I was sure my manager had mispositioned me.

That was the start of the two happiest years I spent in baseball. I hadn't realized how much pleasure and peace of mind there could be in the game when you are closely associated with a manager and club owner who is both a baseball genius and a gentleman of great character.

Not that I suddenly became a pacific ballplayer in my old age. I still played just one way: to win. At forty-one, I felt Mr. Mack had $70,000-plus worth of work coming to him, if I could deliver it.

At a huge cost, Mr. Mack had assembled one of his finest combinations. We had young Jimmy Foxx at first base, Mickey Cochrane behind the plate, Al Simmons in center field, Max Bishop and Joe Boley as a keystone combination, and such pitchers as Lefty Grove, Rube Walberg, Howard Ehmke, Eddie Rommel, and wise old John Picus Quinn, who'd been around since 1909 with his spitball and still won 33 games for us in 1927-28 when past forty years of age. Tris Speaker and Eddie Collins joined us. We were a blend of youthful power and elderly baseball savvy. On paper, we figured to overthrow "Old Fox" Griffith's high-riding Washington Nats and the Yankees, defending champions.

We started slowly. I'll always be happy that I had something to do with snapping our tough luck and helping move the A's into the first division late in April. Up in Boston, we were trailing the Red Sox, 7-1, and Mr. Mack was cleaning off his bench in an effort to get some runs. That day he used eight infielders, five outfielders, three catchers, and four pitchers—20 men.

By the seventh inning, we still were behind, 7-3. I singled, stretched it to a double when the Red Sox outfield failed to hustle, and stole third. Bill Carrigan, managing Boston, relieved Whitey Wiltse and brought in Tony Welzer to pitch. I studied the situation. In some ways, it resembled the set-up in the World Series of 1909, when I stole home on pitcher Vic Willis of the Pirates.

Welzer—like Willis—had a batting rally to quell, and he wasn't thinking of me too specifically.

However, in 1909, we'd had a right-handed batter at the plate, his body screening the catcher's view of third base and somewhat blocking his movement. This time a left-hander was up. It gave catcher Slick Hartley of the Red Sox all the space between the plate and the incoming runner to make the play.

All the same, I decided to go. The A's needed something wild and woolly to happen to spark our budding rally.

As Welzer wound up, I kicked my legs into as much effort as they had left in them. Welzer almost broke his back checking his pitch and throwing to Hartley. My slide was a fallaway, with just a toe left for the catcher to touch, and Hartley pounced on it a split-second too late.

That made it 7–4, and we picked up two more runs the next frame, and went into the ninth tied, 8–8. With Jimmy Dykes on base, I doubled him home. We had the game won, 9–8, if we could stop the Bosox in their half of the ninth.

Alertness beats sheer speed in baseball, as I've preached to young players earlier in this book. With one out, the Bosox got a man, Baby Doll Jacobson, on first base. Phil Todt, a light-hitting infielder, came up. I crept in dangerously close behind Jimmy Foxx at first base. Todt, as I'd hoped, lined a low looper over Foxx's head.

Catching it on the dead run, I kept going to touch first base and double up Jacobson, ending the game.

That was my last steal of home, my last unassisted double play, in a big league game.

Well, it felt mighty good. The old warhorse seemed to be able to run and catch and hit with some remaining usefulness. In a four-game series with the Browns and White Sox, I hit for a .722 average. After 20-odd games, the major league batting-fielding race looked like this:

	AB	H	Pct.	Fielding
Hornsby, Giants	52	24	.462	.990
Cobb, Athletics	62	25	.403	1.000
Ruth, Yankees	48	15	.313	.962
Speaker, Senators	48	14	.292	1.000

I entertained no fond hopes of adding another batting title to the 12 I held, not at my age, and with slugging youngsters such as Harry Heilmann, Lou Gehrig, Al Simmons, and Heinie Manush in the league. My ambition was to finish well up there, add what spark I could to the A's attack and lend Mr. Mack some help with his younger talent. I picked out Al Simmons as a boy who could use some advice. In spring training, he'd been sadly out of shape, overweight.

"How about doing some running with the old man?" I said to Al.

"Okay," said Simmons. I guess he figured that I couldn't set too hot a pace at my age.

I ran him until his tongue hung out. We zigzagged, trotted, walked, galloped and trotted for miles around the park. Al sweated bucketfuls, but firmed up nicely, and worked as hard on his hitting. There were some who wanted to change Simmons' odd foot-in-the-bucket stance. "Leave him alone," I argued. "Even if he hits them standing on his ear, don't ever monkey with that swing."

A fault common to many hard-pressing hitters afflicted Al. I noticed that he became discouraged if he failed to hit in his first two times at the plate. He needed a mathematics lesson.

"If you are .000 the first two times up, you still have two chances left," I pointed out. "It's simple to see that you can still be a .500 hitter in that game. That is, if you bear down extra hard on those remaining chances."

Simmons stuck to his style, took a few other tips from me, and improved his batting mark 49 points between 1926–27, averaging .392 to Harry Heilmann's league-leading .398. Since both were my pupils, and finished one-two, I felt that my theories on batting remained as valid in the jack-rabbit-ball era as they seemed to be in 1906. I still feel that way about it.

Joe Williams, describing an Athletics-Yankee game of the 1927 season, commented on this same point:

"History was made at Yankee Stadium yesterday. Ty Cobb went around the bases in the sixth inning. It marked the 2087th time he had circled the bags, but more enlightening was the method he used—old-fashioned stuff scorned in the Era of Ruth.

"He laid down a bunt, perfectly, which caught Third Baseman Joe Dugan totally by surprise. Cobb slid into first, beating Dugan's hasty throw. How long since you've seen a first base slide?

"Next, when Hale hit a short rap to center field, and when anyone else would have stopped at second, Cobb pumped his aged legs and went for third. Comb's throw to Dugan had him out cold. Locating the ball with a quick glance over his shoulder, Cobb slid left, then contorted himself to the right. There was a geyser of dust and when it cleared, he was seen to have half-smothered the throw with his body, and as Dugan scrambled for the ball, Cobb was up and dusting himself off.

"The whole sequence was beautiful to see, a subtle, forgotten heritage from the romantic past."

No one will know, until now, how much it cost me to suit up each day and match myself against the Harleys, Welzers, and Dugans. By midseason, I was playing on a fast-dwindling reserve. After a game, I'd go directly to my hotel bed, have dinner served there, and relax with some light reading. And I'd stay in that bed until almost noon the next day. I would breakfast in bed, entertain from my bed, and handle my outside business affairs from a bedside telephone. Only when it was time to leave for the park would I rise and dress. Often, before a game I'd turn on a portable phonograph and for thirty minutes relax to Fritz Kreisler's music.

When a game ended, I didn't make the mistake of so many moderns, who fail to realize they are cutting short their playing span. As it goes now, players don't analyze the strain they put on their nervous systems. Entering the clubhouse, they're all sweated up. They dash in, undress, shower, dress, and rush home to the wife and children or to an uptown date. They'll be on a TV show within 45 minutes of playing nine tough innings or conferring with their business manager.

As I used to tell Joe DiMaggio (who could have lasted much longer), "Joe, when you reach the clubhouse, sit down in uniform and light a cigarette. Let the other boys dash for the showers. Let them go—there'll always be soap and hot water left. When the others are all through, take your shower. After that, sit down or lie down and cool out gradually. Take half an hour. Then get dressed and go to your hotel. But don't head for the dining room. Stretch out and read the evening paper or watch TV or simply look out the window for an hour. By that time, your stomach is ready for food. Keep doing this and you'll avoid nervous indigestion, colds, and a lot of other ailments."

There you have it: a small thing, it might seem, but one of the big secrets to my staying power in baseball.

Yes, I know about night baseball, which throws schedules all out of whack. All the more reason the professional athlete should devise ways and means to adjust his body to and from the strain he places on it each day.

Religiously, I had saved myself over two decades, which enabled me to finish with my head up, and not as a hollow mockery of a ballplayer. I see too many once fine players who finish tragically when only in their early thirties.

The Athletics played the Red Sox on May 5 of 1927, a game I won't soon forget. Talk about a riot—this one was a humdinger, with me in the middle of it. In the ninth inning, I tied the score with a long drive near the foul line and over the fence. The ball was fair when it left the park, but Red Ormsby, the plate umpire, ruled that it was foul and called me back from my home run. I jumped all over him. So did Al Simmons. It was such a palpably awful ruling that we jostled Ormsby around. The fans exploded. Bottles and debris filled the air. For almost 15 minutes, there was general hell to pay. Both Simmons and I were indefinitely suspended by the league office.

Down in Detroit, where I hadn't appeared since leaving a Tiger uniform, elaborate plans were afoot for a welcome-home ceremony. The Motor City fans immediately got busy with petitions, demanding that I be reinstated. They raised such a hubbub that Simmons and I were allowed to play in Detroit on May 10.

The people of Detroit did themselves proud, and made me tremendously welcome. Even though I was in an enemy suit, they cheered me in the streets. For a Tuesday game, 35,000 showed up at Navin Field. Ropes had to be strung to handle the overflow outfield crowd. I walked to the ropes and shook hands with as many of the fans as I could reach and thanked them for their loyalty and good wishes.

"Lord bless you, Ty. We never had a doubt about you," one old fellow said to me emotionally.

It was the only reference to the unfortunate episode of 1926 that ever was tossed my way. I am proud of the fact that *not once* during my final two seasons did anyone ever throw at me any word regarding Dutch Leonard's plot to discredit me. The public simply would not dignify it by any mention that it had happened.

We won that day, 6–3, behind Lefty Grove. My double in the

opening inning drove in two runs, which capped a perfect return to the old stamping ground.

Miller Huggins, the pint-size Yankee manager, had a lot to do with New York finally beating us out for the '27 pennant. There was one afternoon when we were two runs behind, but had filled the bases. I was the runner on first, with Eddie Collins running at second, and Sammy Hale the runner at third. The batter hit a high foul. Nig Grabowski, the Yankee catcher, discarded his mask, tore after the ball and caught it on the lip of the Athletics' dugout. At full tilt, he tripped over a low iron railing and, still holding the ball, plunged to a concrete staircase below. As his spikes flashed and he dropped from sight, a player yelled, "My God, he's killed!"

Everyone was horrified. Both benches were up and rushing to the scene.

Not Collins, Cobb, and Hale. Accustomed all our life to making every break work for us, we were off and running. We tagged our bases, lit out and, sensing that home plate wouldn't be protected, raced for paydirt during the confusion. Hale scored. Collins scored. And as I came steaming past third, Grabowski shoved his battered head above the steps. His arm was cocked back and then his face fell.

All his fellow Yanks were so excited that no one was at the plate to receive his throw. So I scored, too—the third run in on a pop foul.

Huggins went into action. He calmly took umpire Tom Connolly aside and said, "The run from third is legitimate and scores. But, Tom, you can't allow Collins and Cobb to score. You see, Grabowski was interfered with."

"What?" I hollered. "Why, he fell head first! The players went down there and pulled him back to the top. They rescued him, that's what!"

Huggins shook his head. "Yes, and in so doing, they blocked, impeded, harried, and bothered him until he was unable to execute the play. You, Cobb, and Collins must go back to your base."

The little devil stood there, so confidently, that Connolly scratched his head and looked uncertain.

"But Grabowski had no play at home!" I argued. "There was no one to take a throw, if he could have made one."

Huggins kept on fast-talking, intrigued Connolly and pried a ruling from him that Collins and Hale had scored, but that I had to return to third base.

I should mention that I represented the winning run. The ruling left the score at 8–8, and, wouldn't you guess it, the Yankees went on in extra innings to win.

Little Hug was a fast thinker.

I had a little fun with the Bambino about this time that I forgot to mention in earlier comments on Ruth. Babe came to bat, swaggering, and waved his handkerchief at our outfielders to move back. He took three swings powerful enough to cause a windstorm and struck out. When I came up next, I pulled the same stunt with a handkerchief. I waved the boys back. Then I bunted, beat it out, and stole second and third. I can't repeat what the Yankees said to me.

The year 1927 remains green and treasured in my memory. While the Athletics finished second, I had the feeling that my friend, Mr. Mack, was closing in on another championship, which he did not once, but three times, in '29, '30, and '31. My personal performance in 1927 was satisfactory: a matter of 175 hits in 134 games, 104 runs scored and another 93 driven in for a .357 average. At forty-one, I could still leg it a bit, if 22 stolen bases was any evidence.

Had we won the flag, an added bonus Mr. Mack had guaranteed me would have brought my earnings close to $100,000. As it stood, the peonage system had been broken. My salary remained an incontestable reminder to other club owners that a new era had arrived for their employees. From now on, the ownership had to pay for what it got. In 1928, Ruth nailed down that point with an $80,000 contract. The day when contracts were dictated by the front office, and not negotiated, was over.

I felt vindicated, in every way.

20

Peace at Last

Biographers of Victor Hugo claim that the French people went down on their knees and thanked God that the poet, philosopher, and dramatist died before he lived long enough to make a fool of himself.

I've been a student of the classics all my life. And although Hugo was far out of my league, maybe I was thinking along those lines the evening of September 17, 1928. Because that day I finally did it.

The newspaper boys covering the Athletics gathered in my hotel room, where I handed each of them a statement:

"Never again, after the finish of the present pennant race, will I be an active player in the game to which I have devoted 24 seasons of what for me was hard labor. I make this announcement today because of the many inquiries constantly coming to me concerning my future plans.

"Friends have urged me to try it one more season so that I could round out a quarter century of continuous service in the American League, but I prefer to retire while there still may remain some base hits in my bat. Baseball is the greatest game in the world. I owe all that I possess in the way of worldly goods to this game. For each week, month, and year of my career, I have felt a deep sense of responsibility to the grand old national sport that has been everything to me.

"I will not reconsider. This is final."

Both my critics and my fans had trouble believing it, and they wagged their heads wisely. But they were wrong. Actually, I had appeared for the last time six days earlier, September 11, at Yankee Stadium. Acting as a pinch-hitter for Jimmy Dykes, I took the last of what must have been something like 60,000 swings at a stitched ball. My life totals read 3033 games, 11,429 at-bats, 4191 hits, 2244 runs, 6294 put-outs, 406 assists, 274 errors, 892 stolen bases, and a career hitting average of .367. It seemed enough to me.

That last season of 1928, which I played for Mr. Mack mostly from a sense of duty, was hellishly hard. My batting eye was almost as dependable as ever, but the legs wouldn't carry me around the garden with speed and timing. Old wounds ached constantly. I literally had to grit my teeth and force myself to run when the chance arose to bunt and beat it out or stretch a single into a double. Luckily, I got out with no serious injuries and with a final season's average of .323 that kept my string of .300-hitting seasons intact back to 1906.

I had feared it would be hard to quit, but found that it wasn't. I only regretted I hadn't made the move four or five years sooner. When the next spring arrived, and the boys left for the training camps, I grew a bit restless. It didn't seem exactly right that I wasn't going along. Once or twice I had to pinch myself to make sure it wasn't a mistake, but it quickly wore off. You're free, I told myself. For the first time since you were eighteen, you can go anywhere and do anything you like.

When I left baseball, I left so fast I didn't even bother to pick up the uniform I'd worn in my last game, a memento I later regretted losing.

In early '29, with my family, I was embarking on the U.S.S. *Roosevelt* for a long vacation in Europe. En route, I stopped in Philadelphia to wish the Athletics luck in the season ahead. As I entered the clubhouse, the press gate custodian, George Brand, grabbed my hand.

"Ty, I've been saving something for you. I talked Mr. Mack out of it last winter."

George handed me my A's uniform. It looked good to me—especially good, since I didn't have to climb into it ever again.

Not long later, I got off a train in the picturesque town of Keith on the Scottish coastland. I'd seen half the museums in Europe and now I was gratifying an urge I'd had for fifteen years. I inquired where I might find Sir Isaac Sharpe, the world-famous trainer of hunting dogs.

The Scot who'd been sent to meet me at the depot by Sir Isaac said, "He'd have been here to greet you in person, sir, but he had to appear at a bazaar at the kirk tonight."

"Could I attend the bazaar?" I asked.

The Scot didn't mind. "If you like, sir."

The weather was down close to freezing, and when we reached the kirk, I found out that the natives didn't bother to heat their meeting places with a thought to tourists. The church was colder than any umpire's heart. Even in a heavy topcoat, I was shivering.

And up walked a little Scottish lass, selling ice cream!

I found Sir Isaac, who was to guide me on a bird-hunting expedition on the celebrated Keith moors, operating a booth which featured displays of plucked wildfowl—partridge, grouse, and pheasant. We shook hands and I suggested that maybe we could move elsewhere and wrap ourselves around a hot toddy.

"Oh, I can't, Mr. Cobb, not until I sell out my birds," said Sir Isaac. "It's for charity."

Only one thing to do. I bought out the whole display and sent the fowl to local hospitals, and, on the way to a warm pub with Sir Isaac, relieved the little girl of her ice-cream stock.

The shooting was a far cry from the way we did it in the red clay hills of Georgia, but it was the big league of upland bird hunting, a pilgrimage place for the world's finest shotgun artists. The challenge of trying my luck here had been gnawing at me since I was a young man. Something like 450 pointers and setters were under Sir Isaac's training. The highly skilled dogs worked out ahead of us through the heather in zones, never crossing over a hedgerow or rock fence from the area assigned them. We had 80,000 acres of the finest birdland anywhere to explore.

Keith was like a whiff of Heaven to a worn-out ballplayer.

No one asked me if I could shoot, but the Scots kept a sharp eye my way when the first covey was flushed. We were shooting behind the butts—a fixed position, with beaters sending the birds your way, which gave the grouse one hell of a start. They bulleted past and I knocked down two with my first shot.

Down in north Georgia, where I'd hunted quail from the time I was knee high to a hedgehog, the birds are fast, too.

Sir Isaac grunted. "I see you're canny enough," said he. "I'll just get back home, because my hip is hurting me, and you enjoy the shoot."

It was as good a compliment as any I'd had from a stadium crowd.

And more welcome, in a way. For all the time I was in Keith, not a lad or a lassie mentioned the word baseball.

21

The Greatest in the Game—
As I Knew Them

One June day of 1939 at Cooperstown, New York, while we were dedicating the National Baseball Hall of Fame and Museum, a group composed of Charley Gehringer, Napoleon Lajoie, Rogers Hornsby, and Eddie Collins gathered to one side for some old-fashioned fanning.

"Since when," said Casey Stengel, "did you ever see four second basemen as good as those fellas collected in one spot?"

I never had. I never would see their like if I lived to be two hundred.

Of the four, I'll take Eddie Collins, hands-down, as my All-Time, All-Star middle baseman. Lajoie was the picture player and a fierce rival of mine; Gehringer, whom I managed and coached, was a phenom; Hornsby batted .358, lifetime, the No. 2 average in the books. None of them quite reached Collins' class, and I'll tell you why.

Hornsby couldn't go in and out to bag those pop flies. He needed help from the shortstop and first baseman, a fatal weakness. Lajoie and Gehringer, great as they were, didn't match Edward Trowbridge Collins as a lightning thinker, strategist, and leader. He was a manager on the field at all times.

I remember the 1917 World Series—John McGraw's Giants against the White Sox. My job was to cover the Series as a reporter—writing

262

my own stuff, incidentally, and not having it composed for me by a professional ghost.

Collins broke up that Series with one of the most heads-up plays I ever watched.

In the sixth game, Eddie singled and worked his way around to third. Joe Jackson was safe at first on an error. Happy Felsch of the Sox hit straight back to Pitcher Rube Benton on the mound. Benton threw to Heinie Zimmerman at third, hanging up Collins between the bag and home plate. Although in a trap, Collins stayed cold as ice. He ducked back and forth between Bill Rariden, the Giants' catcher, and Zimmerman, manipulating a prolonged run-down which would give Jackson and Felsch a chance to advance.

Now, picture the scene: Rariden decided to come up the line and shorten the hotbox Collins was in. The instant he did that, and tossed to Zimmerman, Collins made a dash for home. For all the while he was trapped between Zimmerman and the catcher, watching the ball and the enemy at once, Eddie also was keeping a whole section of the diamond under surveillance. Who was protecting the plate when Rariden moved up the line? Holke, the Giant first baseman? Benton, the pitcher? One of them should have covered, but instead they stood around gawking at the play.

And that's when Collins ran right around Rariden.

What an opportunist he was! Heinie Zimmerman has unfairly gone down in history as author of a classic "bonehead" World Series play, because after taking Rariden's toss, he chased Collins all the way home—in a comically futile attempt to catch and tag him. Zim wasn't the goat, at all. Pin those horns for all time on the men who should wear them: Benton, who was closest to the play, and Holke.

"Who the hell should I have thrown the ball to—Klem?" Zim used to say of the play. Bil Klem was the plate umpire.

Eddie Collins I admire deeply. He broke into major league baseball in 1907 and lasted through 1930—twenty-four years. One of a small handful to make 3000 lifetime hits. In fact, only Hans Wagner, Tris Speaker, and myself collected more. Master of the sacrifice hit with a total of 514—the American League record. Scoffed at home runs— some seasons didn't hit even one over the fence. But look at that lifetime average—.333—and those World Series clutch averages of .429, .409, and .421.

Sloppy and stupid playing drove Eddie wild. He'd blast the team-mate who gave up easy. He wasn't flashy, himself. "He looks like your Aunt Minnie out there," we'd say, "but since when did a ball get past him?" He was an uncanny diagnostician and probably suppressed more potential hit-and-runs, double steals, and squeeze plays than any infielder who ever lived.

That's my second baseman on my All-Star team—the fellow who played his heart out with the White Sox in the 1919 World Series. Eddie was field captain. He kept interrupting the Series games to rally his fielders, consult with his pitchers, to call time and huddle with his catcher, Ray Schalk. He was puzzled that such a great team couldn't make the plays.

Of course, that was the "Black Sox" team which threw the Series to Cincinnati. It half-broke Eddie Collins' heart when he found out what had happened all around him.

In a moment, I'll tell you why Ray Schalk, who was trying as hard to win as Collins, also belongs on any all-time aggregation.

But first I want to finish picking my All-Star infield.

At first base, not Hal Chase, not Lou Gehrig, not Bill Terry, not Jimmy Foxx. My man is George Sisler. His reflexes were unbelievable. Sisler, a pitcher good enough to beat Walter Johnson in his early days, switched to first base and hit a mere .420 one season. Anyone around doing that today? Anyone who can lead his league six times in assists?

Do you know who collected the most base hits in a single season of any player in the majors? My man, Sisler, in 1920 with 257. Despite chronic eye trouble and other ailments, he was the acme of alertness, determination, and shrewdness. In 1922, he was out to break a record hitting streak of mine—40 straight games—when he tore an arm muscle so badly that he could only play one-handed. Sisler couldn't lift his right hand high enough to catch any ball thrown to him above the waist. Even then, he had to lift his gloved hand with his other hand. "Throw the ball to me low, boys," he ordered the St. Louis Browns.

What did he do? He didn't make an error in the next few games, and, swinging almost one-handed, broke my record by hitting safely in games No. 40 and 41.

Sisler—life average .344. The finest first baseman of them all.

At shortstop, no discussion is necessary. Phil Rizzuto, a throwback

264

EDDIE COLLINS was a manager on the field—I rate him ahead of all other second basemen.

I COULDN'T HIT this fellow, the Big Train, until I discovered his one "weakness," a heart as big as all outdoors. I grew to love Walter Johnson, the greatest of pitchers.

STYLIST, tremendous hitter who topped .400 twice, crafty as they ever come—my all-time first baseman, George Sisler.

THE BABE's hitting a single here, something he did very well, and often, despite his home run reputation.

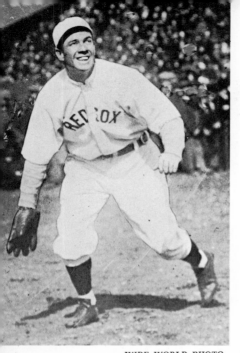

Two SHOTS of Tris Speaker, as a youngste[r]
and as a veteran. "Spoke" topped all de[-]
fensive outfielders and averaged .344 ove[r]
22 years with tricks they never heard o[f]
today.

—I didn't once call Hans Wagner a "krauthead" and have my lip split by him the World Series. That's a fabrication. Honus was a block of granite. You didn't around with him.

IF CHRISTY MATHEWSON was around today, the home-run-crazy boys would get only a batful of ozone. Matty would tie them in knots with his control and stuff. As related here, I saw Matty doomed to die.

GETTYSBURG EDDIE PLANK could doctor a ball until it came dancing up there like a butterfly. Won 325 games.

ᴅɴ'ᴛ ꜱᴇᴇ much of National League Cy
ng, who developed his iron arm splitting
. And I'm glad of it. Cy lasted from 1890
ough 1911 and won 510 games, the all-
e record.

ᴛ ꜱᴏ ᴅᴜʀᴀʙʟᴇ as some, Big Ed Walsh won
games in 1908. King of the wet-ball
ᴏwers. And handsome, too.

OLD PETE ALEXANDER: they said liquor lowered his amazing pitching ability, but they didn't know what really ailed him. Pete was an epileptic, suffered hell on the field.

THE MAN I revered; the man under whom I experienced my two happiest seasons in baseball—Mr. Mack.

type with the Yankees, has been one of the few modern stars to excite my admiration, and there have been others of real class. Luke Appling and Rabbit Maranville score high on longevity. None ever approached Honus Wagner. Weighing past 200 pounds with gorilla arms that grabbed everything, he also was fast enough to lead his league in stolen bases for five years. Led the NL in batting eight times. Played ball in an easygoing manner, unless riled—then look out!

Wagner towers above all other shortstops.

Thus far, I have given you two college men—Collins (Columbia) and Sisler (Michigan)—and a coal-mine laborer, Wagner, who had no schooling. Two were of moderate stature, one a block of granite. One was on the cocky side—Collins; Sisler was quiet and reserved; Wagner was as sweet-natured as a man can be. Collins and Sisler became respected managers of teams. Wagner tried managing, and lasted exactly three days. Honus just couldn't organize things and get tough.

That's baseball. It takes all types to create the records fans marvel at today.

At third base, I take Pie Traynor over many another great one, including Buck Weaver and Jimmy Collins. While it's true that Collins invented lasting techniques for handling bunts and covering territory, Traynor had the better hands and outhit Collins by a wide margin. The Pie Man was a .300-or-better hitter in ten seasons and holds the record for assists and put-outs by a third baseman.

My outfield is Joe Jackson—the greatest natural hitter I ever saw—Babe Ruth, and Tris Speaker. Jackson didn't play by the rules, he played instinctively. He always knew what to do even though he didn't know why it was the right thing to do.

They had a tough time roping Shoeless Joe. Mr. Connie Mack bought him in 1906 for the lavish sum of $325 from the Greenville club of the Carolina Association. One of Mr. Mack's aides escorted Shoeless Joe aboard the first train he'd ever ridden. Next morning, Joe had disappeared from the train.

"They found me back home," Joe used to tell us. "I jest jumped off'n that rattler and beat my way home best way I could. Say, I was skeered of all the noise!"

They recaptured Joe, taught him poise, and he began to wear out the boards on the fences. Babe Ruth patterned his form after Joe. I learned a lot, watching him. Year after year I had Jackson to beat for the bat championship. I honestly believe that with that wonderful, fluid swing of his—batting against the lively ball—that Joe Jackson would hit .450 today.

Long after we were retired, around 1946, I was motoring through Greenville, South Carolina, with Grantland Rice. We'd been to the Masters Golf Tournament at Augusta, and were headed north. I told Grant, "I've got an old friend in this town. Let's look him up."

We asked a policeman where Joe Jackson might be, and found him working in a small liquor store on a side street. I hadn't seen Joe in many years. He stared at me in what seemed to be a blank way.

"How's business?" I inquired, acting like a customer.

"Fine, sir," said Joe, turning his back to arrange some merchandise on the shelf.

"Don't you know me, you old so-and-so?" I said.

Joe spun around and grinned all over his face. "Sure! But I didn't think you knew me after all these years. I didn't want to embarrass you or nothin'.'"

I shook his hand. "Joe, I'll tell you how well I remember you," I said. "Whenever I got the idea I was a good hitter, I'd stop and take a good look at you. Then I knew I could stand some improvement. I don't think I ever saw a more perfect swing than yours."

Old Joe, who died four years later, seemed pleased at my remark.

On my All-Time team, I want two catchers, and they are Ray Schalk and Mickey Cochrane. I have to give Bill Dickey almost an equal nod here. All three, tremendous handlers of pitchers, students of batters, and directors of the defense. If Schalk had hit a bit higher, I would have to rank him in a class by himself. In one three-year stretch, Ray caught the phenomenal number of 404 games. Cochrane caught 120 or more games for ten years. Dickey caught 400 in three straight Yankee seasons.

It helps tremendously to have a first-flight catcher who can work the bulk of the games, squatted down there, absorbing all sorts of punishment from foul balls, flying spikes, loose bats, and pitches that break strangely.

Cochrane was just about as versatile as Schalk. He proved it by catching the varying deliveries of knuckle-baller Ed Rommel, left-hander Rube Waddell, Tommy Bridges, a curve-baller who never won 20 games until Mickey caught him, and Lefty Grove, all speed and temperament.

Mickey suffered one of the worst skull fractures in baseball history in 1937. He should have died, but pulled through. It ended a glorious career far short of its expectancy.

For my pitching staff, I want the greatest sextet ever assembled. Four right-handers, two left-handers.

We start with Christy Mathewson, of course. I've covered Matty in another chapter, so let it suffice that the Mathewson Memorial Gateway leads to the campus of Bucknell University, his alma mater, and that at Cooperstown stands a bust and plaque for a pitcher who was simply sublime.

Walter Johnson and Matty stand about on a par with me. Walter had the greater speed, Matty as much control as Johnson, and a breaking pitch that left batters helpless.

I knew Walter well, although he dueled against me with the Washington club. One night in Detroit, the two of us were zipping along in my car when an officer of the law overhauled us. "Speeding, eh?" said he.

We admitted we had been in excess of the limits.

"It's Cobb, isn't it?" said the cop, staring at me.

"And this is Walter Johnson," said I. "He's pitching tomorrow."

The officer pondered. "Tell you what," said he. "If you'll hit a couple of home runs off Johnson tomorrow, I'll forget about writing you a ticket."

"Done," said I.

Walter didn't pitch the next day, but he kidded me all evening about my boast. So next day, off another Washington pitcher, I got those two homers. Anything to square a traffic tag.

If Walter had been working, I'd probably have gone to the lock-up. In some 60-odd games against him, I had one homer and three triples. Mostly, you tried desperately to get some part of the bat against Johnson's flame ball and beat it out for a single.

Johnson, incidentally, had the most commendable vocabulary of any ballplayer I've known. A true gentleman, he never learned to cuss. When irritated, he'd say, "Goodness gracious!" When really red-eyed, Walter pulled out all the stops. "Goodness gracious—*animal!*" he'd explode. That was Walter's total lexicon of swear words.

In a game, Johnson would throw you two fastballs that scorched your uniform for two strikes, and then would want to throw his "curve," just for the variety of it. My old friend, Muddy Ruel, who was Walter's catcher, wouldn't have the gumption to argue with him after handling his blazing fast one. Muddy would let him have his way, and in would come the "curve." It had just a wrinkle on it. Batters would wait for that one—it was just about their sole chance to touch the Big Train.

"You know, Ty," Muddy tells me, "in the 1924 World Series, Bill Dinneen, the umpire, confessed to me that Walter was so fast that he was doing some lively guessing on where the ball crossed or didn't cross the plate. That's a big admission for an umpire. I didn't tell Bill to get his eyes open. I was having enough trouble following Walter's speed, myself."

Johnson was the fastest who ever lived. This I vouch for.

For durability and work-horse qualities on our staff of right-handers, I want Ed Walsh. His manager on the White Sox, Fielder Jones, had a saying:

"Walsh today, tomorrow and maybe twice on Sunday."

In 1908, Big Ed pitched 42 complete games, 464 innings and won 40 games, records which look greater with every passing year. He won 45.4 per cent of his team's 88 victories in '08 singlehandedly holding Chicago in the pennant race until the final day of the season, when my Detroit team edged out the Sox. In the last nine games the Sox played, Walsh pitched seven times. And won six of them, losing only to Addie Joss's perfect game by a score of 1–0. What a man he was. King of the spitball.

Old Pete Alexander my fourth right-hander, was epileptic through his last ten years of pitching. Most fans don't know that. Sometimes a fit would strike him on the mound. Pete carried a bottle of spirits of ammonia with him. When the seizure came, he'd have to be helped off the field—several times he was carried off—and stretched out in the locker room. Pete would take a whiff of the ammonia, struggle to get control of himself, and head right back out there and resume pitching.

He drank too much liquor, true. But many a time when the fans saw him staggering, Pete was undergoing the torment of epilepsy.

With all that, plus deafness in one ear, Pete won 373 games in his time. Only Walter Johnson and Cy Young did better. Pete's

90 shutouts are second only to Johnson's mark. There isn't a pitcher around today who could equal Pete's efficiency on the hill —or guts. One day for the Phillies, Pete beat the Cardinals in the first game of a double-header. Pat Moran, his manager, told him, "We're going to miss our train out of town, I'm afraid."

"Let me pitch the second game," said Pete.

He did, and won it by a shutout in 58 minutes flat and the Phillies caught their train.

In 1916, he beat Cincinnati, 7–3, in the opener of a twin bill, then shut them out in the second game. As a rookie, he won 28 games, the all-time record. At the age of forty, he won 21 games. There's never been anyone to top Grover Cleveland Alexander for clutch-pitching and drama.

My All-Time left-handers are Eddie Plank and Lefty Grove. Plank won 325 games, Grove 300. I batted against Plank something like 125 times and, believe me, he was tough. Gettysburg Eddie was a thin, fidgety type, an artist at exasperating hitters to the point of braining him. He'd fuss and stall on the mound, hitching his belt, pawing the ground, fiddling around until you were all knotted up— then he'd whip that big curve in there. I hated to see Plank out there as much as any man I ever faced.

Lefty Grove hated to lose as much as I did. That partly accounts for the fact that he still won 300 games after being delayed in the minors for five years when he was well ready for the big league. Grove was one of the four or five fastest pitchers who ever lived, right around the top for competitive zeal and the fellow who in 1931 won 31 games and lost four—a mark that may never be beaten.

That's my line-up, composed entirely of old-timers. It could whip any group you could select from the past twenty-five years of base-ball, without trouble. For one reason, Mathewson, Johnson, Alexander, and the others wouldn't pitch home-run balls the way they're cheaply served today. With their exquisite control, little good enough to tag for four bases would be thrown up there. The .400 hitters in my line-up would take care of the attack nicely—they and my hit-run and sacrifice experts. My defense would pull plays no longer seen. Even if base-running hadn't almost vanished as a fine art, Collins, Wagner, Sisler, and Traynor would be more than capable of stopping the moderns from stealing and taking extra bases. In short, I believe that a line-up featuring such as Bob Feller,

Joe DiMaggio, Stan Musial, Mickey Mantle, Ted Williams, Willie Mays and Duke Snider would stand little show with the men of my era.

The manager of this All-Time aggregation certainly would have a soft berth, but he'd have to be able to cope with the strategy of the opposition leader, handle his stars with understanding and be a thorough master of the old-time game. My selection is Mr. Connie Mack.

He dueled for years with the keenest minds that ever plotted ways to win games. George Stallings, for instance.

That fellow Stallings would make mincemeat of a lot of modern-day managers. In 1914, he lifted a Boston Braves team that was in eighth place in mid-July to a pennant in September. Then he looked for a way to keep his boys on fire through the World Series against Mr. Mack's Athletics.

One phone call, that probably hasn't been revealed before this, did it.

Stallings told his veteran infielder, Johnny (Crab) Evers to phone Mr. Mack from the clubhouse, making sure his players overheard the conversation. Johnny opened the conversation with a pleasantry or two, then said:

"Mr. Mack, we'd like to work out tomorrow. Can we make some arrangements to use your field?"

Evers almost dropped the phone at what was coming over the wire.

"What!" he roared. "You tell us to go roll our hoop? We're the National League champs, and we demand the right to use the grounds for practice!"

Evers turned to Stallings. "He won't let us work out."

Stallings grabbed the phone and rattled off some scorching remarks to Mr. Mack. "We'll beat hell out of you for this!" he shouted. He crashed down the receiver, and turned to his players.

"How do you like that? We're not good enough to use his —— field!"

Well, the "Miracle Braves," who didn't figure to beat Mr. Mack, with his great team, swept the Series in four straight games.

The phone call that worked up the Braves to wallop the A's was a fake. Evers wasn't talking to Mr. Mack, but to a dead line.

No manager, though, equalled Mr. Mack for ability to understand men and get so much effort from them. His was always the velvet hand. He was like a father on the bench. If a pitcher blew up or dogged it, and got the rest of us on the Athletics team down on him, Mr. Mack never showed his own displeasure. While we waited inside the clubhouse to rip the fellow up and down, Mr. Mack would be seated with the pitcher outside, speaking in encouraging, calming terms and urging the player to do better. He was so nice that many "experts" wonder how he ever won a pennant.

He won nine of them, and the World Series five times. That's nice, too.

I remember a night in 1927 when Mr. Mack was in the thick of a pennant fight. Eddie Rommel, who had tailed off badly in his pitching, walked past Mr. Mack in the hotel lobby, where a group of us stood talking. "Good night, boys," chirped Eddie, heading for the elevator. It was curfew time, and Rommel, evidently, was headed for bed like a good ballplayer.

Mr. Mack waited for the elevator doors to close. "Excuse me a moment, Ty," he said. "I'll be right back."

He headed for the alley behind the hotel, and, pretty soon, here came Rommel, climbing down the fire escape.

"Good night, Eddie," said Mr. Mack.

Rommel started back up the ladder. "Good night, Mr. Mack," said he.

Nothing more ever was said about the incident by Mr. Mack. Rommel appreciated it so much that he pitched his head off.

More than once Mr. Mack had to break up a pennant combination because of poor attendance and financial stringency—for which he was panned—and yet he came back with a new combination to win world championships again and again. He was the most outstanding builder of ball clubs we have had. No one could go down into obscure leagues and the colleges, find talent and develop it like Mr. Mack.

With all his niceness, Mr. Mack was a decisive man. I've seen others fail for lack of decision. Nap Lajoie, as a manager, had nine .300 hitters at one time, and couldn't take a pennant at Cleveland. Walter Johnson failed as a manager for the same reason. George Sisler was indecisive—would start to change pitchers and then change his mind and return to his first-base position, often with disastrous results. Tris Speaker, on the other hand, made a very fine manager. Clark Griffith had big success with the old New York

Highlanders, but with all his canniness wasn't successful in many years at Washington. Miller Huggins was both a star player and one of the keenest analysts the game ever saw. He was as important to the rise of the Yankees as a power as any man, including Ed Barrow, Jake Ruppert, and Babe Ruth.

Casey Stengel ranks as one of the great, great strategists and handlers of men. I believe his record of pennants won never will be equaled.

Still, I'll take Mr. Mack to manage my greatest-player line-up. He won his league championship in 1902 and kept on doing it until 1931, a master builder when he was nearly seventy years old.

When he died in 1956, Mr. Mack was almost as old as Moses—well, ninety-three years old, to be exact—and loved by all Americans. And no player who ever worked for him could feel otherwise.

22

A Perilous Moment for the Pastime

They've been trying to fix things that are wrong with my game ever since I can remember, and I fear they'll never succeed.

Commercialism, television, a breakdown of the old order of procedure in trading players and maintaining long-established franchises, the wrecking of traditional league lines by adding new clubs willy-nilly and failure to solve the reserve-clause problem have put the grand old game in jeopardy as we move well into the 1960s. Wild things are happening. The fabric of baseball is crumbling.

Other sports, I'm afraid, will soon put baseball in the shade. As far back as 1932, in the Olympic Games at Los Angeles, a special exhibition of an American pastime was staged. Did we give the world a baseball game? We did not—we gave that Olympic audience an exhibition of football. No one particularly protested or saw much amiss in this. And there you have it. The encroachment of another sport on baseball's season would have been unthinkable once upon a time. Now, pro football opens in August and packs in the fans. Other sports outpromote baseball: hockey, basketball, pro football, and even tournament golf on the professional level. The minor leagues, of course, have been wrecked all over America by wild-eyed, desperate expansion of the majors. The town nine may soon be extinct. Lads who don't live in big cities will grow up without ever seeing a game of professional ball.

The greatest mistake made is the cheapening of all that really was meant to matter when the game of baseball was hammered out by Harry Wright, Albert Goodwill Spalding, Cap Anson, Alexander

Cartwright, Bill Hulbert, Alfred H. Spink, and other pioneers. This is a contest meant to be settled *within* a definitely confined area, bounded by fences. *Within* this geometric area, great feats can take place. *Within* a space where 18 men compete, skill at hitting and handling and throwing the ball is the essence of the activity.

Ball games are not meant to be settled by 250-foot Chinese home runs sailing out of the park, where no play can be made upon them.

In its authentic form, the sport produces runs by base hits, bases-on-balls, sacrifices, bunts, steals, passed balls, errors afield, balks, hit batters, and the various hit-and-run strategies. Fans used to hang open-mouthed over the rails—every play was a breath-taking event and not merely an inconsequential moment within a welter of long hits and carloads of runs scored. Games were tight, low in score. If a player failed to bunt on cue, or threw to the wrong base, or if a manager let a pitcher stay in there overlong, it was a public scandal and the customers held red-hot indignation meetings. Teams fought for runs like tug-of-war teams fight for an inch of turf. It was thrilling, full of heat, sweat and fury.

The version we have today holds runs so cheaply that it's common to see an infield play back and give its opponent a run, even late in the game, when that run means a score, or possible defeat. If this is baseball, my name is not Cobb.

Baseball has become as nonchalant as a vaudeville turn of old, instead of clinging to the fiery drama which is its real metier. People go to games to experience mighty thrills, not to watch the elegant and studied boredom of the actors. Batting has gone swing crazy —whale away as you please, and don't bother to count the mounting strike-outs. Never mind if the league's leading hitters rarely, if ever, sacrifice, or are able to steal a base because they are all power and no versatility. How well, and distastefully, I recall a season when the four highest-priced players—Ted Williams, Stan Musial, Joe DiMaggio, and Ralph Kiner—stole just seven bases among them over an entire season. Old-timer Clyde Milan, with 88 steals, and Eddie Collins, with 81, got away with more thefts in a season than 14 of the 16 American and National League clubs individually produce in a typical year.

The runner loose on the paths, daring the defense to stop him, is the most spectacular sight of all. But why bother to steal today

274

when some humpty-dumpty strong boy can pull a dynamite-laden ball over phony fences to drive in the runners?

Sliding pads have gone out of style—training camp sliding pits, as well. The excuse given is that someone might get hurt. I'll accept that, for the moderns don't know the proper way to slide. I wore pads all the time, specially built, and even then my thighs often were a mass of raw flesh. Harry Salsinger used to say that it took a strong stomach to look at them. Slides force errors, among other things. But even errors aren't important now. Job-lot runs is the whole thing.

If I played today, I'd try to give some of these mechanical men called big-leaguers a hospitalizing case of the jitters. I'd try to do it merely by playing the old established percentages and pulling the unexpected and unorthodox. I'd bunt and fake the bunt, poke-hit and drag them past the pitcher, do delayed steals and bedevil the pitcher with distracting actions on the bases.

I'd work for speed, and never stop working.

Once, when I was well into my thirties, a young newspaperman watched a Detroit rookie win a foot race against me, circling the bases. He thought it was big news and wired home quite a story about how I'd slowed up.

I told the writer not to miss the game next day. In it, I stole four bases.

"Now take a look at the shoes I was wearing in that race," I invited the writer. They were weighted with lead until they were three times as heavy as normal. In introducing weighted shoes, I knew that they would make me work harder, and make me speedier when I switched to regular light shoes.

There are limitless ways to improve, if you use some imagination. That's another quality out of style today.

We find today's slugger asking the ownership for more money. "You only hit .270 last season," says the general manager. "You were slow on the bases, too."

"Yes, but I hit thirty home runs," says the slugger.

He gets the raise.

If I managed a team nowadays, I'd give the fans scientific inside ball they've never seen. How I miss the vanished "phantom" play. On a ball slashed through them, the second baseman and shortstop go through a perfect imitation of a double play. The runner coming down from first, fooled into believing he's out, quits at second. He's prevented from taking another base. And the hidden-ball trick, which requires a master artist. The baseman tucks the ball under his arm, in one variation, while pretending with frantic concern that he's lost it. While he searches the ground, the runner lights out. Crowds used to turn handsprings when they saw a man trapped by this hocus-pocus.

I'd want players less interested in a bonus, a business manager, and a bowling alley than in fighting to win. In my day, a man wasn't safe in his own clubhouse if he'd blown an important game, tempers were that hot. If he failed to run out a hit, he wasn't fined. He had to fight a whole ball club. Mike Donlin, Kid Gleason, Ray Schalk, Pep Young, Frank Chance, and Kid Elberfeld were typical of the hard-bitten, last-ditch fighters on every roster. We used to argue whether tobacco juice or raw whisky was better for a spike cut. Kid Elberfeld rubbed his wounds with both, just to be safe. I've seen Johnny Evers run out a triple with a fractured leg. Today's players are coddled and either can't or won't take hardships. They even want to enlarge home plate, so the pitchers can find it. Pitchers fold up with arm "ailments" and the number of men who can work 300 innings per season is fractional. Joe McGinnity, Ed Walsh, Cy Young, Jack Chesbro, Rube Waddell, Grover Alexander, and many others used to work 350 to 450 innings without a complaint. The 20-game winner is a remarkable personage in the 1960s. He was just ordinary forty years ago.

I'll make a startling prediction. Unless some sharp changes are made, the .300 hitter will become extinct in not many years. Only ten of the 400-odd major players reached .300 or more in 1960. Nap Lajoie could have hit .300 one-handed against the present jack-rabbit ball.

Even more dangerous than the collapse of playing techniques is the trend toward destroying league lines, the wild trading of players between the American and National circuits, manager-swapping, and the destruction of the identity of the rival leagues by creation of new franchises faster than fans can keep up with them. The American fan operates out of loyalty to team and old established traditions. Take that away, and he'll start looking for his entertainment elsewhere.

With the dollar the motive, teams are scheduling far too many

276

spring exhibition games. A ballplayer is like a storage battery. He has just so much energy to expend before he fades and needs re-charging—which isn't possible in the August and September high-pressure days. I was often rapped as a prima donna for staying away from spring training as long as possible. I never pretended to be smart. But I was smart enough to not wear myself out before the season started. I could add up figures. I knew that the 154 games of the regular season were all that counted in the standings, and that I couldn't keep in shape for them if I went stale and tired mentally from too much baseball.

I argue that the major leagues should start spring training two weeks later than at present, then keep the players in Florida, Arizona, and California—under the sun—until a few days before the season opens. Work for condition, not gate receipts. Take a look at how many players fade in the averages and percentages in the final couple of months. You don't see the hustling play after Labor Day, that you did years ago. The boys are playing on ragged nerves be-cause the ownership has ground them down through weeks of spring barnstorming.

Get rid of the intentional base-on-balls. I don't know of any-thing more tiresome. It slows up games, which creep along today, and are another reason baseball is being outpromoted right down the line. In my time we would find bulletins in the clubhouse warn-ing us to speed up the game. In 1920, the longest game in history, 26 innings, pitched by Leon Cadore and Joe Oeschger, was finished in 3 hours, 57 minutes. That constituted almost three nine-inning games. The three-hour nine-inning game we see now should be cut to close to two. This is especially harmful, with so much night ball played. A fan can't afford to get home so late after a long-winded contest.

Let's give the pitcher a break. Enlarge the strike zone to where it used to be measured: from the armpits to the knees. Pitching should be a fine art, not drudgery, with corps of relievers marching in and out boringly and endlessly. Not long ago, I watched a San Francisco-Pittsburgh game in which ten moundsmen were used. In 1960, not one American League pitcher would win more than 18 games. There were only three 20-game winners in the major leagues. That's enough to make any real baseball lover choke.

One final suggestion. In July of 1951, I sat in the witness chair in

Washington to testify before a House Judiciary Committee inquiring into baseball's ailments. Arguments had been raging pro and con as to whether the game should be subject to anti-trust laws and federal intervention of other types. That matter hasn't been solved yet, more than a decade after the boys in Washington began to debate and harangue the public with ideas for new "controls."

"What should we do about changing the game's policies?" I was asked.

"Don't do a thing," I told them. "This is baseball, and you can't take such an institution and place restrictions on it without hurting it."

Let the politicians keep their hooks off the sport of Matty and Rube and the Big Train and Old Pete. If changes are to be made, let baseball men make them. There are still enough of them left with the brains to do what's right. But they had better hurry.

23

"To Plant One Rose—"

The years go on, the years slip by,
The heroes rise, the heroes die,
There'll come a day, not far away,
A day of fans that knew not Ty.

I don't know how many are left who remember me and the men I vied against. I have told my story both for those who do remember and those to whom baseball's Golden Era is a lost and mysterious time. If what is past is only prologue, as wise men believe, then this that I have put on the record is not just ancient history.

If one youngster is moved by my experiences to fight harder than he knows how to fight, but always squarely, for what he wants—to expect bitter condemnation for using his brains as well as muscles to forge ahead of others—then I haven't wasted my words.

A tough, aggressive spirit never hurt anyone. That is, anyone able to rise above the inevitable slurs that such a spirit arouses. Embattled men often forfeit some happiness. But the knowledge that they never backed down from any challenge will warm them forever. The knowledge that they also won out because they were *thinking* men is as fine a reward as any of us could want.

I subscribe to this old bit of philosophy, which I clipped from a sports page fifty-odd years ago:

For acts are but straws on the surface,
While thoughts are the pearls that lie deep;

And these latter count more in the official score
That Recording Angels keep.
And your life is just like a ball game—
We may cheer for the cleanup swat,
But the valuable gink is the one who can think
And who wins on the brains that he's got.

I am well into my seventh decade. Quite honestly, I can testify that I am not burdened with regrets. Would I play it the same way if I had a second chance? Yes, indeed, with an adjustment here and there. I was a boy with a vying nature. As a very young lad, I remember walking a tightrope strung dangerously high across the main street of Royston, Georgia, merely to prove that I could match the bigger boys. I was a man who saw no point in losing, if I could win. That spirit sustained me against cruel and unasked-for punishment when I reached the big league. I was not one who held himself above the rules, but neither did I let anyone throttle or tyrannize me, when the remedy was in my power. I was called a radical, a despot, a bad loser, a dirty player, and worse. Some of these words still hurt.

"Align yourself on the side of right and fear no man," my father told me. Abiding by this, I am here today with some name, some wordly goods, some ability to help others, and some remaining ability to set the record straight about myself.

If I had ever been on the side of wrong, would all this have happened?

I do not believe The Maker would have allowed me so much had I violated my father's creed.

When I played ball, I didn't play for fun. To me it wasn't parchesi played under parchesi rules. Baseball is a red-blooded sport for red-blooded men. It's no pink tea, and mollycoddles had better stay out. It's a contest and everything that implies, a struggle for supremacy, a survival of the fittest. Every man in the game, from the minors on up, is not only fighting against the other side, but he's trying to hold onto his own job against those on his own bench who'd love to take it away. Why deny this? Why minimize it? Why not boldly admit it?

Many a writer has said that I was "unfair." Well, that's not my understanding of the word. When my toes were stepped on, I stepped right back. As a green kid still trying to gain a reputation,

I met pitchers who did everything they could think of to stop me. They didn't hesitate to send a killer-ball hurtling at my head. Suppose their efforts to intimidate me had been successful. The league grapevine rapidly would have carried the news that Cobb's "geezer" was showing and from then on I'd have been a sitting duck in a shooting gallery. I'd have lasted in big-time baseball two years instead of twenty-four. If I'd been meek and submissive, instead of fighting back, the world never would have heard of me.

Certain things the Lord has allowed me to do never would have happened.

On a January day some years back, I stood on a platform before a new brick building in Royston and spoke to a gathering of three thousand old friends and the young folk of my home town.

"I don't believe there'll be any time in my life when I'll be happier than I am today," I began.

"Here I am in the toughest spot I have ever been in. I see so many faces of friends I've known through the years that I can't think of what I wanted to say. When I was a boy here, we had oratorical contests and I memorized my speech, rehearsed my gestures and had it down perfect, so that once I won a contest. Well, I turned from school to baseball. Therefore, I didn't improve my Demosthenesian methods.

"There isn't much I can say. I wish I had the gift. But I want you to know that this building and all that is in it belongs to you people, here where I used to live. It is for you friends for whom I've always had it in my heart."

Then I dedicated the Cobb Memorial Hospital in loving memory of my mother and father.

In that modern hospital in rural Georgia, where none existed for many years, wonderful things are happening today. It was built by funds that came my way because I was a baseball player. Would it stand there if I had defied my God?

I know that it would not.

Neither would there be a Cobb Educational Foundation, which finances high-caliber boys and girls through college in such important fields as medicine, engineering, social sciences, art and research of many kinds. By the several hundred, the Foundation can point to students and graduates whose future deeds for man's good will be immeasurable. All those the Foundation helps are "distress" cases, lacking funds to complete the education they themselves started and have worked hard to maintain.

The distress also would be mine, if I could not lend a helping hand.

Edgar Guest, one of my favorite poets, wrote:

> *For man must live his life on earth,*
>   *Where hate and sin and wrong abound.*
> *'Tis here the soul must prove its worth,*
>   *'Tis here the strength of it is found,*
> *And he had justified his birth*
>   *Who plants one rose on barren ground.**

I sit on a Georgia hill, or by a shimmering California mountain lake, and am happy. The pain that may attack my flesh is eased in so many ways.

I commune often with my God. I ask Him to guide me in all my decisions. Every young fellow should do the same. It will leave him strong, confident, and able to fight for what he clearly sees is right.

The book I once believed that I would never write is finished.

End of game, inning, and time at bat.

---

* Copyrighted. Used by permission of The Reilly & Lee Company.

Ty Cobb died July 17, 1961. The next morning on its editorial page the New York *Herald Tribune* said:

The redoubtable Tyrus Raymond Cobb, sharp of mind and spike, is dead. It would take a long parade of superlatives to re-enact his career, for his were talents of unmatched variety.

Ted Williams could hit, but his running left room for jeers. Pepper Martin could run, but he was no Babe Ruth at the plate. Babe Ruth became the undisputed Sultan of Swat, but nobody wanted him around as a manager. And many is the athlete who lives the well-rounded baseball life but whose efforts to earn an honest living off the diamond end in the poorhouse.

Ty Cobb shone with multilateral brilliance. In baseball (he once held ninety records), and in business afterward (he became a multimillionaire) he scored consistently. After retiring from the game in 1928 his name lived on as a symbol of championship performance. A generation that never came within earshot of his crackling bat argued his prowess and publicized his feats.

It is not for us to say that his aggressive pre-emption of the base paths was or was not in keeping with the book. We'll leave that to the untiring tongues of grandstand umpires.

Of Ty Cobb let it be said simply that he was the world's greatest ballplayer.